Faith-Based War

Religion and Violence

Series Editors
Lisa Isherwood, University of Winchester, and Rosemary
Radford Ruether, Graduate Theological Union, Berkeley,
California

This interdisciplinary and multicultural series brings to light the ever increasing problem of religion and violence. The series will highlight how religions have a significant part to play in the creation of cultures that allow and even encourage the creation of violent conflict, domestic abuse and policies and state control that perpetuate violence to citizens.

The series will highlight the problems that are experienced by women during violent conflict and under restrictive civil policies. But not wishing to simply dwell on the problems the authors in this series will also re-examine the traditions and look for alternative and more empowering readings of doctrine and tradition. One aim of the series is to be a powerful voice against creeping fundamentalisms and their corrosive influence on the lives of women and children.

Published:
Reweaving the Relational Mat
A Christian Response to Violence against Women from Oceania
Joan Alleluia Filemoni-Tofaeono and Lydia Johnson

Weep Not for Your Children: Essays on Religion and Violence
Edited by Lisa Isherwood and Rosemary Radford Ruether

In Search of Solutions: The Problem of Religion and Conflict
Clinton Bennett

America, Amerikkka: Elect Nation and Imperial Violence
Rosemary Radford Ruether

Shalom/Salaam/Peace: A Liberation Theology of Hope in Israel/Palestine
Constance A. Hammond

Forthcoming:
Crying for Dignity Caste-based Violence against Dalit Women
Mary Grey

Faith-Based War

From 9/11 to Catastrophic Success in Iraq

T. Walter Herbert

LONDON   OAKVILLE

Published by Equinox Publishing Ltd.
UK: Unit 6, The Village, 101 Amies St., London SW11 2JW
USA: DBBC, 28 Main Street, Oakville, CT 06779

www.equinoxpub.com

First published 2009

British Library Cataloguing-in-Publication Data
A catalogue record for this book is available from the British Library.

ISBN-13   978 184553 161 4   (hardback)
          978 184553 162 1   (paperback)

Library of Congress Cataloging-in-Publication Data

Herbert, T. Walter (Thomas Walter), 1938-
    Faith-based war : from 9/11 to catastrophic success in Iraq/T. Walter Herbert.
        p. cm. — (Religion and violence)
    Includes bibliographical references and index.
      ISBN 978-1-84553-161-4 (hb) — ISBN 978-1-84553-162-1 (pbk.) 1.
War — Religious aspects — Christianity. 2. Executive power — United
States. 3. United States — History, Military — Religious aspects. 4.
Iraq War, 2003- I. Title. BT736.2.H46 2009
956.7044'31 — dc22
                          2008055836

Typeset by S.J.I. Services, New Delhi
Printed and bound in Great Britain by Lightning Source UK Ltd, Milton Keynes

CONTENTS

For my grandsons,

Zachary Roberts Herbert, Ethan Roberts Herbert, and
Liam Roarke Herbert-Miller

ACKNOWLEDGEMENTS

Because an interpretive study like this one is dependent on truthful first-hand documentation, I want first to acknowledge my gratitude for the work of journalists and investigators that researched the inception, context and execution of the Iraq invasion, and wrote books that amplified and corrected the narrative that the daily media put before us. I am particularly indebted to Andrew Cockburn, David Corn, Mark Danner, Michael Gordon, Chris Hedges, Michael Isikoff, Jane Mayer, Frank Rich, Thomas E. Ricks, Philippe Sands, Ron Suskind, Bernard Trainor, Bob Woodward, and Lawrence Wright.

I also want to acknowledge a pervasive debt to the theological and political works of Reinhold Neibuhr, whose writing I studied and whose lectures I attended when I was a student at Harvard College and Union Theological Seminary.

I am grateful to Southwestern University for budgetary support and the expert secretarial assistance of Kelly Lessard. I have received invaluable comment and counsel provided by the Writer's Group at Southwestern, convened by Gwen Kennedy Neville and including Dan Hilliard, Ed Kain, Suzanne Chamier, Doug Wixson, Ken Roberts, and Laura Hobgood-Oster. Robert Snyder and Eric Selbin, Southwestern colleagues in Political Science, read selected portions of the manuscript and offered expert assistance.

I owe an additional debt to Ken Roberts. We offered a team-taught course on 'England from Colony to Empire' in the Fall semester of 2002 for a group of Southwestern students studying in London, which offered a fortunate vantage from which to view events in the United States preparatory to the invasion of Iraq.

Evan Carton and Warwick Wadlington, longstanding colleagues at the University of Texas, read through two full drafts of the work-in-progress and brought their wisdom and their deep knowledge of American literary culture to bear. Sam Pfiester and Ted Gray are humane and spirited friends who examine economic and political issues from vantage points different from my own; they read the manuscript with care and gave me very helpful responses. So also did my brothers Linton and Carlisle, who have been vigorous and challenging intellectual companions since we were boys together.

I am grateful to Anne Mayer for corresponding with me on key features of the project, to Jim Rigby for talking over theological issues, to Ian Miller for strategic suggestions when I most needed them, and to Rosemary Ruether for inviting me to do it.

My wife, Marjorie Millard Herbert, gave me detailed comment on the full manuscript. For more than four decades our spiritual journeys have been indissolubly intertwined; this book is unthinkable without her inspiration and loving support.

Introduction

FAITH-BASED WAR

Faith-Based War

On 20 September 2001 President George W. Bush addressed a nation still reeling from the atrocity nine days before. 'Each of us will remember what happened that day,' he said. 'We'll remember the moment the news came — where we were and what we were doing.' It was a day of religious vision, Bush explained, when Americans were propelled into a world that lies behind the veil of ordinary experience, where permanent realities become visible. 'Americans have known wars,' President Bush declared, but these were 'wars on foreign soil.' When terrorists killed thousands at the World Trade Center and the Pentagon, 'night fell on a different world, a world where freedom itself is under attack.' On the transcendant landscape opened up by the agony and shock of the moment, the President discerned a compelling drama, an eternal warfare of good and evil in which America plays a leading role. Attacking American soil was an attack on freedom itself, and while the nation had been staggered by the attack, it had also come home to its enduring mission. 'Freedom and fear are at war. The advance of human freedom — the great achievement of our time, and the great hope of every time — now depends on us.' If the nation will now keep faith with the role God had assigned, that of freedom's home and champion, the war can only end in victory. 'Freedom and fear, justice and cruelty, have always been at war, and we know that God is not neutral between them.'[1] The specially called Joint Session of Congress resounded with thunderous applause, and the President's words also rang true with the public at large.

---

1. George W. Bush, 'Address to a Joint Session of Congress and the American People,' United States Capitol, 20 September 2001. www.whitehouse.gov/news/releases/2001/09/20010920-8.html.

In summoning support for the war, the White House skillfully wove together themes of Christian piety and democratic principle, speaking about freedom and God's purposes in ways that sounded authoritative and familiar. Because the case for war drew on a shared vocabulary of public devotion, both secular and devout Americans supported the venture, or found it difficult to frame the reasons for their opposition.

'Christian Americanism' would serve as a crude title for the religious outlook at work here. The attack of 9/11 was experienced as a religious trauma because it violated this common faith, and the administration's response carried conviction because it appealed to the nation's historical self-understanding. Yet in forming and implementing its war policy, the Bush White House followed a militarist religious vision, forcefully advanced by the Christian Right, which gave distinctive meanings to the shared tradition and yielded catastrophic results.

The first chapters of this book treat the conception of America as a 'promised land' occupied by a 'chosen people,' which originated with the Puritan colony at Massachusetts Bay, and was quickly adapted to westward expansion. The 'promised land' came to have a dynamic meaning, that of enlarging the sphere of democracy and freedom and of spreading America's blessings to other societies. This sense of national calling was absorbed into the doctrine of Manifest Destiny and then into a vision of America's worldwide mission that was championed by Theodore Roosevelt and Woodrow Wilson.

The second part of the book treats a corollary myth, that of a hero-figure who plays his part at the line of conflict, where an expanding 'promised land' presses against territory occupied by the not-chosen, to whom the land is not promised, yet who stubbornly insist on keeping to their ancestral ways in their ancestral homeland. This mythology envisions no neutral meeting ground between the parties: instead, the chosen and the not-chosen face each other at a 'frontier' where God's favorites claim their birthright against godless opposition. Tribes in New England, and then across the continent, were compelled to accept the losing part in this drama.

Many wars were required to surmount the armed resistance of resident tribes, from the Puritan victory over the Wampanoags and their allies in 1677 to the defeat of the Apaches in 1886. As this conquest unfolded, it was imagined by the triumphant Anglos as a story centered on the exploits of the 'frontier hero.' In the early nineteenth century, James Fenimore Cooper established the great prototype on which subsequent heroes are patterned, figures who 'are opening the way for the march of the nation across the continent.'[2]

The twin visions — of America as an expanding promised land, and of the frontier hero — are key components of a national faith, and have long shaped America's way of encountering the world beyond our borders. In *Promised Land, Crusader State*, Walter McDougall demonstrates that these doctrines have inspired 'wise and decent' policies as well as 'foolish and brutal' ones. The 'ethnic cleansing' of the continental tribes should not be allowed to stand for the whole American story, McDougall insists, nor should the humanity of the Marshall Plan, or the wisdom of founding the United Nations.[3]

The decision to invade Iraq was animated by an imperialist version of Christian Americanism that has commandeered this broader tradition. George W. Bush blurred assertions of his distinctively aggressive creed into conventional-sounding religious pronouncements, but his heartfelt commitment is nonetheless evident, as is the warm welcome his White House extended to its public advocates. This vision holds that America's conduct toward other nations is consistently and triumphantly innocent, and that American 'freedom' requires access to resources controlled by other societies.

It is well known that Ronald Reagan invoked the Puritan heritage in his vision of America as a 'shining city on a hill.' But Reagan and his political offspring brushed aside the fierce Puritan debate about the meaning of the 'city.' Roger Williams set forth religious principles against which he condemned the colony's treatment of neighboring peoples, but in Reagan's version, America itself becomes the supreme standard of political virtue. The war in Iraq was inspired by this vainglorious dream, and produced a telling caricature of its central icon. The Green Zone in Baghdad was meant to serve as an outpost

---

2. James Fenimore Cooper, *The Pioneers, or The Sources of the Susquehanna: A Descriptive Tale*, with an Afterword by Robert E. Spiller (New York: Signet Classics, 1964), p. 436.

3. Walter A. McDougall, *Promised Land, Crusader State: The American Encounter with the World since 1776* (Boston, MA: Houghton Mifflin, 1997), pp. 2–3.

of the 'city,' projecting the forces of freedom and democracy into the savage wilderness of Iraq; it became instead a cloud-cuckoo-land of self-destructive delusions, abetting the disaster that befell the U.S. occupation.

At its most intense, radical Christian nationalism is grounded on the belief that hatred for God is endemic to the moral constitution of human beings, provoking God's righteous wrath upon all except those saved by Christ. In this view, true Christians are obligated to do their part in executing the divine wrath against evildoers. Biblical passages sometimes express a spirituality of hate, but often include second thoughts. 'Do I not hate them that hate thee, O Lord?...I hate them with perfect hatred,' says Psalm 139; but the psalmist immediately expresses uneasiness about his spasm of loathing. 'Search me, O God, and know my heart!...See if there be any wicked way in me.' Such self doubts do not moderate the moralistic ferocity of the Christian Right.[4]

Jesus expressly rejected teachings of pious hatred: 'You have heard that it was said, "You shall love your neighbor and hate your enemy"; but I say to you "Love your enemies and pray for those who persecute you"'(Mt. 5:43). Rus Walton, a contemporary right-wing partisan, adroitly cancels Jesus's words in driving home the central precept of warrior Christianity. 'Our Savior and our King instructs us to love our enemies. Yes! But nowhere in scripture, nowhere, does the Lord God tell us to love His enemies.'[5] As their scathing rhetorical style reveals, exponents of this creed treat domestic political antagonists, to say nothing of terrorists, as enemies of God fit for destruction.

The New Testament theologian Walter Wink has shown that early Christians believed their salvation had liberated them from intangible forces of spiritual oppression, from what St. Paul called 'principalities and powers' that enthrall mortal souls and foster destructive and self-destructive enterprises. As the leading example

---

4. *The Holy Bible. Revised Standard Version, containing the Old and New Testaments.* Translated from the original tongues, being the version set forth A.D. 1611, revised A.D. 1881–1885 and A.D. 1901; compared with the most ancient authorities and revised A.D. 1952 (New York: Thomas Nelson, 1953). For an unqualified endorsement of the hatred felt by the psalmist see Rus Walton, *Biblical Solutions to Contemporary Problems: A Handbook* (Brentwood, TN: Wolgemuth & Hyatt, 1988), p. 164.

5. Rus Walton, *One Nation Under God* (Nashville, TN: Thomas Nelson, rev. edn, 1987), p. 168.

of such an enchantment, Wink cites the 'myth of redemptive violence,' whose origins he finds in a Babylonian legend of 1250 BCE, where a creator god builds the universe from the body parts of a rival god he has killed. Wink then traces expressions of this violent faith in the exploits of male war gods that spread across the ancient world, and he finds it very much alive today. The 'frontier hero' – who creates the civilized order by killing savages – is an American version of this ancient and abiding mythology. Richard Slotkin explored the origin and development of this recurring legend as a leading feature of American cultural history, independently of expressly religious traditions. Slotkin terms it a drama of 'regeneration through violence.'[6]

The militant Christian Right, far from offering liberation from the myth of redemptive violence, installs Christ as its exemplary hero. St Paul taught that believers should refrain from taking revenge, admonishing them that God has reserved that function entirely to himself (Rom. 12:14–21). The Book of Revelation likewise envisions a post-resurrection Jesus returning to earth to conquer the forces of evil without assistance from the faithful. But in the teachings of the religious right, Christ the divine avenger provides Christians with a model for ethical action in this world. Politics for them becomes the abolition of evil forces by the agents of divine righteousness, and the vision of heroism sustained by this version of Christianity has a substantial representation in popular culture. Clint Eastwood's Dirty Harry, like his Pale Rider, are Christ-figures dealing out post-resurrection wrath upon evildoers.

Key features of the Iraq invasion bear witness to this shared religious outlook: the belief that President Saddam Hussein was an embodiment of 'evil,' justifying the U.S. in waging a 'preventive war'; the trust that a 'shock and awe' campaign would eradicate

---

6. Walter Wink, *Engaging the Powers: Discernment and Resistance in a World of Domination* (Minneapolis, MN: Fortress Press, 1992), pp. 13–32. See also *Naming the Powers: the Language of Power in the New Testament* (Philadelphia, PA: Fortress Press, 1984) and *Unmasking the Powers: the Invisible Forces that Determine Human Existence* (Philadelphia, PA: Fortress Press, 1986). Richard Slotkin, *Regeneration Through Violence; the Mythology of the American Frontier, 1600–1860* (Middletown, CT: Wesleyan University Press, 1973) see also his *The Fatal Environment: The Myth of the Frontier in the Age of Industrialization, 1800–1890* (Norman, OK: University of Oklahoma Press, 1985), and *Gunfighter Nation: The Myth of the Frontier in Twentieth-century America* (Norman, OK: University of Oklahoma Press, 1998).

the evil without the need for a well-planned occupation; and the use of torture against captives. Bush himself plays the role of a frontier hero who acts as an agent of divine wrath, freed from the requirements of human law. Those who planned and executed the invasion of Iraq were not all committed to a Christian version of this mindset, as was President Bush; but they shared a community of moral sentiment in which the unconditional warfare of goodness against evil came to define political conflict. This shared vision blinded the administration, and the public at large, to the perils of the invasion and brought on the catastrophe to which it led.

Catastrophic Success

General Tommy Franks met with the National Security Council on 5 August 2002, to present OPLAN 1003V, a detailed plan for 'regime destruction' in Iraq. The assembled leaders—President George W. Bush, Vice-President Richard Cheney, Secretary of Defense Donald Rumsfeld, Secretary of State Colin Powell, National Security Advisor Condoleeza Rice, and CIA Director George Tenet—discussed the 'Rolling Start' deployment of ground forces and of logistical support, the roles of the air umbrella and of naval firepower, the potential of opening a northern invasion launched from Turkey, the relation of Iraq to the ongoing war in Afghanistan. Then Franks raised some 'difficult questions' under the heading of 'catastrophic success.'[7]

How would the U.S. military respond if Hussein's regime fell more quickly than anticipated, toppled by a military coup, or because Iraqi resistance simply collapsed? With his mastery of logistical requirements, Franks perhaps sensed that the force level planned for the invasion would be insufficient for an occupation, as General Erik K. Shinseki was to assert in public the following February. If so, Franks's oblique warning fell on deaf ears. 'We would continue the operation to restore and maintain order until the Iraqis can govern themselves,' Donald Rumsfeld briskly replied. 'To a person,' Franks comments, 'the NSC concurred'.[8]

Or perhaps General Franks's odd expression was meant as a play on words, alluding to the 'catastrophic failure' that occurs when the structural elements supporting a bridge or a dam suddenly give

---

7. Tommy Franks, *American Soldier* (New York: HarperCollins, 2004), pp. 285–393.
8. Franks, *American Soldier*, p. 392.

way. Franks may have meant that 'catastrophic failure' for the Hussein regime would be a 'catastrophic success' for the United States. It is possible that Franks was as blind as the rest, and had no premonition of the tragedy. If so, his words are an eerie foreshadowing indeed, the signal of a prophetic intelligence unrecognized by the high officials in the room.

In any event, the catastrophe was well underway one year later. On 7 August 2003 the insurgency bombed the Jordanian embassy, followed by the United Nations headquarters in Baghdad on 19 August, killing UN Ambassador Sergio Viera de Mello. Most of the UN staff then left the country. Other institutions giving credibility to the U.S. occupation pulled out soon thereafter, including the World Bank, the International Monetary Fund and Oxfam. In January of 2004 photographs of prisoner abuse at Abu Ghraib focused attention on the U.S. torture program.

L. Paul Bremer III, the chief of the Coalition Provisional Authority, transferred formal sovereignty to an Iraqi regime in June of 2004, but the security situation was so desperate that getting Bremer safely to a flight out of Baghdad became a taxing and intricate operation. U. S. military deaths reached 1000 in September of 2004, and in October the top U.S. weapons inspector announced there was no evidence Saddam Hussein possessed weapons of mass destruction at the time of the invasion. The following November was the deadliest month to date for U.S. forces, with 137 killed.[9]

Two years later the catastrophe could no longer be wished away. Donald Rumsfeld resigned in the wake of Democratic victories in the 2006 elections, and attention turned to salvaging something from the mess. A bipartisan Iraq Study Group, headed by Rep. Lee H. Hamilton and former Secretary of State James A. Baker III, acknowledged a 'grave and deteriorating' situation, and proposed that regional negotiations be initiated, with a view to reducing American involvement. President Bush instead adopted the 'surge,' sharply increasing the U.S. military presence under the leadership of General David Petraeus. Like the Hamilton-Baker proposal, 'the surge' was a recognition that the initial faith-based approach had

---

9. See Thomas E. Ricks, *Fiasco: The American Military Adventure in Iraq* (New York: Penguin Press, 2006), p. 214 and L. Paul Bremer and Malcolm McConnell, *My Year in Iraq: The Struggle to Build a Future of Hope* (New York: Simon & Schuster, 2006), pp. 394–95.

failed, and appointing the pragmatic Petraeus marked the effort to find a new direction. At the time of this writing (March of 2009), the surge has reduced the level of violence, but it remains unclear whether the Baghdad regime can survive, or whether the internal conflicts unleashed by the invasion will erupt once again, should withdrawals begin in earnest.

The war's cost now far outweighs any potential benefits. The outlay of American blood and treasure already exceeds four thousand lives and hundreds of billions of dollars — perhaps as much as three trillion — accompanied by the blow to American prestige and the impairment of military capacity that are already emboldening dangerous adversaries around the globe.[10]

The invasion was catastrophic in ways that we can be certain General Franks did not have in mind. It was a betrayal of America's democratic ideals. America does not rule client states directly, but even when managed through military treaties and trade pacts, imperial dominion entails exercising governance over people who have no opportunity to give or withhold consent.[11] The White House programs of surveillance and prisoner interrogation have included systematic violations of democratic principle. Chalmers Johnson has argued that the invasion strengthens the reasons to fear that democracy in America may at length be sacrificed to the cause of empire.[12]

This book treats the invasion as a religious catastrophe, of the sort portrayed in tragic drama, where a price is paid for the perversion of religious truth. A startling downfall carries heroic figures from power and prestige down to humiliating defeat, and the downward slide is often hastened by the reckless fury that is unleashed — as for King Oedipus and King Lear — when the ruler's vainglory is affronted, a transaction making plain that arrogance

10. See Joseph E. Stiglitz and Linda J. Bilmes, *The Three Trillion Dollar War: The True Cost of the Iraq Conflict* (New York: Norton, 2008).

11. See Joseph E. Stiglitz, *Globalization and its Discontents* (New York: Norton, 2003), pp. 222-29, 247-52.

12. Chalmers Johnson, *Nemesis: The Last Days of the American Republic* (Henry Holt: New York, 2006). Jacob Weisberg, *The Bush Tragedy* (New York: Random House, 2008); Philippe Sands, *Torture Team: Rumsfeld's Memo and the Betrayal of American Values* (New York: Palgrave Macmillan, 2008); Jane Mayer, *The Dark Side: The Inside Story of How the War on Terror Turned into a War on American Ideals* (New York: Doubleday, 2008).

and moral blindness drive the protagonist to fatal over-reaching. The malice of enemies plays a part, but the disaster befalling the tragic hero is mostly self-inflicted. The principle actors in the Iraq catastrophe — President Bush, Vice-President Cheney, Secretary of Defense Rumsfeld — were not brought down because a jealous god resented their arrogance, but because religious delusions blinded them to the realities they faced.

Their imperialist and anti-democratic version of Christian Americanism was not invented in the Bush White House, nor will it pass from the American scene now that another regime has taken power in Washington. As America becomes more vulnerable on the world stage, and suffers the inevitable economic and military humiliations, a new cast of characters will appear, eager to sponsor further applications of this self-destructive creed.

Throughout this book I use the term 'Christian' descriptively, referring to institutions, officials and opinions that mark themselves as Christian, and I have followed common practice in referring to the Christian God as 'He.' I myself do not subscribe to this practice, or to much of what passes as 'Christian' belief. This poses a problem that requires attention now.

In order to treat perversions of religious truth, it is necessary to invoke a religious standard. Imperial maintenance can be measured against well recognized criteria, and democratic values are encoded in American law; to propose a comparably exact criterion against which to judge departures from religious truth would require defining that truth in unambiguous declarative terms.

But religious truth ultimately refuses to be fixed into language, at least for me. It involves encounters with a living mystery that takes place on scheduled and unscheduled occasions — encounters with texts, with other people, and with presences that are evoked by art, by landscapes and seascapes. Shared action for the sake of social justice provides such occasions, and sacred ritual sometimes provides a context for them. By the accident of my birth and rearing, biblical stories are central to my religious life, much as they are for Muslims and Jews — the other 'peoples of the book.' These spiritualities now merge, however, into sacred stories and active pieties within Taoism, Hinduism and Buddhism, along irregular coastlines of interaction. My journey has led me to a place shared by many others, where sharp boundaries no longer surround a Christian heritage.

I was born to a devout family in an overwhelmingly Protestant community and took the faith to heart in boyhood and adolescence. I majored in Biblical Studies at Union Theological Seminary in New York City, and served three years as a campus minister before starting my career as a student of American literature and culture. I think of ethical and religious questions in a Christian language, as I think of them in the English language, because it is the language native to me, which I have applied myself to understand and to use with care. Like other traditions, Christianity can offer sound ethical instruction and communion with divine presence, but it can also be used to confer the legitimacy without which power arrangements, just or unjust, cannot sustain themselves.

Commonplace profanity is often scolded for 'taking the Lord's name in vain,' but there is an immeasurably more grievous offense. Exponents of the Christian Right typically claim that their opinions about God rest on the absolute authority of scripture, or the direct revelations of the Holy Spirit. Yet, the effect of these claims is to evade responsibility. We are all answerable for the way we read holy texts, and the way we interpret moments of mystical awareness, and this responsibility compels the acceptance of uncertainties that are shunned by those who seek the comforts of blind unquestioning faith. Religious authoritarians offer those comforts by pretending to certainties they do not possess.

Like those of other creeds, Christian fanatics distinguish themselves by their contempt for those who disagree, their principled refusal to engage in reasoned arguments, and the frequent collisions between their claims and the factual realities before them. When this book criticizes such failings, no theological standard of judgment is required. On the rare occasions when I invoke my own faith, I've adapted the ancient Jewish practice that refrains from uttering the name of God, using 'hashem' [the name] in its place. I've chosen to use, when necessary, the unpronounceable 'G*d.'

Loyal Americans are called upon to defend the democratic traditions violated by the Bush White House, but also face an enduring agenda that is native to religious life, that of keeping faith with a sacred reality that transcends the authority of national governments. Christians enjoy no monopoly on the articulation of such faith, but share the effort with Jews, Muslims, Hindus, Buddhists and with honest souls whose devotion does not find a home in any extant tradition. We need sustenance for the quiet difficult business of loving justice and seeking truth, to meet the responsibilities we discharge as citizens of a nation whose pre-eminent global power will inevitably pass from the scene. Adherents of religious traditions must live faith responsibly, to renew and amplify the spiritual resources available to oncoming generations. This book is written in hope of contributing to these efforts, explaining how ardent devotion to a misplaced faith led to catastrophe in Iraq.

Chapter One

AMERICAN BLINDSPOT

Religious Trauma

'Are you watching television?' our son-in-law asked, when we picked up the telephone. Our daughter, he told us, had been called to jury duty at City Hall, about a hundred yards from the World Trade Center. We turned on the television and watched as the second plane struck the second tower, making it obvious this was deliberate. It was hours before we learned our daughter was alive, that she had walked northward after she made it to the street — past Tribeca, Greenwich Village, Midtown, Central Park, all the way to Morningside Heights — looking back only once.

My confusion and shock momentarily took on a primal intensity, as though an unknown killer had singled out my daughter, and had struck at her through a blindspot in my world. What had happened was unthinkable. Thousands suffered what I only feared, bearing the death of loved ones that day with the same incredulity; the tidal wave of rage and grief reached far beyond stricken families, flooding the national consciousness.

The blasted Manhattan cityscape took command of the video imagery, as TV coverage fostered a national effort to absorb the shock, and hinted at ways to understand it. The images themselves became the meaning of the event: the collapsing towers, streets filled with wreckage, rescue vehicles and snaking fire hoses; the famous skyline mangled — with a foul cavity thrust between the tall buildings and the Statue of Liberty offshore. A violated New York became the central emblem, eclipsing the wounded Pentagon and the remains of United Flight 93.

September 11 took form in the public mind as the defilement of a gleaming American city. Matching the criterion for a successful terrorist attack set forth in Joseph Conrad's *The Secret Agent*, it possessed 'all the shocking senselessness of gratuitous blasphemy' against a target the public holds sacred.[1] Our collective response was not rooted in any particular affection for the twin towers. Citizens with little conception of world trade were stricken because the buildings stood tall in the Manhattan cityscape.

Americans have taken to heart a nation where 'alabaster cities gleam, undimmed by human tears,' and—following a more ancient sacred tradition—a nation that serves as 'a city on a hill,' ordained by God as a showcase for the virtues of his chosen people. The atrocities of 9/11 inflicted a religious trauma because of the blasphemy against this distinctively American sense of the sacred. We will discuss the traditions underlying this religious temperament more fully in due course, but our pathway toward understanding the subsequent political tragedy leads first through the obverse of this vision, the blindness of 9/11.

'Why do they hate us?' Americans asked. Those who noticed that the World Trade Center bespeaks global capitalism, or that the Pentagon symbolizes the nation's worldwide military reach, had scant context in which to place those facts.

Al Qaeda? Most Americans had never heard of it, to say nothing of seeing its significance. Five days before the attack, the President himself had brusquely dismissed warnings that a major Al Qaeda operation was imminent, as had Condoleeza Rice earlier that summer. We learned that Osama Bin Laden resented the placement of American military bases in Saudi Arabia; but what sane person— Muslim or otherwise—would share this resentment?

This was the blindspot through which the attacks had come, our inability to recognize that American actions around the world arouse resentment. Terrorism, for all its unspeakable cruelty, is not unfathomable; it is a commonplace of human strife. A time-honored maneuver of the weak, terror tactics were adopted by rebels in the American colonies expressing resentment for British rule.

Most Americans are unaware of the worldwide system of military bases that the United States continues to maintain on foreign soil, bases developed to contain the Soviet threat that were kept in place long after the threat disappeared. Americans would be gravely offended by the presence of such installations on American soil. Imagine the furor that would be aroused if Russian military bases

---

1. Joseph Conrad, J. H. Stape, and Michael Newton, *The Secret Agent: A Simple Tale* (London: Penguin, 2007), p. 27.

in Massachusetts and Texas operated on terms that immunize Russian soldiers from prosecution for violating American laws. When the predictable scandals at U.S. overseas bases provoke angry demonstrations, however, Americans are shocked and insulted.

Chalmers Johnson explains that 'blowback' is a term coined by the CIA, and defines it as 'the unintended consequences of policies that were kept secret from the American people.'[2] It was first used in an 'after-action' report on the U.S. role in overthrowing the democratically elected government of Premier Muhammad Mossadegh in Iran, and the subsequent installation of the Shah.[3] This venture produced a reservoir of resentment much larger than American planners recognized; there was great surprise in official circles when the Ayatollah Khomeini overthrew the Shah in 1979, and established a regime of anti-American fundamentalists. The vast majority of Americans, of course, knew nothing about our part in the removal of Mossadegh. Yet unwelcome consequences also follow from policies that are not secret, but remain invisible to the public eye.

Carlos Fuentes once remarked that our nation should be called 'The United States of Amnesia.' Every Mexican schoolchild knows about the Treaty of Guadeloupe Hidalgo, under which the United States doubled its territory at the expense of Mexico, adding California, Utah, Nevada, Colorado, Arizona, New Mexico and Texas. This treaty, signed after the Mexican War, made the United States a continental nation, but very few American college graduates know about it.[4]

Niall Ferguson celebrates American empire, strongly in contrast to Johnson, but is likewise struck by this pattern of blindness. Writing in the wake of the 9/11 attacks, Ferguson argues that military predominance, coupled with America's dominant role in economic globalization, makes it 'functionally, if not self-consciously, an empire,' and he issues a warning against 'the perils of being an

2. Chalmers A. Johnson, *Blowback: The Costs and Consequences of American Empire* (New York: Henry Holt & Co, 2000), p. 8.

3. Chalmers A. Johnson, *Nemesis: The Last Days of the American Republic* (New York: Henry Holt & Co, 2006), p. 2.

4. Carlos Fuentes and Alfred J. Mac Adam, *The Crystal Frontier: A Novel in Nine Stories* (trans. Alfred Mac Adam; New York: Harcourt Brace, 1997), p. 57.

"empire in denial."'[5] The champions of earlier empires knew that they were hated by the peoples over whom they ruled, as captured in the Roman motto *Oderint dum metuant*, meaning 'Let them hate, so long as they fear.' Ferguson notes that the success of earlier empires depended on 'an imperial cast of mind' that Americans lack.[6]

Like Rudyard Kipling, Ferguson is eager for the United States to maintain a version of the worldwide Anglophone empire that the British established, reminding us that Kipling wrote 'The White Man's Burden' in 1899 to encourage American empire-building in the Philippines. But Americans are alarmingly unwilling to accept this burden, Ferguson complains, especially the bitter frustration that results when the imperialist is repaid with resentment for the benefits he confers. Kipling calls it 'the blame of those ye better, the hate of those ye guard.'[7]

The wide disagreement between Johnson and Ferguson defines the outer boundaries of a vigorous debate about American global power, which provides a real-world context within which a retaliatory strike such as 9/11 can be appraised. But our national leadership did not take such questions into account. At a news conference one month after the attack, President Bush made a point of asking himself the question:

> How do I respond when I see...[this] vitriolic hatred for America? I'll tell you how I respond: I'm amazed. I'm amazed that there is such misunderstanding of what our country is about, that people would hate us. I am, I am — like most Americans, I just can't believe it. Because I know how good we are.[8]

The atrocity of 9/11 remained for the President a blasphemy, calling for a counter-attack that would demonstrate the God-ordained self-evident American goodness that our enemies somehow hadn't understood. Getting the message out would require not only an

5. Niall Ferguson, *Colossus: The Rise and Fall of the American Empire* (New York: Penguin Press, 2004), p. viii.

6. Ferguson, *Colossus*, p. 29.

7. Rudyard Kipling, 'The White Man's Burden' in Rudyard Kipling and Irving Howe, *The Portable Kipling*, The Viking Portable Library (Harmondsworth [Middlesex]: Penguin Books, 1982), p. 603.

8. George W. Bush, 'President Holds Prime Time News Conference', The White House News and Policies, 11 October 2001. http://www.whitehouse.gov/news/releases/2001/10/20011011-7.html.

attack in Afghanistan, where Al Qaeda training camps were located, but also — such is the alchemy of affronted vainglory — a ferocious military onslaught against Iraq, which had no part in 9/11. The blind self-righteousness expressed in the President's vision of America became blind hatred when it was insulted, and emboldened him to aim the nation's military power at an extraneous target.

Three days after the 9/11 attacks, President Bush led a prayer service in Washington's National Cathedral, which might have provided an occasion to assuage the shock and grief, so as to face the challenges before us. Instead, the service kept the trauma alive by reasserting the vanity that gave rise to it. The President declared that America's mission was 'to rid the world of evil,' a single phrase that set the religious perspective of the White House response. It means that evil is incarnate in America's enemies, is wholly absent from our own character, and can be eradicated by military action. This non-feasible charter served to justify the morally indefensible and strategically self-destructive invasion of Iraq.

Yet the administration did not initiate the Iraq war in defiance of the public will. Popular support for the President stood at 86 percent following 9/11, and remained near 66 percent during the early months of the war.[9] The White House gained a measure of justification from the claim that Saddam Hussein possessed weapons of mass destruction, which collapsed when it turned out Iraq possessed no such weapons. But the leadership shifted to a new justification, claiming that our mission was not self-defense, but implanting democracy by force in an Iraq that had never known democracy. The President's public support did not then melt away. On the contrary, his claims retained enough plausibility to confound political opponents, and gain him re-election in 2004.

The prayer service at the National Cathedral summoned up the vision of America that would carry authority with the public beyond the point at which the war could be justified as self-defense. It featured two famous hymns, 'Onward Christian Soldiers' and 'America the Beautiful' which evoke the themes dominating the religious mythology at stake here. 'Onward Christian Soldiers' celebrates Christian warrior-saints prevailing in an apocalyptic

---

9. Glenn Greenwald, *A Tragic Legacy: How a Good vs. Evil Mentality Destroyed the Bush Presidency* (New York: Crown Publishers, 2007), pp. 1, 5.

crusade, in which 'the cross of Jesus' serves as a military standard leading God's chosen into the battle against evil:

> At the sign of triumph, Satan's host doth flee;
> On then Christian soldiers, on to victory![10]

Bush defined the war on terror in just such terms: 'This will be a monumental struggle of good versus evil, but good will prevail' he said on the day after 9/11.[11] And the vision of Bush as a warrior saint, leading the forces of freedom and democracy against Satanic evil, came to the center of administration rhetoric.

'America the Beautiful' evoked the sacred America that was violated on 9/11. The Big Apple, intact and splendid, was felt in retrospect as a sacred cityscape, the Statue of Liberty beckoning all who wish to live in freedom, with towering monuments of human fulfillment lining the great avenues. It was the gleaming alabaster city, to whose stainless virtue was added a myth of invulnerability.

Not since the British burned the White House in the War of 1812 had a national landmark been desecrated by foreign attack, and a repetition had long seemed unimaginable. In the late nineteenth century, as the carnage of the Civil War was fading from memory, and with no comparable rival to challenge the federal authority, Secretary of State Richard Olney declared that the 'infinite resources' of the nation 'combined with its isolated position render it...practically invulnerable.'[12] Flanked by oceans east and west, with weaker neighbors on the northern and southern borders, the nation seemed providentially secured from foreign invasion. The myth of American invulnerability was joined to a myth of American virtue, as if the nation deserved the divine favor shown it, so that the shock of 9/11 carried an implicit accusation. Ordinary Americans were haunted by the fear that our seemingly impregnable position was an illusion, that divine protection had failed.

---

10. Sabine Baring-Gould, 'Onward, Christian Soldiers,' in United Methodist Church (U.S.), *The Methodist Hymnal: Official Hymnal of the United Methodist Church* (Nashville, TN: Methodist Publishing House, 1966), p. 305.

11. George W. Bush, 'Remarks by the President in Photo Opportunity with the National Security Team', The White House News and Policies, 12 September 2001. http://www.whitehouse.gov/news/releases/2001/09/20010912-4.html.

12. Ferguson, *Colossus*, p. 42.

Judged against the White House faith, such self-doubt was anathema. There was an abundance of deceit and media manipulation in the actions through which the administration took the nation to war, but it is important to remember that these devious methods served an ardent and heartfelt piety. The administration did not invent their delusionary version of the common faith, and there is no reason to believe they invoked its classic expressions insincerely. The key players — Bush, Cheney, Rumsfeld — were thrown back on their core convictions in the trauma of the moment, and on their intuitions of the public mind. They have never imagined that the invasion of Iraq was unjust, but this does not mean they could explain their purposes openly.

* * *

Toppling the regime of Saddam Hussein was on the Bush Administration's agenda from the outset. At the first meeting of the National Security Council in January of 2001, discussion turned promptly to how Iraq is 'destabilizing the region,' so that removing Saddam would be necessary to reshaping it. CIA Director George Tenet produced a large grainy aerial photograph of an Iraqi industrial facility, saying it possibly showed a factory for the production of chemical or biological agents for use in weapons.[13]

The outline for ensuing policy was thus already visible: Hussein's regime, a force for international violence and disorder, is producing weapons of mass destruction. These claims were not new, but had been promoted by neoconservatives in the Republican right wing for several years. The Project for the New American Century had written an open letter to President Clinton in January of 1998 calling for an invasion, and Clinton shortly thereafter signed a bill making 'regime change' in Iraq a goal of US policy.

Richard Clarke, Bush's anti-terrorism advisor during his early months in the White House, raised the threat posed by Al Qaeda with Deputy Secretary of Defense Paul Wolfowitz in April of 2001, five months before the attacks. A leader among neoconservatives, Wolfowitz brushed off Clarke's concern about Bin Laden, insisting that Iraq posed a far more serious terrorist threat. Clarke retorted

---

13. Ron Suskind, *The Price of Loyalty: George W. Bush, the White House, and the Education of Paul O'Neill* (New York: Simon & Schuster, 2004), pp. 72–73.

that the intelligence community had no evidence that would support such a view.[14]

The neoconservative appraisal of Saddam Hussein had been embraced by candidates Bush and Cheney before their election. Otherwise it would not have been placed on the opening-day agenda of the NSC. But this view had been kept carefully out of sight because of the problem Richard Clarke represented. Too many people—veteran intelligence professionals and ordinary voters alike—simply wouldn't believe it.

The Project for a New American Century addressed this problem in a report issued a year before 9/11 which called for a revolutionary transformation in policy, but lamented that public support for such a change could not be summoned, 'absent some catastrophic catalyzing event—like a new Pearl Harbor.'[15]

The administration seized upon September 11 as just such a catalyst. That afternoon, after surveying the damage to the Pentagon in the late morning, Secretary of Defense Rumsfeld held a staff meeting, at which he recognized the attack might provide the sought-after opportunity to remove Saddam Hussein. As notes from the meeting indicate, Rumsfeld was aware that Osama Bin Laden's Al Qaeda was responsible. But the moment seemed promising nonetheless: 'hit S.H. [Saddam Hussein] @ same time—not only UBL [Usama Bin Laden].'[16] Later that day, President Bush made a telling entry in his diary: 'The Pearl Harbor of the 21st Century took place today.'[17]

Comparing 9/11 to Pearl Harbor 'was not an exaggeration,' wrote Bob Woodward, since in 1941 Hawaii wasn't even a state, and the enemy carrying out the 9/11 attack was a 'shadowy' presence with 'no country or visible army.'[18] This remarkable misjudgment, by so respected and seasoned an American journalist, is evidence of the spiritual trauma afflicting the nation at that time. The attacks of 9/11 were perfidious and destructive, but they didn't severely injure

14. Ron Suskind, *The One Percent Doctrine: Deep Inside America's Pursuit of its Enemies Since 9/11* (New York: Simon & Schuster, 2006), pp. 76–77.

15. Donnelly, Thomas *et al*, 'Rebuilding America's Defenses', Project for a New American Century Website, September, 2000. http://www.newamericancentury.org/RebuildingAmericasDefenses.pdf, p. 51.

16. Bob Woodward, *Plan of Attack* (New York: Simon & Schuster, 2004), p. 25.

17. Woodward, *Plan of Attack*, p. 24.

18. Woodward, *Plan of Attack*, p. 24.

the Pacific Fleet, threatening to leave the Pacific Ocean at the disposal of a Japanese imperial power that had already scored major triumphs in the Far East, and was allied with Nazi Germany, whose march of conquest had not as yet been checked.

September 11 was not a material impairment of American power. It was a symbolic affront, contradicting fantasies about America that had become articles of faith, and the Bush Administration placed this affront in the foreground as it broadcast a vision of Saddam that could be used to justify an invasion.

But at this early stage it was obvious such a vision was not yet generally accepted by the public. On Saturday, 15 September, Bush and his chief advisors met at Camp David and decided against an immediate attack on Iraq, and Vice-President Cheney put his finger on the reason why it would be unadvisable. 'If we go after Saddam Hussein,' he said, 'we lose our rightful place as good guy.'[19] The justification had yet to be assembled, Cheney recognized, and his way of putting this point signaled the vision of 'good guy' vs. 'bad guy' that would become increasingly dominant as the administration built its case, the same dichotomous vision evoked at the National Cathedral the day before as 'Christian soldiers' opposing 'Satan's hosts.' 'We won't do Iraq now,' President Bush told Condoleeza Rice on the following day; 'we're putting Iraq off.'[20]

But how could public support for such a project be generated? How could the 'Pearl Harbor' shock be translated into a willingness to remove a foreign head of state who had nothing to do with the attack? How could the invasion be sustained when it was discovered that Hussein lacked weapons of mass destruction with which to supply Al Qaeda, or any other non-state terrorist organization?

The answer was a vision of the terrorist threat that endowed Saddam with supernatural properties: capable of building and operating factories for the production of biological, chemical and nuclear materials, and for their incorporation into deliverable weapons without leaving clear-cut evidence for fly-over and satellite surveillance to spot, or for on-the-ground investigators to uncover. Hussein's terrifying dark magic also supposedly permitted him to establish a dependable working relationship with Al Qaeda, whose radical Islamic faith rendered Hussein's secular regime anathema.

19. Woodward, *Plan of Attack*, p. 25.
20. Woodward, *Plan of Attack*, p. 25.

A vision of infinite and supernatural evil made these impossible claims plausible: it is a vision incorporating biblical and theological themes, which imagines that America is hated by evildoers because it is good. 'War has been waged against us, by stealth and deceit and murder,' the President declared at the National Cathedral, 'they have attacked America because we are freedom's home and defender.'[21] Bush did not concern himself with American shortcomings, or require his government to develop policy alternatives in the light provided by some measure of self-criticism. There was nothing for Americans to learn about ourselves from the disaster, except that we'd been horribly wronged; there was no reason to inquire into social conditions abetted by our policies that might have prompted the terrorists to commit their crimes; there was no precursory failure on our part at all — not even a failure of intelligence — that needed to be faced and resolved.

In classical Christian theology Satan hates the goodness of God because it is goodness. Likewise here: the attacks were motivated by hatred of American virtues. Against this shadowy, shape-shifting cosmic evil, no evidence is necessary, no debate required: its perfidy is obvious to the eye of faith. Whether proven or unproven, the actions of the Iraqi regime did not serve, for the American leadership, as evidences of Saddam's capabilities or intentions, but as confirmations an evil nature recognized *a priori*. The public at large — represented by a substantial majority in Congress — was beguiled by this invocation of the shared mythology, and accepted its mistaken practical implication, namely that Saddam posed an unacceptable material threat.

The singing of 'Onward Christian Soldiers' at the National Cathedral was not pious window-dressing; it defined the rhetorical strategy soon to unfold. But its vision of Christian soldiers fighting the minions of hell gained political traction because Americans embraced the doctrine of 'America the Beautiful.' Ultimate realities were now in play because the sacred landscape, stretching from 'sea to shining sea' had been desecrated. The reasons for the invasion of Iraq arise in good measure from the requirements of this religious outlook, an American vision of evil implied by a specific conception of American sanctity.

21. George W. Bush, 'President's Remarks at National Day of Prayer and Remembrance', The White House News and Policies, 14 September 2001. www.whitehouse.gov/news/releases/2001/09/20010914-2.html.

America the Beautiful

Katherine Lee Bates was prompted to write 'America the Beautiful' in 1893 when she ascended Pikes Peak, after traveling by railroad to Colorado from her home in New England. Gazing eastward across the Great Plains, Bates received a powerful inspiration, and her poem testifies to a conviction nearly all Americans share, not only that America enjoys divine protection, but that the body of the nation itself is charged with divine energy.[22] Francis Scott Smith's 'My Country, Tis of Thee' likewise celebrates the landscape as a sacrament, resonating with 'sweet freedom's song.'[23] Martin Luther King's '"I Have a Dream" Speech' proclaims 'Let freedom ring!' and envisions resounding mountainsides in a panoramic sweep across the continent: 'Let freedom ring from the prodigious hilltops of New Hampshire...from the snow-capped Rockies of Colorado...from the curvaceous slopes of California.'[24] The common faith, affirmed in these classic expressions, beholds the body of the nation itself the visible sign of an invisible divine truth.

It is important to recognize that 'America the Beautiful' repeatedly emphasizes the need for ethical self-criticism. As the poem recites the nation's sacred history, each episode triggers a prayer for national reform. The 'pilgrims,' who beat a 'thoroughfare of freedom...across the wilderness,' did not impart moral perfection, but provide a model of conscience-stricken supplication: 'America, America, God mend thine ev'ry flaw; Confirm thy soul in self control, thy liberty in law!'[25]

Bates invokes the 'liberating strife' of the Civil War in order to criticize the corruptions of her own American era, the 'Gilded Age' when holders of great wealth purchased candidates for office. Bates prays that self-serving greed give way to public service and respect

22. Dorothy Whittemore Bates Burgess, *Dream and Deed; The Story of Katharine Lee Bates* (Norman, OK: University of Oklahoma Press, 1952), pp. 101–102.

23. Samuel F. Smith, 'My Country, 'Tis of Thee,' United Methodist Church (U.S.), *The Methodist Hymnal: Official Hymnal of the United Methodist Church* (Nashville, TN: Methodist Publishing House, 1966), p. 547.

24. Martin Luther King, Jr., '"I Have a Dream" Speech', U.S. Constitution Online, www.usconstitution.net/dream.html.

25. 'America the Beautiful', United Methodist Church (U.S.), *The Methodist Hymnal: Official Hymnal of the United Methodist Church* (Nashville, TN: Methodist Publishing House, 1966), p. 543.

for sacred ideals. 'May God thy gold refine,' she writes: 'Til all success be nobleness, and ev'ry gain divine!'

Bates concludes her pageant with the World's Columbian Exposition of 1893, which she had visited in Chicago on her way West. Scheduled to take place on the four hundredth anniversary of Columbus's 'discovery,' the exposition celebrated the progress of American civilization. A vast 'White City' of faux-marble buildings displayed technological and civic triumphs of AngloAmerican society, and featured performances of Buffalo Bill's Wild West, which were organized to dramatize the upward procession from the 'savage' state in which the continent was found, through the conquest of the wilderness by civilizers, to the establishment of orderly, lawful and productive communities, crowned ultimately by the White City itself. Yet Bates marks this festival of self-satisfaction as an occasion for self-critical reflection:

> Oh beautiful, for patriot's dream
> That sees beyond the years
> Thine alabaster cities gleam
> Undimmed by human tears!
> America! America! God shed his grace on thee,
> And crown thy good with brotherhood, from sea to shining sea![26]

Bates invokes the alabaster city as a transcendant ideal, lying 'beyond the years.' It was meant as a standard against which American realities should be judged, not an allusion to any actual American city, least of all—for a New Englander like Bates—New York City. The 'good' of national wealth and power was not a sufficient achievement, until 'brotherhood' crowns it.

Yet these high-minded sentiments turn us toward the dark side of Bates's vision. Notice that her moral admonitions address the way in which AngloAmericans treat one another, not other peoples and nations. Failures of 'self control,' and the 'nobleness' with which financial 'gain' should be refined into civic virtue, are moral concerns that do not apply to non-white aliens, in particular those who resist the juggernaut of American progress. Invoking an American paradise 'undimmed by human tears' did not prompt Bates to reflect on the Trail of Tears, the forced expulsion of the Cherokees in 1838.

---

26. 'America the Beautiful.'

Bates accepts the vision dramatized in Buffalo Bill's Wild West, that America's coast-to-coast empire marks the triumph of civilization and freedom over savage darkness. Blindness to the systematic injustice of this conquest is inherent to the 'America' her poem celebrates.[27]

Organized tribal resistance to AngloAmerican expansion in the West had been crushed in the decades before Bates's 1893 visit to Pikes Peak: the struggle of the Navajo and the Mescalero Apaches ended in the early 1860s, with Kit Carson starving out the Navajos in 1864 at the Canyon de Chelly. The Red River War of 1874–75 ended with the confinement of Comanches, Kiowas, Apaches, Cheyennes and Arapahos in reservations; Sitting Bull led his contingent of Lakota Sioux into submission in 1881; the Apache leader Geronimo was captured in 1886; the last of the recalcitrant Dakota and Lakota Sioux were decimated in the nightmare at Wounded Knee in 1890.[28]

Bates does not notice these morally wrenching scenes, although they were required for the achievement of an America stretching from sea to shining sea. Victory over Plains Indians, aided by the slaughter of the great buffalo herds, had been necessary to the completion of the Intercontinental Railroad in 1869, and the Northern Pacific in 1883, which enabled Bates to make her journey.[29] Bates asks God to shed his grace on an America whose 'brotherhood' does not include the tribes.

27. See Richard Slotkin, *Gunfighter Nation: The Myth of the Frontier in Twentieth-century America* (Norman, OK: University of Oklahoma Press, 1998), pp. 63–69.

28. For armed resistance to Anglo expansion see the following: Dan L. Thrapp, *The Conquest of Apacheria* (Norman, OK: University of Oklahoma Press, 1967), pp. 358–60 for Geronimo; Robert Marshall Utley, *The Indian Frontier of the American West, 1846–1890*. Histories of the American Frontier (Albuquerque, NM: University of New Mexico Press, 1984), pp. 256–61, for Wounded Knee; p. 84 for Navajos at Canyon de Chelly; pp. 174–78 for the Red River War; Robert Marshall Utley, *The Lance and the Shield: The Life and Times of Sitting Bull* (New York: Henry Holt, 1993), pp. 229–32. For a recent discussion of Cherokee Removal see Robert Vincent Remini, *Andrew Jackson & His Indian Wars* (New York: Viking, 2001).

29. For a recent discussion of the Transcontinental Railroad see Stephen E. Ambrose, *Nothing Like It in the World: The Men Who Built the Transcontinental Railroad, 1863–1869* (New York: Simon & Schuster, 2000). For the Northern Pacific see Kurt E. Armbruster, *Orphan Road: The Railroad Comes to Seattle, 1853–1911* (Pullman, WA: Washington State University Press, 1999).

As she gazed eastward from Pikes Peak—if the day was clear and she knew where to look—Bates could have spotted the site of the Sand Creek Massacre of 1864, where a volunteer Colorado militia under the command of John M. Chivington, a former Methodist preacher, attacked an encampment of old men, women and children. They were Cheyennes and Arapahos, whose fighting males were elsewhere on a hunting trip. Chivington paid no attention to the peace signals—an American flag and a white flag—prominently displayed on the lodge of the Cheyenne chief. The grotesque mutilation of the corpses, as well as the subsequent public display of body parts—including pubic scalps—shocked the nation.[30]

Bates, an English professor at Wellesley College, was doubtless well aware of this atrocity, but it becomes invisible on the American landscape she envisions. It is the 9/11 blindspot that rendered otherwise morally alert Americans incapable of imagining why other nations might harbor resentments against American projects.

'America the Beautiful' is pervaded by a fine moral sensibility, and it is possible to bring this consciousness to bear on the injustices committed by AngloAmericans against non-whites in other societies. Such a sensibility was doubtless aroused when news of Sand Creek reached Wellesley College. It is aroused today as Americans reconsider American policies overseas that inspired a terrorist blowback, to say nothing of the photographs from Abu Ghraib. But at President Bush's prayer service no such application was included. Instead 'America the Beautiful' was made to sustain the moral luxury of bypassing questions about American culpability, how injustice and oppression inherent in certain of America's overseas projects have contributed to violent hostility directed against us.

The song is all too well suited to celebrating an America that does not exist, an America that is hated, if at all, only by those who hate goodness.

Here, for George W. Bush, were the ingredients of a compelling vision: primal American innocence assaulted by supernatural malice, as visibly personified in Saddam Hussein. President Bush came to

30. See 'Sand Creek Massacre,' www.lastoftheindependents.com/sandcreek.htm and Robert Marshall Utley, *The Indian Frontier of the American West, 1846–1890.* Histories of the American Frontier (Albuquerque, NM: University of New Mexico Press, 1984), pp. 86–98 for Sand Creek.

believe that he was divinely required to unleash the fateful lightning of God's terrible swift sword, to abolish that evil from the face of the earth. As the President broadcast this vision, a substantial majority of Americans concurred.

It is important to grasp the international doctrine that is hidden within the ethical precepts of 'America the Beautiful.' It holds that God will bless America's foreign wars, if Americans meet the ethical obligations they owe one another. This deep-running tradition is likewise implicit in Buffalo Bill's pageant of civilization triumphing over savagery: AngloAmericans are God's chosen people, to whom He will provide decisive military assistance so long as they obey His law.

The attack on the World Trade Center brought to bear this powerful mythology as well, the vision of America as a 'city on a hill.' The blasphemy against America's sacred ideals refocused a set of convictions that had first been asserted in the Puritan seventeenth century, when Englishmen in the Massachusetts Bay Colony debated their sacred entitlements and their international mission. Ronald Reagan placed the classic Puritan metaphor at the heart of the rhetoric through which he inaugurated the political movement that culminated in the regime of George W. Bush.

For Reagan 'the shining city' offers a supreme standard of justice and freedom not subject to judgment by any criterion beyond itself. The Puritans by contrast considered that their 'city' was under exceptional divine scrutiny, and they differed sharply among themselves about God's appraisal of the project. The Puritan debates explore Christian justifications for the use of military force and struggle with axiomatic biblical and ethical traditions that are eclipsed by Reagan's cheerful nationalist sanctimony. The Puritan controversies illuminate fundamental religious issues at stake in the Iraq War, as well as forming a background against which to appraise the distorted White House vision of America's God-given role.

Chapter Two

Defending God's Chosen

City on a Hill

In the 1920s a college dropout from Chicago was unloading oil drums from an American vessel on the Congo River when a vision of America came to him and gave him a lifelong mission. He then went back to college to study American history.[1] Perry Miller eventually produced a shelf of scholarly books that have shaped the national soul because they provide a convincing explanation of its origins and character. Implausible as it may sound, Ronald Reagan's invocation of the 'city on a hill' would never have happened without Miller's work.

Looking back three decades later, Miller contrasted his youthful self to Edward Gibbon, who was inspired to write *The Decline and Fall of the Roman Empire* as he gazed at the concatenated ruins of two great Empires, that of Rome and of medieval Christendom. Miller was moved to study the inception of empire, not its collapse.

'Thrust upon me' Miller writes, was 'the mission of expounding what I took to be the innermost propulsion of the United States, while supervising, in that barbaric tropic, the unloading of drums of case oil flowing out of the inexhaustible wilderness of America.'[2]

In the 1920s the oil business was not a marker of America's increasing dependence on other nations. For Miller the fuel drums spoke of America's autonomous power to project its own special character worldwide; he understood that control of oil counted for more than low prices for fuel to run cars and heat homes. With the advent of mechanized warfare in the twentieth century, oil has acquired geopolitical significance of the first order. Kevin Phillips observes that petroleum has been 'the all-important fuel of American

---

1. Perry Miller, *Errand into the Wilderness* (New York: Harper, 1956), p. vii.
2. Miller, *Errand into the Wilderness*, p. viii).

global ascendancy,' much as coal sustained British hegemony in the nineteenth century.[3]

When Perry Miller was unloading the oil drums in the 1920s, roughly 10 billion barrels of oil were being discovered per year, most of it in the United States. By 2005, 5–6 billion barrels were discovered per year, while 30 billion were used up, and U.S. production had long since peaked.[4] Among U.S. interests in the Middle East today, oil is paramount, and played an unstated role in the invasion of Iraq.[5]

Miller himself understood that abundant oil reserves in America promised global dominion. 'Even then,' Miller continued, 'I could dimly make out the portent for the future of the world, looking upon these tangible symbols of the republic's appalling power.'[6] But how would that power be directed? What distinctive signature would it bear?

Miller's quest for the 'innermost propulsion of the United States' drove him to study the Puritan colony at Massachusetts Bay, and his work established that colony as the primordial America. All rival claimants to primacy have taken subordinate places— Spanish missions in the Southwest, Cavaliers in Virginia, Quakers in Pennsylvania, to say nothing of the dozens of peoples who occupied the continent before the European advent. The 'origins of the American self,' so it is commonly taught, are to be found among the English Puritans who settled on the Atlantic seaboard.[7]

At the core of the Puritan story is 'A Model of Christian Charity,' a sermon that John Winthrop preached on the deck of the Arbella, flagship to the fleet of seventeen vessels that brought the first contingent of Massachusetts Bay settlers in 1630. Winthrop defines the Puritan obligation as two-fold: first, the community is to

3. Kevin Phillips, *American Theocracy: The Peril and Politics of Radical Religion, Oil, and Borrowed Money in the 21st Century* (London: Penguin Books, 2007), p. xi.

4. Charles Weeden of Weeden & Co. cited in Phillips, *American Theocracy*, p. xxv.

5. For discussions of this issue see Chalmers Johnson, *The Sorrows of Empire: Militarism, Secrecy, and the End of the Republic* (New York: Henry Holt and Co., 2004), pp. 226–34; Joseph E. Stiglitz and Linda Bilmes, *The Three Trillion Dollar War: The True Cost of the Iraq Conflict* (New York: W.W. Norton, 2008), pp, 116–20; Andrew J. Bacevich, *The New American Militarism: How Americans are Seduced by War* (New York: Oxford University Press, 2005), pp. 175–204.

6. Miller, *Errand into the Wilderness*, p. ix.

7. For a challenge to this imputed myth of origins, see James D. Drake, *King Philip's War: Civil War in New England, 1675–1676* (Amherst, MA: University of Massachusetts Press, 1999), pp. 2–13.

establish a 'Bible Commonwealth', where God's truth and justice will prevail, and all members will fulfill their places within a shared bond of love. 'We must be willing to abridge ourselves of superfluities, for the supply of other's necessities...We must delight in each other; make others' conditions our own; rejoice together, mourne together, labor and suffer together.'[8]

Like 'America the Beautiful,' Winthrop's sermon emphasizes the justice and compassion God's people must show one another; but Winthrop is far more explicit about the linkage between these virtues and the collective mission with which God has charged them.

The primary Puritan obligation was international, taking place on a European stage amid the struggles of the Protestant Reformation. In Great Britain and across the European continent, communities within the Calvinist tradition were redefining how Christians are obliged to live, and seeking the political power required to sustain such a life against the opposition of Catholic rulers. English Puritans had been at odds with the Church of England, which attempted to blend reformation ideals with Roman Catholic practices. Puritans intended that the exemplary community in New England, living strictly in accordance with biblical precepts, would provide an inspiration to the international effort and a model for others to follow. This would happen if, but only if, the community remained faithful to the ethical duties God had set forth to govern their life together.

Winthrop sounded the warning. Should the lust of wealth and power supplant Christian virtue, terrible punishment would follow. If we 'shall embrace this present world and prosecute our carnal intentions, seeking great things for ourselves and our posterity, the Lord will surely break out in wrath against us.'[9] The Puritan community would then become a notorious disgrace for other nations to despise, not a model for them to follow.

> For we must consider that we shall be as a city upon a hill. The eyes of all people are upon us. So that if we shall deal falsely with our God in this work we have undertaken, and so cause him to withdraw his present help from us, we shall be made a story and a by-word through the world.[10]

8. John Winthrop, 'A Model of Christian Charity', http://history.hanover.edu/texts/winthmod.html, p. 12.
9. Winthrop, 'A Model of Christian Charity', p. 11.
10. Winthrop, 'A Model of Christian Charity', p. 12.

As though foretelling the disgust that Bush's America awakened in conscientious and loyal Americans, and in friends of democratic freedom around the world, Winthrop declared that moral failure will 'shame the faces of many of God's worthy servants, and cause their prayers to be turned into curses upon us.'[11]

The long-range carrying power of Winthrop's language in American political discourse results from circumstances no Puritan could foresee. The failure of the Puritan Revolution in England meant that the Church of England's elaborate system of compromise would prevail. No longer would reformist Protestants abroad search for models to guide a root-and-branch restructuring of national religious life. 'Having failed to rivet the eyes of the world upon their city on the hill,' Miller comments, the Puritans 'were left alone with America.'[12]

The Puritans could likewise not foresee that English-speaking peoples on the American continent would eventually exercise the 'appalling power' that the United States attained in Perry Miller's lifetime three centuries later. Having been forced to the margins of international life, the Puritans inaugurated an American story that would give prophetic force to their earliest dreams. The Puritans saw their own mission as the fulfillment of an ancient biblical promise, in which God chose a nation—alone from all the peoples of the earth—to be his very own.

The moral arrogance and blindness of the Bush Administration were rooted in exactly this doctrine. Believing their enterprises were authorized by God, the Massachusetts Puritans believed that God's devastating wrath would fall upon any who threatened the community from without, or obstructed its God-ordained expansion, and further believed that the Puritans themselves would serve as agents of that wrath.

Alternative Cities

From its origins, Christianity has defined itself as the fulfillment of God's promise to Abraham, that his descendants would be God's chosen people, destined to occupy a 'promised land.' Calling Jesus 'Christ', or 'Messiah', means that he is 'anointed', as kings were

---

11. Winthrop, 'A Model of Christian Charity', p. 12.
12. Miller, *Errand into the Wilderness*, p. 15.

anointed in ancient Israel, and thus designates him as the savior that the people of Israel envisioned when they passed under foreign rule. Jesus was born in Palestine during a period of recurrent peasant revolts against Roman oppression, and the movement he led was perceived by the Romans as yet another outbreak of resistance.[13] The rebellious Jews lacked the military resources necessary to expel the Romans, yet early Christian believers claimed Jesus as the 'Messiah' nonetheless. Some relinquished the dream of a political restoration, and others counted on the fulfillment prophesied in the Book of Revelation, that Jesus would return equipped with supernatural deadly force, to overturn the Romans and establish an everlasting kingdom for the faithful.

The Massachusetts Bay Puritans conceived themselves as God's chosen—Christian inheritors of God's covenant with Abraham—and visualized the place of their new world settlement as the 'promised land.' Just as ancient Israel was liberated by God from Egyptian bondage, taken into a covenant at Mount Sinai, and led through the desert to their appointed land, so the Puritans had escaped Anglican piety under a Catholic monarch, had passed through the wilderness of waters, and now sought to live out the covenant in the land God had prepared for them. But a disagreement soon erupted about the meaning of this shared faith, and the justification it provided for the use of armed force.

Roger Williams was banished from Massachusetts Bay after he challenged the colony's governing authority on two critical points. He denied that the English had an inherent legal right to occupy the 'promised land', instead of obtaining that right in fair negotiations with Americans—Narragansetts, Mohegans, Wampanoags, and Pequots—who occupied it before they arrived. Christians had inherited God's covenant with Israel only in a spiritual sense, Williams argued, as a standard of Christian spirituality and collective life. There was no unbroken transmission of divine authority from ancient Israel to Massachusetts, giving the

---

13. For discussions of this context see Richard A. Horsley, *Jesus and the Spiral of Violence: Popular Jewish Resistance in Roman Palestine* (Minneapolis, MN: Fortress Press, 1993); Richard A. Horsley and John S. Hanson, *Bandits, Prophets & Messiahs: Popular Movements in the Time of Jesus* (Harrisburg, PA: Trinity Press International, 1985); John Dominic Crossan, *The Historical Jesus: The Life of a Mediterranean Jewish Peasant* (New York: HarperCollins, 1991).

government in Boston a pre-emptive right to use force against the resident tribes. On the same ground Williams claimed that the government of the colony had no right to force conformity with orthodox belief by making dissent a crime.

'Williams was not merely a social nuisance,' Miller observes, 'but a real danger to the very structure of [Puritan] society. Any government in its right mind would and should exterminate him.'[14] How was the 'city on a hill' to live in strict obedience to God's law, if it had no power to enforce that law? Belief in the Puritans' status as God's chosen people becomes a poetic figment, not a political fact, absent a legitimate and enforceable claim to land. The Puritan claim, backed by the authority of God, must extinguish alternative claims, including those of prior inhabitants. In practice the Massachusetts Bay Puritans did not at first exercise this pre-emptive right, but entered into various treaties and alliances while holding their ultimate entitlement in reserve.

The banished Williams lived out his debate with the Boston leadership from his exile in the Rhode Island colony, which he founded on land that he purchased from the Narragansetts and where freedom of conscience was guaranteed.

Williams established Providence—an alternative city on a hill, with an alternative vision of the proper relation between religious doctrine and state power. Williams's teachings on freedom of religion were incorporated into the United States constitution and carry authority today. On the pre-emptive claims of the English to lands occupied by American tribes, Williams's vision survives as a vital tradition of opposition, challenging a long history of expropriation by force.

The man who pronounced the sentence of banishment against Williams was himself subsequently condemned by the Bay Colony, and expressed his gratitude for Williams's alternative city: 'the most wise God hath provided [Providence] as a refuge and receptacle for all sorts of consciences.'[15] As conflict with the tribes forced the Bay Puritans to live out the military implications of their creed, this

14. Perry Miller, 'Roger Williams, An Essay in Interpretation,' in Roger Williams, *The Complete Writings of Roger Williams*, (7 vols; New York: Russell and Russell, 1963), vol. 7, p. 8.

15. Roger Williams, 'To Major [John] Mason, June 22, 1670' in 'Letters of Roger Williams' in J. Hammond Trumbull (ed.), *The Complete Writings of Roger Williams* (7 vols; New York: Russell and Russell, 1963), vol. 6, p. 345.

accolade concerning religious freedom revealed its broader meanings. Providence became a refuge for Christians who could not accept the atrocities perpetrated by the Massachusetts Bay Puritans, and rejected the religious justifications provided for it.

Amalek

The writers of the Hebrew Bible understood that a god who promises exclusive title to land must equip the children of promise to remove rival claimants — the not-chosen — by force. God's covenant with Moses included His agreement to meet this responsibility: 'I will drive out before you the Amorites, the Canaanites, the Hittites, the Perizzites, the Hivites, and the Jebusites'(Exod. 34:11).[16]

Maintaining a sovereignty — whether a tribal alliance, a Bible Commonwealth, or a modern nation — entails meeting security requirements. If hostile military action cannot be countered by negotiation, it must be answered in kind. Whether the chosen people initiate such action or respond defensively, divine authority justifies the large-scale killing that follows.

Biblical teachings about God's love and forgiveness implicitly condemn the horrors of war. The Hebrew Bible speaks of God's tenderness toward strangers and sojourners in the land; the Book of Jonah, like the Book of Ruth, portrays divine compassion for those not among the chosen. Jesus is likewise famous for the injunction to 'love your enemies,' quoted in Winthrop's sermon, a maxim impossible to reconcile with slaughtering them. In Christian communities these conflicting features of biblical teaching live uneasily with one another, so that pious accounts typically conceal the carnage of warfare.

Winthrop's sermon touches obliquely on this uncomfortable issue. Warning that God's covenant with the Massachusetts Bay settlers is especially strict, Winthrop makes a biblical allusion that modern readers are unlikely to catch, which captures the chronic distress about faithfulness and slaughter. It's an allusion that came to haunt

16. *The Holy Bible. RSV, containing the Old and New Testaments. Translated from the original tongues, being the version set forth A.D. 1611, revised A.D. 1881–1885 and A.D. 1901; compared with the most ancient authorities and revised A.D. 1952* (New York: Thomas Nelson, 1953).

the imagination of the Puritans, becoming code language for the horrific violence they deployed against the 'not-chosen'.

Here are Winthrop's words:

> When God gives a special commission he looks to have it strictly observed in every article. When he gave Saul a commission to destroy Amalek, He indented with him upon certain articles, and because [Saul] failed in one of the least, and that upon a fair pretense, it lost him the kingdom, which should have been his reward, if he had observed his commission.[17]

Winthrop relies on his listeners' knowledge of 'Amalek,' shying away from the grisly particulars.

The Amalekites were a tribe that opposed the entrance of the Israelites into the promised land, and King Saul's commission was to 'utterly destroy all that they have; do not spare them, but kill both man and woman, infant and suckling, ox and sheep, camel and ass' (1 Sam. 15:3). Saul performed this task, except he spared Agag, the king of the Amalekites; and he also permitted his soldiers to spare the best of the livestock. This seems provisionally forgivable to Winthrop, because the livestock was kept alive for use in a formal sacrifice, at the ceremonial center in Gilgal.

Samuel, the priest at Gilgal who had conveyed God's commission to Saul in the first place, now conveyed the divine rebuke: 'because you have rejected the word of the Lord, he has also rejected you from being king'(1 Sam. 15:23). Then Samuel called for Agag to be brought to him, and Agag came along 'cheerfully,' thinking 'surely the bitterness of death is past,' whereupon Samuel 'hewed Agag in pieces before the Lord in Gilgal' (1 Sam. 15: 32–33).

The God who chose the Israelites, and promised them a land of their own, orders the total annihilation of a people already in residence, and his chief priest brings the atrocity to a climax with human sacrifice: Agag dismembered before the Lord in place of the oxen, sheep and lambs.

Winthrop invoked this story as a warning to the Puritan leadership: God is always poised to unleash a merciless assault against any who displease him, typically at the moment least expected, when the impious — like Agag — are filled with cheerful self-confidence.

---

17. Winthrop, 'A Model of Christian Charity', p. 11.

In his epic history of New England, the *Wonder-Working Providence of Sion's Saviour* (1654), Edward Johnson characterizes the Puritans as the army of Christ, fighting to throw off 'their long servitude' to Roman Catholics. Their oppressors, in keeping with the established narrative, make the mistake of scorning the Puritans' 'low condition, little number, and remoteness of place' only to have the Lord Christ bring 'sudden and unexpected destruction upon them.'[18] Christians have nothing to fear if they are underdogs, Johnson teaches. The faithful sailing for the American 'wilderness' will be 'landed among barbarous Indians, famous for nothing but their cruelty.' But they can take inspiration from Christ's ultimate victory against the assembled might of every godless polity on earth, when he comes again 'to destroy Antichrist and give the whore double to drink the very dregs of his wrath.'[19]

Fear of God's explosive fury may have haunted the consciences of Puritan leaders, but it also entitled them to massacre those they visualized as 'Antichrist' or the 'Whore of Babylon.' This doctrine may seem archaic, very remote from American foreign policy in the twenty-first century. But its terms are clearly audible in exhortations that had a powerful influence in the Bush White House. 'Our government has the right,' said Jerry Falwell, 'to bring wrath upon those who would do evil.'[20]

Winthrop recognized that the Puritan community could not survive without military force; the Arbella itself was equipped with 28 great guns. Yet Winthrop also counted on the military assistance that Christ would provide if His Puritan warriors were found worthy. If 'we keep the unity of the spirit in the bond of peace' his shipboard sermon declares, 'we shall find that the God of Israel is among us, when ten of us shall be able to resist a thousand of our enemies.'[21]

Such hopes were put to the test in 1637, when Massachusetts Bay and the Connecticut Colony joined forces to confront the Pequots, who had resisted encroachments on their territories.

18. Edward Johnson, 'Wonder-Working Providence of Sion's Saviour in New England (selection) in James E. Miller, Jr, (ed.), *Heritage of American Literature*, (2 vols; New York: Harcourt Brace, 1991), vol. 1, pp. 109–14, (p. 110).

19. Johnson, 'Wonder-Working Providence', p. 113.

20. Jerry Falwell, *Listen, America* (New York: Bantam, 1981), p. 85.

21. Winthrop, 'A Model of Christian Charity', p. 12.

Major John Mason described the Pequots as 'a great people, being strongly fortified, cruel, warlike, munitioned, and the English but a handful in comparison.' Mason accuses the Pequots of 'outrageous violence' and of promoting a 'quarrel against the English, who had never offered them the least wrong.'[22]

The Puritans were greatly alarmed when they learned that the Pequot leadership was negotiating an alliance with the Narragansetts, and appealed to Roger Williams for assistance. Soon after his arrival in New England, Williams had cultivated a sympathetic interest in the local tribes, and had schooled himself in their language. He lived with the Narragansetts during his midwinter flight from the Bay colony to Rhode Island, and it is unlikely he would have survived the ordeal without their aid. Yet, he was appalled by the revenges taken by Pequots against Connecticut settlers, and found it alarming 'to lodge and mix with the bloody Pequot ambassadors, whose hands and arms reeked with the blood of my countrymen.'[23]

Williams succeeded in bringing the Narragansetts and the Mohegans into alliance with the Puritans, which fundamentally shifted the balance of force. Yet for the Puritans at this crisis, the heart of the Pequot trouble lay elsewhere. It lay in their relation to God. Were they to be expelled from the land that God had marked out for His covenant community? Or was their virtue sufficient to merit divine aid? 'Blessed be the Lord God of Israel,' Mason exulted when victory had been achieved. 'The Lord was pleased to smite our enemies...and to give us their land for an inheritance.'[24]

The decisive moment in the struggle came when the English exterminated the inhabitants of the Pequot fort at Mystic River, including women and children. The English attacked just before dawn, and soon found it frustrating to fight the warriors amid the closely packed dwellings within the palisade, whereupon Mason determined that 'we must burn them; and immediately stepping into the wigwam...brought out a firebrand, and...set the wigwams

---

22. John Mason, *A Brief History of the Pequot War: Some Grounds of the War Against the Pequots*, (2 pages), Humanities Web Website, (http://www.humanitiesweb.org/human.php?s=n&p=l&ID=20) p. 2.

23. Williams, 'To Major [John] Mason, June 22, 1670', p. 338.

24. John Mason, *A Brief History of the Pequot War: An Epitome or Brief History of the Pequot War*, (15 pages), Humanities Web Website, (http://www.humanitiesweb.org/human.php?s=n&p=l&ID=20) p. 2.

on fire.' The fire being set to windward, the flames did 'swiftly over-run the Fort, to the extreme amazement of the Enemy, and the great rejoicing of our selves.'[25]

Mason now ordered his soldiers, as well as Narragansett and Mohegan allies, to disengage and surround the fort, so as to shoot down any who tried to escape the inferno. 'Thus were they now at their wits end,' Mason wrote, 'who not many hours before exalted themselves...But God was above them, who laughed his enemies and the enemies of his people to scorn, making them as a fiery oven.'[26] Pequots who managed to flee were captured by the Puritans for execution or enslavement. In the subsequent military operations against what remained of the tribe elsewhere, the Pequots' sovereignty was terminated.[27]

Devout Christian souls in Massachusetts and in England were troubled by the stories of burning women and children, and the leaders were pressed to explain. William Bradford viewed it as a human sacrifice, like that of Agag.

> It was a fearful sight to see them thus frying in the fire...and horrible was the stink and scent thereof; but the victory seemed a sweet sacrifice, and they [the English fighters] gave the praise thereof to God.[28]

John Underhill, the commander from Massachusetts Bay, likewise faced the dilemma of God's agents obliterating an entire community. 'Why should you be so furious? (as some have said). Should not Christians have more mercy and compassion?' Yet Underhill insisted that the biblical accounts of clearing the promised land offered sufficient justification. 'I would refer you to David's war,' he declared.

> When a people is grown to such a height of blood and sin against God...He hath no respects to persons, but harrows them and saws them, and puts them...to the most terriblest death that may be. Sometimes the Scripture declareth women and children must perish with their parents...We had sufficient light from the word of God for our proceedings.[29]

25. Mason, *A Brief History of the Pequot War: An Epitome*, p. 6.

26. Mason, *A Brief History of the Pequot War: An Epitome*, p. 7.

27. Alfred A. Cave, *The Pequot War* (Amherst, MA: University of Massachusetts Press: 1996), pp. 144–51 discusses the attack in detail.

28. Neal Salisbury, *Manitou and Providence: Indians, Europeans, and the Making of New England, 1500–1643* (New York: Oxford University Press, 1982), p. 224.

29. Salisbury, *Manitou and Providence*, p. 222.

The Hebrew Bible, like the Christian Bible, does not speak with a single voice; but the scriptures contain a powerful tradition supporting Underhill's claim. The familiar biblical formulation 'Lord God of Hosts' does not allude only to hosts of angels, but to ranks of soldiers and chariots, the military hosts with which ancient near eastern peoples fought their wars. The 'Song of Moses', in Exodus 15, marks the formation of the chosen people, enabled to escape from bondage in Egypt because God destroys the pursuing Egyptian army. 'The Lord is a man of war,' proclaims the culminating verse (Exod. 15:3).

The writers of the New Testament did not bear responsibility for the survival of a political community, and had no access to military force. But the author of Revelation envisioned the military triumph of the resurrected Christ, a victory heralded by mystical figures of divine war making, who wield the power to kill with sword, famine and pestilence (Rev. 6:7). These passages provide support for Christians who see the invasion of Iraq as God's vengeance against evil.

For Roger Williams, the destruction of the Pequots did not demonstrate God's goodness toward His people, but the Puritans' abandonment of God in preference for an idol of material self-indulgence. 'However you satisfy yourselves with the Pequot conquest,' he writes to Major John Mason,

> yet upon a due and serious examination of the matter, in the sight of God, you will find the business at bottom to be…a depraved appetite after the great vanities, dreams and shadows of this vanishing life, great portions of land, land in this wilderness…This is one of the gods of New England, which the living and most high Eternal will destroy and famish.[30]

These words echo Winthrop's shipboard sermon, where the 'city on a hill' would face divine wrath, if Puritans abandoned their Christian obligations, so as to 'embrace this present world and prosecute our carnal intentions, seeking great things for ourselves and our posterity.'[31]

Because of the mystical and biblical associations surrounding 'land,' it is easy for people of our own day to miss the fact that for Puritan farmers it was a prime economic resource. The wealth

---

30. Williams, 'To Major [John] Mason, June 22, 1670', p. 342.
31. Winthrop, 'A Model of Christian Charity', p. 11.

produced from land ramified through the entire seaboard economy, much as the wealth represented by petroleum ramifies today, a force so all-pervasive as to become virtually invisible until the supply falls short.

Yet to Williams, it seemed 'a prodigy or monster' that Christian people should fall victim to their materialist cravings, making war to serve greed. 'What are these leaves and flowers, and smoke and shadows, and dreams of earthly nothings…Alas, and what is all the scuffling of this world for?'.[32]

Williams had aided the Boston Puritans in their conflict with the Pequots, but he did not see the war as a triumph of divine vengeance, and he repudiated the claim that the Amalek legend justified the slaughter at Mystic Fort.[33] Like most wars, Williams believed, it resulted from a shameful spiritual and moral failing. 'All the contentions and wars of this world,' he declared are 'generally but for greater dishes and bowls of porridge,' for which Christians all too eagerly sell the abundant life that faithful service can provide, even if economic resources are small.[34]

Williams visualized the Rhode Island colony as a city remaining faithful to the calling that Massachusetts Bay had defiled:

> the matter with us is not about these children's toys of land, meadows, cattle, government & c. But here, all over this colony, a great number of weak and distressed souls, scattered, are flying hither from Old and New England. The most high and only wise [God] hath, in his infinite wisdom, provided this country and this corner as a shelter for the poor and persecuted, according to their several persuasions.[35]

Soon after he wrote these words Williams was pressed into service to forestall a dangerous new conflict between the Puritans and the tribes. Yet his efforts were unavailing, and he concluded sadly that 'it is not possible to keep peace with these barbarous men of blood.'[36] The ensuing 'King Philip's War' was a major crisis for the Puritan community, potentially a fulfillment of William's prophecy that the Eternal would 'destroy and famish' self-styled Christians who

---

32. Williams, 'To Major [John] Mason, June 22, 1670', p. 343.
33. Cave, *The Pequot War*, p. 159.
34. Williams, 'To Major [John] Mason, June 22, 1670', p. 343.
35. Williams, 'To Major [John] Mason, June 22, 1670', p. 344.
36. Edwin S. Gaustad, *Roger Williams: Prophet of Liberty*, Oxford Portraits (New York: Oxford University Press, 2001), p. 53.

worshipped the 'smoke and shadows' of transitory wealth. Williams himself was not spared: the town of Providence was burned, including Williams's own house, and he was reduced to depending on his son for support.

Williams was no utopian; he was prepared to recognize that armed conflict was at times necessary. But this does not mean that he adopted the dominant theory, that Christians had a right to visit God's judgment on enemies of His chosen people, and that victory in war showed that God Himself had joined the battle, because His people had proved worthy of His aid.

King Philip's War inspired a new religious vision in Massachusetts Bay to justify the English use of force, a mythology given classic expression in the story of an English woman who lived among the Narragansetts as their captive. Williams's view stands out clearly against this evolving tradition of divinely authorized war-making, and is based on a closer and more knowledgeable relationship with the Narragansetts.

Before pursuing those issues, however, it will be useful to sketch the two versions of the 'city on a hill' that are at stake in the disagreement between Williams and Massachusetts Bay.

In the Massachusetts Bay version, the city serves as a bastion for those showing their Chosenness by conforming their minds and consciences to the edicts of the religious authorities. In exchange for relinquishing their moral autonomy they are given freedom to expand their wealth at the expense of the not-Chosen.

Roger Williams by contrast envisioned a city which provides for those who want freedom of conscience in ordering their own lives, keeping just and equitable relations with their neighbors among the tribes, as among the English. Members of the community bear an obligation to bring their best estimate of the divine will into a collective debate about community policies.

Williams's city is exemplary, exerting influence on other communities because its way of living is visible at a distance—the original meaning that Winthrop rightly saw in the biblical passage about the city on a hill. The Massachusetts Bay city focuses on its adherence to a prescriptive righteousness, and its pre-emptive claim to land, and becomes a launching pad for predation, as authorized by the God who has chosen them, and backed by the promise of that God to amplify the military power required.

The Massachusetts Bay version, despite its biblical origins and its impact on America's sense of national destiny, is a religious delusion. It is untrue that G*d has granted any community a pre-emptive right to economic resources possessed by others, or that the success of the community making such a claim results from military assistance from on high. The Williams version, by contrast, is as realistic as the efforts of the faithful can make it, sometimes requiring the use of military power, but never as God's wrath visiting divine punishment on behalf of his chosen. God's judgment, for Williams, falls on both parties to every conflict, and finds virtue and wickedness on both sides. Williams did not hold that enemies who join in armed conflict are equally culpable, or that doing battle cannot be justified: but neither combatant is free of injustice, and fit to qualify as an instrument of God's righteousness.

The conflict between these two versions of the city has been revived in our own time. It is echoed in the dispute between Ronald Reagan and Jimmy Carter, as we shall see, when Carter argued for the economic sacrifices necessary to end America's dependence on foreign oil, which Reagan succeeded in branding 'gloom and doom.' Crucial support for the Bush Administration, moreover, came from a group of religious leaders who aspired to the status of the Massachusetts Bay theocrats. Jerry Falwell's appraisal of the American moral failings that invited the 9/11 attack ignores the shortcomings of American foreign policy, and focuses instead on lifestyle issues: 'the abortionists, and the feminists, and the gays and the lesbians' had aroused God's displeasure, so that he allowed the forces of evil to penetrate the shield God had erected to keep America safe. Falwell also blamed the American Civil Liberties Union, marking his clear opposition to the views of Roger Williams.[37]

Falwell's remarks seemed wildly irrational to many mainstream Americans, and he quickly retracted them. But his thinking fit perfectly within the classic paradigm: as God's chosen people, Americans enjoy divine favor and gain the hatred of infidels. God offers protection from foreign attack, but only so long as Americans obey His law in their relations with one other. When His indignation is aroused by flagrant immoralities, God revokes the protection and 'allows' the minions of Satan to have their way with us.

---

37. John F. Harris, 'God Gave U.S. "What We Deserve," Falwell Says', *The Washington Post*, 14 September 2001.

The restoration of God's favor, by this logic, renews the national right to the assets controlled by the not-chosen. But restoration is in doubt until the community has been tried in battle. The decision to invade Iraq, and the manner in which the war was waged, rested on the religious vision that the Massachusetts Bay Puritans worked out in their relation to the American tribes, especially as they confronted the threat of complete destruction.

Chapter Three

LIMITLESS DIVINE SANCTION

Land of Promise

The Pequot War was not a war of conquest initiated by the governments of the Connecticut or Massachusetts Bay Colonies. Settlers at the edges of those colonies, together with Dutch settlers, made their way incrementally and often without explicit official authorization into territories that the Pequots held, and the Pequots sought to discourage this by similarly incremental reprisals. This pattern of mounting local conflict, resolved by a crushing armed response from the white community, was to be repeated across the continent during the Anglo-American expansion that reached the Pacific in the 1840s and was completed in the 1880s. Likewise prophetic was the fact that kidnappings, killings and house-burnings inflicted by the Pequots seemed like wanton unprovoked atrocities to the English, who believed that their economic expansion followed from doing God's will.

In addition to devout attendance on public and private worship, Englishmen labored in their divinely appointed callings. They built dwellings, cleared the land of rocks and trees, prepared the soil for planting, sowed and harvested; they set up as blacksmiths, wheelwrights, and shoemakers. Woodland trails became thoroughfares threading outward from the seaports, as the faithful carried articles for trade to the hinterland, or sought timber for construction in the towns, or for export to shipbuilding centers in England. Puritan traders also acquired furs and tobacco for the domestic market and for export.

The prosperity that resulted from these enterprises was taken as a sign of God's favor, and Winthrop's Arbella sermon set out the definition of 'charity' under which Englishmen were to retain that favor by sharing the proceeds equitably amongst themselves, refraining from the accumulation of great wealth in the face of poverty suffered by fellow-Puritans. In addition to aiding the unfortunate, successful Puritans were enjoined to devote their profits not to ostentatious display, but to the enterprises that had produced them. They were early exemplars of the Protestant Ethic, an ethos of personal self-denial and capitalist re-investment, in which economic expansion is intimately intertwined with obedience to God's law.

As they pursued their opportunities the English made use of agricultural skills, organizational capacities, and access to profitable overseas markets. These generated a larger food supply, and supported larger populations, than the American tribes had ever been able to sustain. 'The whole earth is the lord's garden,' Winthrop observed,

> & he hath given it to the sonnes of men, with a generall Condicion, Gen: 1:28. Increase & multiply, replenish the earth & subdue it…Why then should we stand hear striveing for places of habitation…and in ye mean tyme suffer a whole Continent, as fruitfull & convenient for the use of man to lie waste without any improvement.[1]

Winthrop's vision of the whole earth as the Lord's garden marks a fundamental shift of doctrine, which was incorporated into the American sense of chosenness, and the Puritan appraisal of economic success.

As they began to reckon more directly with the land before them, the Puritans came to think of themselves not as Englishmen, seeking to remake English society, but as 'Americans.' They came to see 'the city on the hill' not only as a conspicuous location for their divine experiment, but also as a staging ground for dynamic expansion westward. The 'promised land' now became the 'land of promise,' God's chosen people vindicating their claim to the territory not only because God wanted them to build a model community, but through the fruits of their labor in the workaday callings to which God had appointed them. They had a right to the land, because they could make the most of it; they could 'improve' the garden that God had provided, which was otherwise going to waste.

As this tenet of the national faith evolved, the ideal of freedom developed new meanings. Finding freedom from Anglican rule, or from theocratic oppression in Massachusetts Bay, invoked a limited

---

1. Walter A. McDougall, *Promised Land, Crusader State: The American Encounter With the World Since 1776* (Boston, MA: Houghton Mifflin, 1997), p. 83.

charter of divine sanction, enough to underwrite a new colony. The God-given right to a 'land of promise' authorized a far more expansive conception of freedom. If the chosen people are entitled to exploit the land without hindrance from the not-chosen, their freedom depends on removing those hindrances, if necessary by force.

Winthrop's language places no geographic limit on Puritan expansion. Winthrop never dreamed of the actual wealth and extent of 'the whole Continent,' but his conception of Puritan entitlement foreshadows the doctrine of Manifest Destiny under which Anglo-American dominion was extended to the Pacific in the nineteenth century, at the expense of the peoples who occupied it when the Puritans arrived. Winthrop's invocation of 'the whole earth' is likewise prophetic, foretelling the enlargement of this doctrine to its current global extent.

By Roger Williams's standard of judgment, this shift in the outlook of the Massachusetts Bay colonists magnified their primary failing. Not only were they possessed by a 'depraved appetite after the great vanities, dreams and shadows of this vanishing life,'[2] they fatally exaggerated the divine commission that sponsored economic expansion. The Massachusetts Bay version of the Protestant Ethic viewed resident tribes who obstructed their ambitions as fit for destruction. Christian faith was now to justify warfare in the service of expanding economic interests, with no limits imposed by the claims of the original Americans. Perry Miller was right to see Massachusetts Bay, not Roger Williams and his enclave, as establishing the vision of America that would yield 'appalling power' in the twentieth century.

As Eric Hobsbawm notes, America's contemporary overseas empire draws its character from the processes of continental expansion.[3] America establishes no permanent settlements abroad, except in the limited form of military bases, nor does our nation assert legal sovereignty over foreign lands, or accept the administrative responsibilities of direct rule. Young men in American colleges, as Niall Ferguson laments, do not train to become colonial

---

2. Roger Williams, *The Complete Writings of Roger Williams* (7 vols; New York: Russell & Russell, 1963), vol 6, p. 342.

3. E. J. Hobsbawm, *On Empire: America, War, and Global Supremacy* (New York: Pantheon Books, 2008), p. 73.

administrators.[4] These realities give credibility to the claim, often repeated by George W. Bush, that America has no empire.

The underlying truth is abundantly illustrated in Walter Nugent's *Habits of Empire*, which discusses three phases of American empire-building. Nugent shows that the overseas acquisitions of the late nineteenth century, like the project of globalization that followed World War II, enlarge upon the massive enterprise of continental expansion that was initiated in the late eighteenth century and completed by 1850. 'The habit-forming imperialism of pre-Civil War days' may not be familiar to contemporary Americans, Nugent writes, but it was momentous for the nation's subsequent history.[5] Building a continental empire became the model for America's exercise of global power.

If other nations possess resources that are 'fruitful and convenient' for the use of Americans, and which Americans can employ better than they, American corporations inherently represent 'freedom' when they operate overseas to exploit those resources. They need not trouble themselves whether the government of the host nation enjoys the consent of the governed. Such corporations expect to receive the support of the United States government if democratic movements in the host country threaten their activities, and this too is represented as the defense of 'freedom.' Because America is God's chosen nation, as that doctrine evolved in Massachusetts Bay, American 'free enterprise' is a God-given right, and it trumps claims of freedom that are grounded in the practice of democratic governance.

The Book of Joshua (1:4) appears to place firm geographical limits on the 'promised land,' beyond which the chosen people are never to trespass, but the nineteenth-century transfer of that doctrine to the American continent wipes away any limits the scripture may imply. An ideology supporting global dominion is thus implicit in the core doctrines of the Massachusetts Bay colony, providing not only the permission to acquire resources controlled by other communities, but a religious entitlement that functions today as a potent article of popular faith. 'What is our oil doing under their sand?' asks the sardonic Texas bumper sticker.

4. See Hobsbawm, *On Empire*, p. 74 and Niall Ferguson, *Colossus: The Rise and Fall of the American Empire* (New York: Penguin Books, 2004), p. xx.

5. Walter Nugent, *Habits of Empire: A History of American Expansion* (New York: Alfred A. Knopf, 2008), pp. xv–xvi.

For this ideological system to be persuasive, however, it must succeed in rendering invisible the aggression implicit in the enterprises of God's chosen, as they make demands on other nations and seek access to their resources. To Roger Williams this aggression was obvious following the war against the Pequots, however dimly the Massachusetts Bay Puritans may have perceived it. Four decades later, in 1675, the English were given further evidence of tribal resentment, a massive insurrection that threatened the survival of the Puritan community and forced a redefinition of its place in the American wilderness.

The myth of the 'western frontier' was born in the ensuing war. After the war, the Puritans no longer mingled with resident tribes in a bi-cultural civil community; on the contrary, they now envisioned themselves living behind a contested boundary, against which their expansive enterprises necessarily pressed. Beyond that boundary lay a huge domain of recalcitrant savagery. The menace of this situation was likewise absorbed into an elaborate new mythology, with the English project taking the form of a helpless captive woman.

Wine of Astonishment

The tribes making up the rebel confederation shared the Algonquian language, and were bound together by ties of kinship. These groups chronically fought each other, sometimes in alliance with Puritans. Mohegans and Narragansetts, for example, aided Underhill and Mason in fighting the Pequots, and their horror at the Mystic slaughter contributed to the gathering conviction that if conflict with the Puritans seemed imminent, tribal groups must decisively choose sides.[6]

Complex scheming and shifting alliances preceded the emerging coalition. Accustomed to vying with each other for advantage, the tribes had entered into treaties with Puritan communities, who likewise competed among themselves to obtain tribal concessions.

---

6. James D. Drake, *King Philip's War: Civil War in New England, 1675–1676* (Amherst, MA: University of Massachusetts Press, 1999), argues cogently that this conflict had a 'civil war' dimension, with tribal groups offering military support to the English. No English group, as Drake notes on p. 78, intervened militarily on behalf of the tribes. Drake demonstrates conclusively that the actual texture of the conflict was incomparably more complex than the Christian doctrines that were projected into it.

The insurrection was ignited by a quarrel between the Plymouth Colony and the Wampanoags, culminating on 20 June 1675 when Metacom, the Wampanoag leader, attacked the Puritan town of Swansea.[7] Over the next months tribal groups determined how they should respond, now that a major conflict with the English was in the offing, and by October the Puritans found themselves at war with a coalition in which the Wampanoags were joined by Nipmucks, Agawams, and Narragansetts. Puritan towns across the region came under attack.[8]

The English were taken off guard. Enthralled by the doctrines that made their economic expansion virtuous in their own eyes, they were blind to its impact on the tribes. They were astonished — much like modern-day Americans — by the blowback.

The Puritans referred to Metacom as 'King Philip,' and 'King Philip's War' remains the accepted name for the conflict that followed, which nearly succeeded in uprooting the Bible Commonwealth altogether. Half of the Puritan communities were wrecked if not destroyed outright; colonial treasuries were virtually exhausted; seaborne trade was halted; one eighth of the white population was killed in battle, or killed on their farmsteads, or died of starvation and exposure. Substantial numbers of women and children were taken into captivity. In proportion to the twenty-first century U.S. population of some 300 million, this was tantamount to a loss of 37 million citizens. But the impact on Puritan New England was substantially greater, Richard Slotkin writes, because of its small size. The war 'posed a real threat to the colony's continued prosperity, perhaps even to its survival.'[9]

Never since King Philip's War has the tenure of God's Chosen on the American Promised Land stood in greater danger, but the English eventually prevailed against the tribal coalition, destroyed its capacity for armed conflict, killed or enslaved the remnants of the population, and took over the disputed land.

* * *

7. Richard Slotkin and James K. Folsom, *So Dreadfull a Judgment: Puritan Responses to King Philip's War: 1676–1677* (Middletown, CT: Wesleyan University Press, 1978), pp. 26, 30–32.

8. Drake, *King Philip's War*, pp. 75–108.

9. Slotkin and Folsom, *So Dreadfull a Judgment*, p. 4.

The shock of this terrible war also prompted the colonists to refashion their conception of the community as God's chosen, forging the core principles of their Puritan faith into a new configuration. The classic statement of this new vision is not a sermon. It was a story, recounted by Mary Rowlandson, concerning her experiences as a prisoner of the Narragansetts. It is a story of hellish evil, the suffering of the righteous soul, and her eventual deliverance. For Rowlandson, however, the righteous are also unrighteous. Her narrative vividly portrays a fiercely intelligent woman of troubled conscience who is unable to rest in a secure understanding of her distresses.

Rowlandson's work established the first distinctively American literary genre, the 'captivity narrative,' which retained its popularity throughout the eighteenth and nineteenth centuries, with a famous twentieth century revival in *The Searchers*, starring John Wayne. The genre makes the captive's personal story into a story of the community as a whole. Entering the promised land, the children of promise simultaneously enter a prison; they are held in bondage by agents of a bloodthirsty regime that controls the land that belongs by right to the settlers. The superior military and economic power of the English disappears from sight in these narratives; they become victims, desperately awaiting redemption by their God.[10]

Explaining how the tribes came to occupy New England, Cotton Mather stated that, 'The Devil decoyed those miserable savages [hither] in hopes that the Gospel of the Lord Jesus Christ would never come here to destroy or disturb His absolute empire over them.'[11] As the Narragansetts devastate Rowlandson's home, accordingly, she sees Satan's slaves re-establishing his empire: 'Oh, the roaring and singing and dancing and yelling of those black creatures in the night, which made the place a lively resemblance of hell.'[12]

10. See Alden T. Vaughan and Edward W. Clark, *Puritans Among the Indians: Accounts of Captivity and Redemption, 1676–1724*, John Harvard library (Cambridge, MA: Belknap Press, 1981).

11. Charles M. Segal and David C. Stineback, *Puritans, Indians, and Manifest Destiny* (New York: Putnam, 1977), p. 182.

12. Mary Rowlandson, 'The Sovereignty and Goodness of God, together with the Faithfulness of His Promises Displayed; Being a Narrative of the Captivity and Restoration of Mrs. Mary Rowlandson,' in Alden T. Vaughan and Edward W. Clark, *Puritans Among the Indians: Accounts of Captivity and Redemption, 1676–1724*, John Harvard Library (Cambridge, MA: Belknap Press, 1981), pp. 29–75, p. 36.

The Narragansetts captured Rowlandson and held her for eleven weeks until she was ransomed. 'There were five persons taken in one house'; Rowlandson recalled,

> the father and the mother and a sucking child they knocked on the head; the other two they took and carried away alive...[Another] running along was shot and wounded and fell down; he begged of them his life, promising money...but they knocked him in the head, stripped him naked, split open his bowels.[13]

Rowlandson views these horrors as punishment for her sin, and the war itself as punishment for the sin of the community. 'Oh, that My people had hearkened unto Me and Israel had walked in My ways,' Rowlandson writes, echoing God's lament (in Ps. 81:13–14) over the plight of His people at the hands of a triumphant enemy.

> I should soon have subdued their enemies and turned My hand against their adversaries. But now our perverse and evil carriages in the sight of the Lord have so offended Him that instead of turning his Hand against them the Lord feeds and nourishes them up to be a scourge to the whole land.[14]

The English destroy corn crops, in hopes of starving the tribes into submission, but the tribes survive by eating things 'that a hog or dog would hardly touch...They would eat horses' guts and ears, and all sorts of wild birds which they could catch; also bear, venison, beaver, tortoise, frogs, squirrels, dogs, skunks, rattlesnakes, yea, the very bark of trees.' In this way the Lord 'preserve(d) them for His holy ends and the destruction of many still amongst the English.'[15]

The narrative as a whole centers on Rowlandson's spiritual trial, which culminates after her six-year-old daughter dies, and she fears becoming deranged. When her captors show her the child's grave, however, she finds the means of her redemption. 'There I left that child in the wilderness and must commit it and myself also in this wilderness condition to Him who is above all.'[16]

God's redemption is inherent in Rowlandson's 'wilderness condition,' because 'the wilderness' is located on the same biblical

---

13. Rowlandson, 'The Sovereignty and Goodness of God', p. 33.
14. Rowlandson, 'The Sovereignty and Goodness of God', p. 69.
15. Rowlandson, 'The Sovereignty and Goodness of God', p. 69.
16. Rowlandson, 'The Sovereignty and Goodness of God', p. 39.

landscape as the 'promised land.' God's punishment does not remove the faithful from His world; it gives them a vantage from which their true possession can be glimpsed. The promised land is the inevitable destination of their passage through the wilderness, so long as their faith sustains the trials to which their sin had subjected them.

Rowlandson's narrative defines the war with the tribes as a re-enactment of the biblical pageant: chosen people passing through the wilderness on their way to the promised land. This vision denies legitimacy to the resistance of the tribes and fails to understand that the Puritan colony is invading a social arrangement deserving respect; it obscures the economic contest from which the warfare arose, and the military contest by which it was resolved. The captivity narrative—taking its place as a classic definition of America's character and mission—reconfirms and perpetuates the religious delusion on which the Massachusetts Bay colony was founded.

Rowlandson sees the Narragansett defeat as yet another version of Agag's fall, exultant security giving way to horror and dismemberment.

> [They] triumphed and rejoiced in their inhuman and many times devilish cruelty to the English…They would [threaten to] knock all the [English] in the head, or drive them into the sea, or make them fly the country, thinking surely Agag-like, "The bitterness of death is past." [But then God] takes the quarrel into His own hand, and though they had made a pit in their own imaginations as deep a hell for the Christians…yet the Lord hurled them into it. And the Lord had not so many ways before to preserve them, but now He hath as many to destroy them.[17]

Rowlandson's bloodthirstiness is conditioned by an impulse to self-searching that does not end with the Puritan victory. Far from feeling morally edified by her afflictions, Rowlandson remains stunned and confused. The Lord had given her, she says, 'the dregs of the cup, the wine of astonishment.'[18]

> I can remember the time when I used to sleep quietly without workings in my thoughts whole nights together, but now it is other ways with me. When all are fast about me and no eye open but His who ever

17. Rowlandson, 'The Sovereignty and Goodness of God', pp. 69, 70.
18. Rowlandson, 'The Sovereignty and Goodness of God', p. 75.

waketh, my thoughts are upon things past…Oh, the wonderful power of God that mine eyes have seen, affording matter enough for my thoughts to run in that when others are sleeping mine eyes are weeping![19]

Rowlandson's anguish results from a core impulse of Puritan spirituality, turning the spotlight of moral inquiry upon herself and her community, ready to identify and acknowledge failings, and to learn from them. Yet as it takes center stage, Rowlandson's conscientious suffering reinforces the spiritual blindness of her community. Many among the defeated tribes suffered torments far worse than Rowlandson's, and there were many reasons for the war, not only the 'perverse and evil carriages' of which the Puritans were guilty in their dealings with one another.

Rowlandson's 'wine of astonishment' is an intoxicant, producing an exalted and delusory consciousness that provides an escape from moral reality. The 'captivity narrative' may teach self-awareness on questions of personal morality, or teach justice on social issues within the community, but it offers a spurious justification for the predatory enterprises of the community as a whole in relation to other communities.

Before King Philip's War, the tribes and the English communities formed a blended interdependent society, living among one another in a civil totality that embraced a wide variety of collaborative and competitive relationships. James D. Drake argues that the tribal insurrection deserves to be considered a 'civil war' that abolished this composite order and replaced it with a dramatically altered situation. The colonists 'no longer viewed themselves as living or settling among the Indians…but perceived a military border demarcating English settlement from wilderness.' Towns at that border were now seen 'as forming the single edge of a westward expanding society.'[20] The dramatic figure Rowlandson created, that of the terrified woman captured by demonic savages, played a key role in the unfolding mythology of the frontier. Her plight calls for the intervention of a male hero, expert in the use of firearms, who executes divine justice. The role of 'frontier hero,' as we shall see, was taken up by George W. Bush, as he went to war with Iraq.

19. Rowlandson, 'The Sovereignty and Goodness of God', pp. 74–75.
20. Drake, *King Philip's War*, p. 173.

Rival Traditions

Roger Williams also lived among the Narragansetts, but not as a prisoner of war. On the contrary, he found refuge among them after the Massachusetts Bay colony banished him. Williams correctly anticipated that the authorities in Boston would seek to deport him, so he risked his life on an arduous midwinter journey by foot, finding sustenance among Narragansett communities as he dodged English settlements on his way toward Rhode Island. Williams owed his life to the Narragansetts, and the experience unsettled his expectations. 'It is a strange truth,' he remarked, 'that a man shall generally find more free entertainment and refreshing amongst these barbarians, than amongst thousands that call themselves Christians.'[21]

Williams's experience offers scant support for Romantic illusions about the Narragansetts, or other resident tribes, as Noble Savages. Williams himself eventually recognized that belligerent hard-liners had taken control of Narragansett policy, and would have to be countered by force. But this does not cancel the sympathetic appreciation he developed for the Narragansetts, or his warm personal friendship with the sachems, Canonicus and Massasoit, who showed him hospitality.

Williams's writing stands in a counter-tradition that accords human dignity to non-White and non-Christian peoples. 'Having of one blood made all mankind,' Williams asserts, God provides the Americans with mental and ethical capacities matching the English. Williams believed that Englishmen and Americans were equally 'children of wrath,' equally disposed to rebellion against God and to disorder in their communal lives.[22] He was sharply aware of the Narragansetts' capacity for violence, but did not see this as the keynote of a savage character that entitled the English to take control of their resources.

These 'wildest of the sons of men' did not live in violent chaos, Williams noted, but had 'cast themselves into [a] mold or form of government' so as to create civil order.[23] He admired the

21. Roger Williams, 'A Key into the Language of America' in J. Hammond Trumbull (ed.), *The Complete Writings of Roger Williams* (7 vols; New York: Russell & Russell, 1963), vol. 1, pp. 61–221, p. 106.

22. Williams, 'A Key into the Language of America', p. 141.

23. Williams, 'A Key into the Language of America', p. 167.

'sociableness' of the Narragansetts, how they 'love society, family, cohabitation, and consociation of houses and towns together.' He found that they enforced 'the high and honorable esteem of the marriage bed,' that they punished adultery, as well as murder and robbery.[24] The result was a degree of civic harmony and interpersonal consideration that put the English to shame.

> When Indians hear the horrid filths,
> Of Irish, English men,
> The horrid oaths and murders late,
> Thus say these Indians then.
>
> We wear no clothes, have many gods,
> And yet our sins are less:
> You are barbarians, pagans wild,
> Your land's the wilderness.[25]

Williams mastered the Narragansett language, and as he became fluent, he sought to assist his fellow Englishmen by publishing *A Key into the Language of America: Or, a Help to the Language of the Natives in That Part of America, Called New-England. Together, with Brief Observations of the Customs, Manners and Worships, etc. of the Aforesaid Natives, in Peace and War, in Life and Death.*

Notice that Williams's title designates the natives 'in that part of America called New-England.' He does not make the mistake of assuming that the local tribes merge indiscriminately into others, lacking qualities to distinguish them from tribes inhabiting the rest of the continent. Williams includes the names by which various sub-groups within the Narragansett societies designated each other. He reports their puzzlement over the whites' calling them all 'Indians' but notes they were prepared to accept it.[26]

However harmless it may have seemed to the Narragansetts, this practice carried an ominous portent. As the English became 'Americans' the resident tribes became 'Indians,' and this set a pattern that came to include the myriad other indigenous peoples that English-speaking society supplanted.

The opponents of the Puritans were not 'Indians,' nor were the adversaries of AngloAmericans in the frontier warfare of the ensuing generations. 'Indians' are a figment of the imperialist imagination,

---

24. Williams, 'A Key into the Language of America', p. 135.
25. Williams, 'A Key into the Language of America', p. 167.
26. Williams, 'A Key into the Language of America', p. 82.

and are now found beyond our shores, as American interests have encroached upon faraway peoples.

Robert Kaplan celebrates the power of this homogenizing vision as he describes Fort Leavenworth, Kansas, planted in 1827 by Colonel Henry Leavenworth in 'Indian Country' on the western bank of the Missouri River, when he discovered that the eastern bank specified by his orders lay in the floodplain. The fort swiftly became the base camp for scouts and exploring expeditions, as well as for troops headed to the Mexican War in the 1840s, and to the war on the Northwest tribes following the Civil War, whereupon Leavenworth provided support for the building of the transcontinental railroad.[27]

Technological innovation has allowed Leavenworth to maintain its position on the Indian-fighting frontier of America's global power, Kaplan claims. The fort has now become a major center for the creation, revision and application of America's strategy worldwide. 'When the United States intervenes overseas,' Kaplan notes, 'the phones and computers at Leavenworth work overtime'.[28]

'Indians,' as a blanket term for continental populations hostile to American expansion, has now been incorporated into a global world-picture. Kaplan enthusiastically describes 'imperial maintenance' taking place in 'far-flung corners of the earth' where 'individual marines, soldiers, airmen and sailors…[are] interpreting policy on their own, on the ground.' As Kaplan visited these outposts of empire, he was greeted with a refrain that carries back to Fort Leavenworth in the nineteenth century, and to the Puritans in the seventeenth. '"Welcome to Injun Country," was the refrain I heard from troops from Colombia to the Philippines, including Afghanistan and Iraq…The War on Terrorism was really about taming the frontier.'[29]

When it comes to imperial policy, what matters is that all these peoples and cultures resist U.S. encroachment. Local tactics may be adapted to the differences between Sunnis and Shiites, much as the Puritans played off Narragansetts against Pequots: but their shared

---

27. Robert D. Kaplan, *An Empire Wilderness: Travels into America's Future* (New York: Vintage Books, 1999), p. 4.

28. Kaplan, *An Empire Wilderness*, p. 6.

29. Robert D. Kaplan, *Imperial Grunts: The American Military on the Ground* (New York: Random House, 2005), p. 4.

status remains: they are 'Injuns,' the not-chosen, wrongfully obstructing divine purposes in America's Promised Land.

* * *

Roger Williams's counter-tradition also has significant descendants, however, who hold that the understanding of alien societies depends on a sympathetic appreciation of the life they lead, and respect for their rights. Williams's commitment to freedom of conscience found welcome in the movement supporting human rights that arose in the eighteenth century, and was enshrined in the American Declaration of Independence. Deism and more liberal versions of Christianity gained authority in the early national period because of their opposition to the theocratic Calvinism that the Massachusetts Bay Puritans held dear.

The Unitarians, who triumphed at Harvard College in the 1830s, produced in turn the Transcendentalist movement led by Ralph Waldo Emerson, Henry David Thoreau and Margaret Fuller, and both of these movements produced searching social criticism that challenged imperialist ideologies justifying the subjugation of peoples who resisted American expansion westward.

William Ellery Channing, the Unitarian leader who encouraged the Transcendentalist reformers, could see that an essential driving force behind conflicts with the tribes was the seizure of their territories by Europeans, abetted by the moral arrogance that counted such seizure as the fault of the tribes, or the result of some providential force in history granting the American promised land to whites, not to people of color.

Writing to Henry Clay in 1837, Channing declared that the nation should adopt a policy of 'serious, resolute restraint,' laying 'an immediate curb on [the nation's] passion for extended territory.' The continent is 'vast enough' for 'the growth of ages,' affording ample opportunity for reasonable and just accommodation with the resident populations. He denounced the rapacious 'career of acquisition and conquest' and the racist delusions advanced to justify it.[30]

30. William E. Channing, 'Letter to Henry Clay, 1837,' in John Morton Blum, William S. McFeely, Edmund S. Morgan *et al* (eds.), *The National Experience. Part One, A History of the United States to 1877* (New York: Harcourt Brace, 7th edn, 1989), p. 276.

Before the term 'Manifest Destiny' was coined, Channing summarized and rejected its essential claim, that an automatic process of historical development was unfolding westward, 'that the Indians have melted before the white man, and the mixed degraded race of Mexico must melt before the Anglo-Saxon.' That fantasies of America's moral pre-eminence should be invoked to deny the rights of native peoples struck Channing as a fundamental perversion: 'Away with this vile sophistry!' he protested, 'We boast of the progress of society, and this progress consists in the substitution of reason and moral principle for the sway of brute force'.[31]

In the twentieth century, ethical and intellectual commitments descending from Roger Williams were incorporated into scientific methods indispensable for the understanding of foreign societies. The anthropological fieldwork pioneered by Bronislaw Malinowski showed that truthful analysis requires an anthropologist to live among the people under study, to learn their language, and to see the world — so far as possible — from the 'native point of view.' The suspension of commonplace preconceptions that is required for such study has now become standard practice in a broad range of historical and sociological disciplines, where gaining an imaginative appreciation of other societies, or earlier eras in our own society, is expected of every serious student. Foreign language study is required in colleges and universities for this reason, that it provides a 'key' as Williams called it, for entering an unfamiliar world.

Following the deceptive euphoria generated by the swift fall of Baghdad, U.S. forces were bewildered by the sudden emergence and startling successes of the insurgency, which Thomas Ricks attributes to the lack of such cultural knowledge. 'After years of talking about its information superiority, the Army suddenly was in an inferior position. It didn't speak the language, it didn't understand the culture, it didn't know much about the enemy, and it seemed all too often to be the last one to know what was going on.'[32]

The Puritans thus bequeathed a tradition in debate with itself, with contrasting versions of 'the city on a hill' and of the pathways

---

31. Channing, 'Letter to Henry Clay, 1837', p. 276.
32. Thomas E. Ricks, *Fiasco: The American Military Adventure in Iraq* (New York: Penguin Press, 2006), p. 302.

toward an accurate understanding of the peoples whom the English settlers encountered in America. Central to Puritan piety was a self-questioning conscience, and the readiness to acknowledge fault. The Massachusetts Bay Puritans were theocrats, and are famous for their cruel intolerance: their persecution of the Quakers, their virtual extermination of the tribes, and their banishment of Roger Williams and Anne Hutchinson. But the broader Puritan community includes these dissidents, and their descendants in later American history, who carry forward a tradition of passionate ethical self-examination, and the moral appraisal of public policy.

Within this complex religious heritage are two variants with distinctive ethical and intellectual axioms. The variant originating in Massachusetts Bay grants Americans a God-given pre-emptive right to resources controlled by other peoples; the rival tradition recognizes that others possess inherent human rights that demand respect. The view that Americans are 'chosen people' entitled *de novo* to the resources of a 'promised land' estimates the character of other peoples in accordance with their conformity with this standard. Those who resist American claims are defined by that resistance, as enemies of the divine promise. The tradition descending from Roger Williams, by contrast, holds that knowing other peoples cannot happen if this self-centered ideology takes precedence.

It is true, of course, that accurate knowledge of other peoples does not necessarily entail respect for their rights. As Thomas Ricks's comment indicates, it can be deployed as military intelligence whether the war in question is morally defensible or not. Conversely, the ignorance resulting from ideologically distorted pictures of an enemy can wreak havoc with any military enterprise, just or unjust. The war in Iraq provides an example of bad intelligence confounding a bad cause, and it is the purpose of this book to argue both parts of that claim.

Americans should aspire to make our country a 'city on a hill' worthy of emulation, and worth fighting for, in keeping with the conviction that G*d creates no second-class human beings, none whose welfare is rightly sacrificed to sustain any claim to land or other resources put forward by His/Her presumptive chosen ones. It is not enough to lament the systematic cruelty justified in Christian terms by the imperialism of our Massachusetts Bay forebears, however, or to celebrate the ethical and religious acuity of Roger Williams.

A moral disaster afflicts the nation in our own time. We must identify the religious delusions at work today — which gave plausibility to the erroneous claims of the administration — and demonstrate the ways in which those delusions shaped the disaster on the ground in Iraq.

Chapter Four

THE FIRE OF FREEDOM

The Shining City as God

Ronald Reagan inaugurated the political movement that sponsored the ascent of George W. Bush to the presidency and gave strong support to his policies. A key component of this triumph was Reagan's revival and recasting of John Winthrop's vision of America as the promised land occupied by God's chosen people. After eight years as President, Reagan concluded his farewell speech with a meditation on Winthrop's city on a hill. 'I've spoken of the shining city all my political life,' he explained, 'but I don't know if I ever quite communicated what I saw. But in my mind it was a tall proud city built on rocks stronger than oceans, wind-swept, God-blessed.'[1]

Reagan's city is proud and overbearing; its conspicuous position does not impose obligations upon Americans but projects invulnerable spectacular prestige, a paradise of 'commerce and creativity' that is an irresistible magnet for those 'with the will and the heart to get here.' It dares peoples 'from all the lost places of the world' to muster the courage necessary to claim the divine blessing available in the city, and not elsewhere.[2]

Reagan's shining city does not offer obedience to an inscrutable and demanding God, but itself occupies a position of god-like pre-eminence. Reagan acknowledges no transcendant standard of justice against which national conduct might be judged. The nation may have internal failings, but in its dealings with other societies, America is itself the God from whom all blessings flow, its own character providing the ultimate criterion of political virtue. Reagan's

---

1. Ronald Reagan, 'Farewell Address to the Nation', Ronald Reagan Presidential Foundation Website, January 11, 1989. www.reaganfoundation.org/reagan/speeches/farewell.asp.
2. Ronald Reagan, 'Farewell Address to the Nation'.

strongest moral condemnations are reserved for those who refuse to subscribe to this ideal.

As he became President, Reagan's triumphant vision swept aside Jimmy Carter's appraisal of America's prospects, as put forward in his famous 'Crisis of Confidence' speech of 1979. Carter's evangelical Protestant faith informed his summary of the crisis, as well as the solution he proposed; but while Reagan was not devout, politically active evangelicals found his doctrines appealing, and turned away from Carter to support him and the movement he inaugurated. The core religious support for George W. Bush arose from the evangelicals' romance with Reagan, and their response to the resulting disappointments.

The clash of religious perspectives at stake in the disagreement between Reagan and Carter reframed the debate between John Winthrop and Roger Williams in twentieth century terms. Carter explained that America's crisis of confidence had arisen because the false gods of materialism had seduced and betrayed the American people. 'Too many of us now tend to worship self-indulgence and consumption...But we've discovered that owning things and consuming things does not satisfy our longing for meaning. We've learned that piling up material goods cannot fill the emptiness of lives which have no confidence or purpose.'[3]

Carter accordingly issued a call to confession and repentance: 'we must face the truth, and then we can change our course.' He acknowledged that 'shocks and tragedies' had sapped the national spirit—the Kennedy assassinations, the 'agony of Vietnam,' Watergate—but declared that Americans could regain their self-respect by summoning the moral resources required to surmount a looming new crisis.[4]

The unrestrained craving for material goods had led the nation into an 'intolerable dependence on foreign oil,' Carter declared, and he warned explicitly against the dangers of presuming an entitlement to petroleum resources that are controlled by other nations. 'Down that road lies a mistaken idea of freedom, the right to grasp for ourselves some advantage over others'.[5]

---

3. Jimmy Carter, 'The "Crisis of Confidence" Speech', *American Experience*, PBS. (www.pbs.org/wgbh/amex/carter/filmmore/ps_crisis.html).
4. Carter, 'The "Crisis of Confidence" Speech'.
5. Carter, 'The "Crisis of Confidence" Speech'.

Roger Williams likewise taught that human fulfillment is 'not about these children's toys of land, meadows, cattle,' and that freedom is not an unfettered quest for economic resources.[6] The freedom honored in Rhode Island, and violated at Massachusetts Bay, was a spiritual right, according to which human beings seek divine wisdom 'according to their several persuasions,' and accept the limitations entailed by recognizing the rights of others.

Carter proposed to lead Americans to the 'true freedom' that is gained through self-discipline. His proposals were rigorous and extensive, including import quotas, a windfall profits tax, a legal requirement on utility companies to cut their use of oil by 50 percent, standby gasoline rationing, and an admonition to American citizens individually to use carpools and public transportation, obey the speed limit, and reset household thermostats. 'There is simply no way to avoid sacrifice,' he declared, on the pathway toward 'more freedom, more confidence, and much more control over our own lives'.[7]

Carter's speech is now derided as a political blunder of the first magnitude, opening his presidency and the Democratic Party to devastating counterattack. Carter's summons to national repentance, redemption and sacrifice was quickly subjected to caricature; it became known as his 'malaise' speech, even though Carter never used the word, and Democrats for years thereafter were accused of 'gloom and doom.'

Carter had proposed that the nation itself, and the political disposition of the American people, was due for reformation. Reagan's vision of the 'shining city' brooked no such moral self-searching; for him, Carter had committed an unforgivable sin against the nation's stainless and triumphant virtue.

Reagan's climb to national prominence began in 1974 with a speech repudiating claims that the arrogance of power had propelled the nation into the Vietnam debacle. 'We are not a warlike people,' he declared, a year before the fall of Saigon, 'nor is our history filled with tales of aggressive adventures and imperialism.' Reagan described 'the lesson of Vietnam' in terms that have a bitter ring today: 'that never again will young Americans be asked to fight

6. Roger Williams, *The Complete Writings of Roger Williams,* (7 vols; New York: Russell & Russell, 1963), vol. 6, p. 345.

7. Carter, 'The "Crisis of Confidence" Speech'.

and possibly die for a cause unless that cause is so meaningful that we, as a nation, pledge our full resources to achieve victory as quickly as possible.' America met defeat in Vietnam because our forces were not permitted to win, Reagan implied, not because their deployment was a mistake.[8]

The sinfulness that threatens America, Reagan insisted, is the refusal to offer America unconditional worship. Instead of rejoicing in the nation's supernal and immaculate virtue, such heretics measure America's conduct against a higher standard and find moral shortcomings. Reagan called it 'the decayed and degraded state of moral and patriotic feeling.' Reagan condemned the schooling of the young, when it draws attention to the destructive aspects of American capitalism, and to the need for federal programs to remedy the hardships they impose. Since he thought the true freedom of Americans is their sacred right to pursue boundless material abundance, Reagan especially condemned those who expressed concern over environmental damage, jeering at the 'boards, commissions, bureaus and agencies' that work to restrict corporate polluters and instill civic self-discipline, claiming that they 'sacrifice freedom for some fancied security'.[9]

What's needed is not governmental action to organize collective self-sacrifice, for the sake of economic self-sufficiency, but measures that will liberate the engines of capitalist expansion from the burdens of government regulation. Enlarging on themes implicit in John Winthrop's teaching, Reagan believed that American freedom is the unhindered pursuit of wealth, and his 'shining city' has a pre-emptive right to whatever resources can be applied to increasing its wealth and power. His message found a ready audience in the American people.

For President Carter, as the historian Dan T. Carter noted, 'the science of governing was a willingness to engage in an endless struggle to control man's sinful nature.'[10] Ronald Reagan's faith was,

8. Ronald Reagan, 'The Shining City Upon a Hill', http://originofnations.org/books,%20papers/quotes%20etc/Reagan_The%20Shining.

9. Reagan, 'The Shining City Upon a Hill'.

10. Dan T. Carter, *From George Wallace to Newt Gingrich: Race in the Conservative Counterrevolution, 1963–1994.* The Walter Lynwood Fleming Lectures in Southern History (Baton Rouge, LA: Louisiana State University Press, 1996). Cited in Kevin Phillips, *American Theocracy: The Peril and Politics of Radical Religion, Oil, and Borrowed Money in the 21st Century* (New York: Penguin Books, 2007), p. 186.

by contrast, a jamboree of moral self-congratulation. For him, it was anathema to consider Vietnam as a moral failure and America's energy dependence as a result of unsustainable self-indulgence. Spiritual integrity and nationalist zeal were synonymous in the Reaganite faith, which to him was the inner meaning of the Christian faith. He chafed at governmental regulations that forbad children to offer Christian prayers at school. 'We have not dealt falsely with our God,' Reagan declares, directly echoing Winthrop, 'even if He is temporarily suspended from the classroom'.[11]

A familiar religious delusion is at work here. Great world religions—Taoism, Hinduism, Judaism, Christianity, Islam—have all provided the ideologies required by aggressive political regimes, notably during the ages of European expansion, including the conquest of the Americas. Sects within Christianity, as within Islam, have invoked divine favor upon regimes going to war against adherents of competing sects. Yet, these faith traditions also offer a larger vision. Their core truths have survived the collapse of nations and empires, and teach the dire consequences that await political regimes that claim divine status for themselves. The Hebrew prophets, like Jesus, Muhammad and Lao-tse, were at odds with the prevailing political order when they received their profoundest insights; their central teachings are perennially renewed because they are so often violated, with the recurrent horrible results.

Christian Soldiers

The invasion of Iraq was shaped by a militant Christian piety that emerged within the Reaganite tradition. Reagan succeeded in recruiting evangelicals to his cause, but with George W. Bush their views came to the center of American foreign policy.

As Andrew Bacevich explains, the war in Vietnam was opposed by leaders of the mainline Protestant denominations and the Roman Catholic Church, but found consistent support among Protestant Evangelicals, who followed Billy Graham in believing that God endorsed 'the American Way of Life,' especially in its battle against 'godless Communism.' Evangelicals viewed anti-war activism as simply another vice, within the general culture of revolt against authority that flourished in the 1960s and 70s—drugs, sex and rock

11. Reagan, 'The Shining City Upon a Hill'.

'n roll, followed by women's liberation and the quest for homosexual rights. To conservative Christians, Bacevich notes, 'all of these developments testified to a nation turning away from God,' and Jerry Falwell took the lead in 1979 to form the Moral Majority, a political opposition in which 'pro-family' and 'pro-life' were identified with 'pro-American.'[12]

Billy Graham had offered a generalized evangelical blessing to patriotic office-holders from Eisenhower forward. But disenchantment with Jimmy Carter led the new evangelical leadership to detach their movement from the Democrats altogether; they became the 'Religious Right' within the Republican Party. When religious conservatives discovered that Reagan was an unreliable champion of the 'lifestyle' policies they most treasured, they turned their energies to gaining political power, not just seeking to influence those in power. Pat Robertson's quest for the Republican nomination for the presidency, after Reagan's retirement, was the most visible instance of this new development.

In the process of seeking positions of power in local school boards, mainline churches, and on the national stage, the Religious Right refashioned traditional evangelical politics, giving it a militant edge suited to their role as champions of Christian virtue attacking an insidious and pervasive evil. Vehement Christian moralism is a minority stance in American society, however, so the quest for office required the Religious Right to devise campaigns in which their candidates' true convictions and intentions remain hidden.

In this crusade, remarks Kevin Phillips, 'stealth is a major premise, furtiveness a byword. The Christian right usually does not like to acknowledge what it is doing or where.'[13]

Faithful to this tradition, George W. Bush has used 'double-coding' in his speeches, using expressions and phrases like 'wonder-working power' and 'killers of innocents' to connect with his militarist Christian supporters while concealing his attitudes from the public at large.[14] Bush's first campaign for the Presidency gave little hint of the radical policies he would adopt once he gained

12. Andrew J. Bacevich, *The New American Militarism: How Americans are Seduced by War* (New York: Oxford University Press, 2005), pp. 126, 175–204.

13. Phillips, *American Theocracy*, p. 215.

14. Bruce Lincoln, *Holy Terrors: Thinking About Religion After September 11* (Chicago, IL: University of Chicago Press, 2006), p. 31.

office. Political pundits were startled that he governed as though he had an overwhelming right-wing mandate, rather than a minority of the popular vote; but Bush's practice was simply an especially visible instance of this well-developed strategic style.

In covering the politics of the Christian Right, the media has focused mainly on 'life-style' issues—abortion, euthanasia, divorce, homosexuality—and on the battle to install creationism and Christian prayer in the public schools. This emphasis has deflected attention from an equally momentous feature of this bellicose Christian moralism—namely its embrace of American military power as a God-given means of vanquishing evil abroad.

In 1980 Falwell decried 'permissiveness and moral decay' as a problem of national security, because America is becoming a nation whose 'morals are corrupted, so that its people have no will to resist wrong...[and] we are in a precarious position for takeover.' With the collapse of the Soviet Union in 1989, the threat of 'takeover' subsided, but after 9/11 the menace of foreign evil reappeared, giving new relevance to Falwell's remedy: American military power directed by political leaders whose vision is informed by the true faith. 'A political leader, as a minister of God,' Falwell proclaimed, 'is a revenger to execute wrath upon those who do evil.'[15]

There can be little doubt that these words informed the thinking of the Protestant Evangelicals in the Bush White House. They echo the words of St Paul in Romans 13, the central New Testament text on God's ordering of state power and the duties of men who hold public office. Like Falwell, those attending White House prayer meetings would have taken this chapter as literal divine instruction concerning the proper use of force by the state, including military force. An official 'beareth not bear the sword in vain,' Paul declares; 'he is the minister of God, a revenger to execute his wrath on him that doeth evil.'[16]

Jerram Barrs elaborated on this key contention as he sought to inspire a Christian crusade against godless communism, and outlined a broadscale theory of righteous punishment that rang true for the

---

15. Jerry Falwell, *Listen, America* (New York: Bantam, 1981), pp. 6–14, 84–85.

16. *The Holy Bible Containing the Old and New Testaments and the Apocrypha: Translated out of the Original Tongues with the Former Translations Diligently Compared and Revised, by His Majesty's Special Command* (New York: Cambridge University Press, nd). Subsequent citations of the King James Version appear in the text as KJV.

Bush White House. The 'punishments that God requires men to hand out' are not meant to be 'educational,' nor are they aimed at 'rehabilitation.' Like domestic offenders, foreign foes become appropriate targets for the 'just vengeance required by God.' Barrs asserts that 'the whole foundation for human government in Scripture is that God executes retribution and he requires government as his representative on earth to do the same...When a government punishes the evildoer with the sword of vengeance, it is acting as God's servant and fulfilling the very task for which God appointed it.'[17]

This conviction—that the President as Commander-in-Chief is charged with bringing God's retribution upon evildoers—has large implications for the planning and execution of the invasion of Iraq. Michael Lienesch explains that it lies at the heart of a 'crusade theory of warfare'[18] that supercedes the 'just war' theory that was developed over centuries within Roman Catholicism and the major Protestant denominations. The term 'crusade' derives from adopting the cross of Christ as a battle standard for the righteous, which was the practice of European Christians invading the Near East from the eleventh century onward, and continues to provide inspiration in the hymn 'Onward Christian Soldiers.' The attendant theory provides a broad and flexible rationale justifying war. What would deserve condemnation as an unprovoked war of aggression under 'just war' theory easily passes muster as a 'crusade.'

'Crusade theory' removes the need to ask whether a war is fought in a just cause (*jus ad bellum*) or with just means (*jus in bellum*), and requires only that the conflict appear to the righteous as a drama in which God's appointed state officials discharge their obligation to punish evil. Far from insisting that war must be waged only as the last resort, crusade theory justifies 'preventive war,' which is launched against evildoers in the absence of an immediate military threat, under a leader wielding the sword of vengeance against the wicked.

Fred Barnes, editor of the neocon *Weekly Standard*, reported that this understanding of the President's God-given role defined the

17. Jerram Barrs, *Who are the Peacemakers? The Christian Case for Nuclear Deterrence* (Westchester, IL: Crossway Books, 1983), pp. 18, 23, 24, 28.

18. Michael Lienesch, *Redeeming America: Piety and Politics in the New Christian Right* (Chapel Hill, NC: University of North Carolina Press, 1993), p. 216.

sense of mission that came upon George W. Bush after 9/11. At a meeting on 19 September, Bush nodded in agreement when James Merritt, then President of the Southern Baptist Convention, announced that God had appointed him to meet the crisis. '"I believe you are God's man for this hour,"' Merritt said. "God's hand is on you."'

Barnes then sized up the archetypal drama. When evil struck the nation, it made evident the divine intention at work in Bush's unlikely rise to power, how he was chosen rather than his more qualified brother Jeb, and was defeated in the popular vote, but then placed in office by the Supreme Court. 'The stage was set,' Barnes concluded, 'for Bush to be God's agent of wrath.'[19]

The affront to national self-righteousness that was inflicted on 9/11 thus became the birthplace of sanctimonious hate. Because the conflict between satanic evil and god-like goodness is absolute, there can be no negotiation between the parties, and preventive attacks launched by the godly are self-evidently justified. 'For the Christian,' writes Rus Walton, 'there can be no neutrality in this battle: "He that is not with Me is against Me"(Matthew 12:30). Not only must we resist, we must go on the offense.'[20] Certain that he was doing the Lord's work, President Bush echoed this language in his address to the nation on the following day. 'Either you are with us, or you with the terrorists,' he declared; 'freedom and fear, justice and cruelty, have always been at war, and we know that God is not neutral between them.'[21] Versions of 'going on the offense' have likewise become a staple of presidential rhetoric. 'Our nation saw the face of evil,' he said on the fifth anniversary of 9/11, and 'since that day, America and her allies have taken the offensive.'[22]

19. Fred Barnes, 'Man with a Mission: George W. Bush Finds His Calling,' *The Weekly Standard*, 30 September 2001. http://www.freerepublic.com/focus/f-news/536853posts.

20. Rus Walton, *Biblical Solutions to Contemporary Problems: A Handbook* (Brentwood, TN: Wolgemuth & Hyatt, 1988), p. 166.

21. George W. Bush, 'Address to a Joint Session of Congress and the American People,' United States Capitol, 20 September 2001. http://www.whitehouse.gov/news/releases/2001/09/20010920-8.html.

22. George W. Bush, 'President's Address to the Nation,' 11 September 2006. http://www.whitehouse.gov/news/releases/2006/09/20060911-3.html. For other instances see 'Debate Transcript, September 30, 2004: The First Bush-Kerry Debate.' http://www.debates.org/pages/trans2004a__p.html; 'President Bush Welcomes President Karzai of Afghanistan to the White House' 26 September 2006.

Protestant exponents of this bellicose piety have joined forces with Roman Catholic 'theocons' and with Jewish (and secular) 'neocons.' For this ecumenical assemblage, evil is not a theological category, it is the living presence of unqualified revolting hatefulness, with the Nazi holocaust and the mass murders ordered by Stalin serving as classic instances. Such evil makes no rational calculation of risks, and will not be contained by fears of military retaliation. Where evil appears in our own society, so the doctrine holds, it is not amenable to psychological healing, sociological remedy, or philosophical correction. Divine forgiveness may be available to those who repent, but the only faithful response to unrepentant wickedness is 'wrath.'

The vengeance then required is defined by the tradition of apocalyptic vision that Jews and Christians share, an absolute collision between God's triumphant justice and the forces of evil. In March of 2003, on the eve of the invasion of Iraq, a devotee of Jewish apocalypse declared that Bush 'should know that he is led by G-d in this...The actual war in Iraq is part of G-d's endtime judgment and His plan to remove the evil all over the world...This is an explanation of the determination of George Bush to go to war against Iraq and to destroy the evil.'[23]

Within the Religious Right, Chris Hedges has noted, doctrines of divine vengeance inform a spirituality that strongly resembles the bloodthirsty self-righteousness of the Stalinist and Nazi murderers they detest. This mentality is hypervigilant toward moral failings, but not in order to admit the fallen 'into a moral universe where they have a criminal's right to be punished and rehabilitated. They are seen instead...as pollutants, viruses, mutations that must be eradicated to halt further infection and degeneration within society. This sacred violence...allows its perpetrators and henchmen to avoid moral responsibility for their crimes. The brutality they

http://www. fas.org/irp/news/2006/09/wh092606.html; 'President Bush Discusses Global War on Terror,' Address at the Pentagon, 19 March 2008. www.whitehouse. gov/news/releases/2008/03/200803 19-2.html. Byron York, 'Bush on Iraq: "If We Can't Win, I'll Pull Us Out,"' *National Review*, 25 October 2006. http://www.article. nationalreview. com/print/?q=ZDg4M2N1ZjdkMWY0M23EyMzUw ZDE3OT.

23.'The War in Iraq Prophesied in the Bible: A Part of the Endtime Wars and G-d's Judgment,' http://www.templemountfaithful.org/phprint.php.

carry out is sanctified, an expression of not human volition but divine wrath.'[24]

The leaders of the Bush Administration did not invade Iraq as an exercise in 'preventive war' solely because they were animated by this religious tradition, and considered Saddam Hussein a consummate evildoer. Strategic doctrine, promoted by the American Enterprise Institute and the Project for a New American Century, likewise urged that the United States should 'act against' emerging threats 'before they were fully formed,'[25] for the sake of attaining a greatly strengthened global dominance, and the material benefits that would result. Yet such ambitions, styled as enlarging the sphere of American freedom, are fully consistent with the crusader doctrines of Christian Americanism; and they could never have been fulfilled, absent religious legitimation sufficient to bring the American public along. Bush himself did not endorse these views purely for the sake of war propaganda, but in keeping with his heartfelt convictions.

The war in Iraq was not only an effort to abolish evil, however; it was also driven by a constructive vision, that of creating an outpost of American freedom in a wilderness where unfortunate souls were suffering oppression under Saddam Hussein. Iraq was to become a model of democracy for other nations in the region to follow, itself a 'city on a hill' that would transmit into this wilderness the irresistible divine energies that had shaped America.

The President as Mystic

George W. Bush is a practical politician, and in Karl Rove had at his elbow one of the most skillful tacticians in American public life. The resultant use of religion for political advantage was uncommonly adroit. When Bush spoke directly of his faith for evangelical audiences, he was able to consolidate their support, yet escape being marked as a religious fanatic himself because of the common assumption he was merely pandering to their interests. Yet, sincere religious convictions lay beneath—and indeed animated—his

24. Chris Hedges, *American Fascists: The Christian Right and the War on America* (New York: Free Press, 2006), pp. 31–32.

25. David Bromwich, 'The Co-President at Work,' *The New York Review of Books*, 20 November 2008, p. 30.

cunning. 'I always laugh when people say George W. is saying this or that to appease the religious right' remarked John Ellis, a Bush cousin. 'He *is* the religious right.'[26]

In discussing his presidential ambitions with the Texas preacher James Robinson, Bush revealed the meditative consciousness through which he seeks God's will: 'I feel like God wants me to run for President. I can't explain it, but I sense the country is going to need me...I know it won't be easy on me or my family, but God wants me to do it.'[27] Notice that Bush's sense of God's purpose is intuitive and as yet incomplete; he sees that he is meant to run for the office, but he doesn't see why. It's not that the country needs him now, but it will need him in the future, somehow. Something will happen to reveal the divine purpose in full. But what?

There is good reason to believe that Bush became President with this question still unanswered. After the election, his closest advisors remained uneasy about the personal quirks that conveyed his internal doubts: his scrambled diction, his awkward attempts at cuteness, his belittling nicknames for colleagues. He gave the impression of a man unsure what to do with the awesome power placed in his hands. He spent an inordinate amount of time on vacation from the intimidating duties of his job.

The attacks of 9/11 then made clear what God had in mind. His biographer Robert Draper describes the transformation that followed. 'All the man's undersized, self-conscious ways — the smirk, the reedy defensiveness, the exaggerated imperiousness of his executive stroll — had collapsed into this new persona, which seemed in fact not to be a persona but instead a natural habitat, waiting for his ownership all this time. He was a war President now, and perfectly at ease with the role.'[28] A poll of Christian conservative leaders two months after 9/11 revealed a consensus that God had foreseen the disaster, and had provided exactly the leader that the hour of crisis required.

President Bush became more certain of his role as the agent of God's purpose following the defeat of the Taliban in Afghanistan and the 'Mission Accomplished' speech celebrating the dazzling

---

26. Phillips, *American Theocracy*, p. xxxvii.

27. Phillips, *American Theocracy*, p. xxxiv.

28. Robert Draper, *Dead Certain: The Presidency of George W. Bush* (New York: Free Press, 2007), pp. 165–66.

early success in Iraq. He now spoke with confidence about his interactions with the Almighty, explaining them in June of 2004 to a group of top Palestinian officials: 'I'm driven with a mission from God. God would tell me, "George, go and fight those terrorists in Afghanistan." And I did, and then God would tell me "George, go and end the tyranny in Iraq"...and I did. And now again, I feel God's words coming to me, "Go and get the Palestinians their state and get the Israelis their security in the Middle East." And by God, I'm gonna do it'.[29]

The words of God arrive in stages. They take form in the course of prayerful reflection over a period of time, culminating in a moment of clear conviction. It is an intuitive and largely non-verbal process of gathering and hardening certainty on an issue over which he meditates.

This in itself is not remarkable. Christians and believers of other traditions go through a similar inward process. Gandhi and Martin Luther sought divine guidance, and the Dalai Lama spends hours every day in meditation, calming his mind so as to focus more clearly on his public and administrative duties. Many devout souls approach rabbis, imams, gurus and Christian priests and pastors to get help with important decisions, and lead lives of devout meditation. But sincerity of heart provides no guarantee against delusion. On the contrary, piety may glamorize ignorance and confused thinking with a specious cosmetic of divine authorization.

Bush's intuitive broodings take place in the absence of disciplined study and analysis, and without knowledgeable debate involving persons who have different points of view. Instead of incorporating the troublesome uncertainties of reasoning into the work of policy formation, Bush excludes them for the sake of maintaining his religious intuitions intact. Secondly, once the determination of divine will has been arrived at and articulated—the largely non-verbal meditative process giving way to 'George, go and end the tyranny in Iraq'—it is accepted as impervious to argument. After the arrival of God's words, the only acceptable response is resolute unquestioning faith. Unshakable optimism and inner peace are benefits that Bush derives from his pious cocksureness, but at the cost of systematic blindness to the realities upon which presidential power must be exercised.

29. Phillips, *American Theocracy*, p. xxxviii.

The shock of 9/11 precipitated George W. Bush into a profound experience of this spirituality, in which he made the worst of his mistakes with the strongest certainty of doing God's will. Surveying a large body of documentary evidence, Kevin Phillips concludes that the fundamental constituents of Bush's Middle East policy were forged in this 'period of personal theocracy' with the invasion of Iraq as its centerpiece.[30] Some believe that Bush abandoned his evangelical allegiances when he failed to follow through on the 'faith-based initiatives' that were supposed to reshape domestic policy. But the invasion of Iraq was itself 'faith-based,' grounded in the President's mystical consciousness.

* * *

You've got to understand my mindset,' Bush declared in April of 2002, as his administration built public support for the War in Iraq.

> We've got to act on behalf of the little ones. We've got to secure the world and this civilization as we know it from these evil people. We just have to do this. And that includes making sure that some of the world's worst leaders who desire to possess the world's worst weapons don't team up with faceless, al Qaeda-type killer organizations. We owe it to the future of this country to lead a coalition against nations that are so evil, and at the same time, desire incredibly evil weapons.[31]

There is an urgent subsurface panic in these words, with their incantatory repetitions: 'evil people', 'world's worst leaders', 'worlds worst nations', 'nations that are so evil', 'incredibly evil weapons.' But the President touches the core of his faith in such litanies, because they put him in touch with the vein of intuition that set him on the trail of Saddam Hussein, and reinforced his confidence even as the ostensible reasons for going to war against Iraq fell apart. Bush's allusion to 'the little ones', invokes the framework within which Bush feels his inescapable obligation. 'Whoso shall offend one of these little ones that believe in me,' says Jesus at Mt. 18:6, 'it were better for him that a millstone were hanged about his neck, and that he were drowned in the depth of the sea'(KJV).

---

30. Phillips, *American Theocracy*, p. xiii.

31. Ron Suskind, *The One Percent Doctrine: Deep Inside America's Pursuit of its Enemies Since 9/11* (New York: Simon & Schuster, 2006), p. 99.

Bush's vision of his presidential duty is shaped by the piety we found at work in the lives of Massachusetts Bay Puritans, in which God's explosive wrath plays a dual role. It menaces faithful souls who fail to comply with divine commands, but if the faithful are obedient it will fall upon the evildoers who threaten them. Bush must discharge the duties of the presidency in keeping with the requirements of an eternal drama, in which divine vengeance is provoked by ceaseless recurring offenses.

Within this mindset the War on Terror is not a policy; it is a mystical consciousness, in which the President visualizes an unfathomable shape-shifting antagonist against whom combat can never end. Political entities like Al Qaeda and Iraq are not the real enemy, but only a temporary locale in which it has manifested itself. As Bush made clear in his address to Congress on 20 September 2001, 'our war on terror begins with Al Qaeda, but it does not end there...Freedom and fear, justice and cruelty, have always been at war.'[32] Thus Bush articulates the axioms of his working faith. In making war on 'terror,' he sets his face against the 'fear' that is the metaphysical antagonist of 'freedom.' If the conquest of Iraq had succeeded, Bush's war would have scored only a temporary victory; the war itself can never come to an end, so long as this consciousness governs the assessment of America's foreign policy options.

When his outlook is challenged by facts and reasoning, Bush answers by invoking the 'evil' of Saddam Hussein. Bob Woodward recalls an interview in which he asked how Americans should respond to the discovery that weapons of mass destruction were not found in Iraq, eight months after the invasion that was justified by the claim that those weapons posed a threat.

"Was the President misled?" Woodward asks.
"No."
"Did he mislead the country?"
"No...The answer is absolutely not."

There had once been such a weapons program in Iraq, and it could possibly have been started up again, and this gives the President a way to communicate the mindset that drives him.

32. Damon Linker, *The Theocons: Secular America Under Siege* (New York: Doubleday, 2006), p. 128.

"And so therefore, given that, even if that's the very minimum you had, how could you not act on Saddam Hussein, given his nature."

Woodward replies delicately that this reply doesn't sound like "the voice of realism," to which Bush promptly replies.

"The realism is to be able to understand the nature of Saddam Hussein, his history, his potential harm to America."[33]

Mystical certainty thus passes for realism, and President Bush becomes impatient with the failure of critics to appreciate the 'nature' of Saddam, how his 'evil' imposed on the President an inescapable divine obligation.

In May of 2002, as it became obvious an invasion was under discussion, Helen Thomas pestered Press Secretary Ari Fleischer with questions about what rationale could support such an action. Bush's claim that the region would be 'better off' without Saddam Hussein, Ms. Thomas insisted, provided no justification for going to war. When Fleischer related this challenge to the President, he responded to the ethical objection by changing the spiritual register.

Legal and philosophical arguments about 'just war' did not apply: what mattered was Bush's visceral revulsion at evil. 'Did you tell her I don't like motherfuckers who gas their own people?...Did you tell her that I don't like assholes who lie to the world?...Did you tell her I'm going to kick his sorry motherfucking ass all over the Mid East?'[34] The aides who were present recognized correctly that this outburst conveyed the President's sincere conviction.

For George W. Bush, the reality of Saddam Hussein was illumined by the fire of his inner vision. Bush calls it his 'instinct' or his 'gut,' terms that give an air of the commonplace to a mystical temperament. 'Instinct' and 'gut' sound like the qualities of a quarterback, or a big-game hunter, but for Bush they are the means of his communion with a divine reality that lies beyond the grasp of mere rationality, a communion that yields true conclusions that defy logic and empirical verification.

In March of 2002, the British government recognized that the Bush Administration was 'now considering regime change' in Iraq. But they looked upon the proposed invasion as a practical enterprise

---

33. Bob Woodward, *State of Denial* (New York: Simon & Schuster, 2006), pp. 488–89.

34. Michael Isikoff and David Corn, *Hubris: The Inside Story of Spin, Scandal, and the Selling of the Iraq War* (New York: Crown Publishers, 2006), p. 3.

not as a mystical drama, and set about contemplating 'what sort of Iraq we want.' They weighed alternative approaches against possible outcomes. The installation of 'a Sunni strongman' ran a 'strong risk of the Iraqi system reverting to type. Military coup could succeed military coup until an autocratic Sunni dictator emerged.' Such a dictator, like Saddam, might try to develop WMD. Another possible 'end state' would be a 'broadly democratic government': this would 'require the US and others to commit to nation building for many years,' and the resultant regime would likely 'seek to acquire WMD and build up its conventional forces, so long as Iran and Israel retain their WMD and conventional armories.'[35] When these concerns were checked against the disposition of the Bush White House, diplomats found little to reassure them: 'There was little discussion in Washington' the report concluded, 'of the aftermath after military action.'[36]

This state of things did not mean that Bush lacked a vision of what his action would produce: he dreamed of a democratic Middle East, with Iraq itself as a 'city on a hill' catalyzing the transformation. As the initial rationale for the invasion was refuted, Bush appealed to this bedrock of his faith. Addressing the Republican National Convention in 2004, Bush explained that he had launched the nation upon a divine project, not just an American project. 'Freedom is not America's gift to the world,' he proclaimed, 'it is the Almighty's gift to every man and woman.'[37] The Reagan/Bush conception of freedom underlies this claim, such that America's unencumbered quest for limitlessly expanding wealth will somehow enrich all other nations. International conflicts over limited resources, and debates about their equitable distribution, are extraneous to this vision: the determining struggle takes place between those who obey God's call, and those who oppose it.

In his Inaugural Address in January of 2005, after Bush had acquired the political authority required to continue his war policy, he explained that his own dedicated struggle, and that of the

35. Mark Danner and Frank Rich, *The Secret Way to War: The Downing Street Memo and the Iraq War's Buried History* (New York: New York Review of Books, 2006), pp. 103, 112–13.

36. Danner and Rich, *The Secret Way to War*, p. 89.

37. George W. Bush, 'President's Remarks at the 2004 Republican National Convention', The White House News and Policies, 2 September 2004. http://www.whitehouse.gov/news/releases/2004/09/20040902-2.html. p. 7.

U.S. military, was not the driving force that would make regime change in Iraq yield a victory for freedom. America's efforts have only

> lit a fire, a fire in the minds of men. It warms those who feel its power; it burns those who fight its progress. And one day, this untamed fire of freedom will reach the darkest corners of our world.[38]

Bush ostensibly disavows the claim that America is 'a chosen nation,' acknowledging that 'God moves and chooses as He wills.' But he asserts that America has been charged with executing a divine will that he himself unerringly discerns. 'History has an ebb and flow of justice,' the President declared, 'but history also has a visible direction, set by liberty and the Author of Liberty.'[39]

In discussing the stated American objectives for a war in Iraq, the British high officials had complained that '"regime change" does not stack up. It sounds like a grudge between Bush and Saddam.' What's needed is to 'depersonalize the objective,' they argued, placing the issues on a broader plane of national policy. The British thus failed once again to grasp the mystical context. To American high officials, 'Bush' and 'Saddam' were not figures in a personal feud, despite the fact that the President was persuaded that Hussein had tried 'to kill my dad.'[40]

In the sacred drama presiding over 'the ebb and flow of justice' Bush and Saddam had become typological figures, embodiments of Good and Evil. They represent supernatural forces locked in eternal conflict, as the cause of God's freedom makes headway in course of history. Bush theology recognizes that God's faithful must encounter moments of testing, but also holds that the ultimate victory belongs to God. The posture of reverent lowliness, as the President prayerfully seeks guidance from the inscrutable Author of Liberty, was linked to his confidence that supernatural power would flow through his actions, if he received that guidance and followed it.

A key to the religious perspective that George Bush brought to the presidency can be found in Ron Suskind's famous 2004 report

38. George W. Bush, 'President Sworn-In to Second Term', The White House News and Policies, 20 January 2005. http://www.whitehouse.gov/news/releases/2005/01/20050120-1.html.

39. Bush, 'President Sworn-In to Second Term'.

40. Danner and Rich, *The Secret Way to War*, pp. 141–42.

on an interview with a White House official, generally supposed to
have been Karl Rove. Here is Suskind's account:

> The aide said that guys like me were "in what we call the reality-based
> community," which he defined as people who "believe that solutions
> emerge from your judicious study of discernable reality." I nodded
> and murmured something about enlightenment principles and
> empiricism. He cut me off. "That's not the way the world really works
> anymore," he continued. "We're an empire now, and when we act, we
> create our own reality. And while you're studying that reality —
> judiciously, as you will — we'll act again, creating other new realities,
> which you can study too, and that's how things will sort out. We're
> history's actors...and you, all of you, will be left to just study what
> we do."[41]

Here the seeming humility of Bush's religious sensibility reveals
its fatal arrogance, that of believing reality itself is malleable in his
hands. Imperial hubris breeds delusions that acquired religious
reinforcement in the Bush Administration. The militant evangelical
tradition — coupled with neocon/theocon religious bigotry —
beguiled George Bush before he entered the White House,
and became overwhelmingly potent in his mind and heart as he
struggled with the trauma of 9/11. Karen Hughes, on whom he
relied for cogent statements of the presiding spiritual drama, put it
succinctly: 'On September 11, Americans saw the face of evil. This
administration will overcome evil with good.'[42]

41. Ron Suskind, 'Faith, Certainty, and the Presidency of George W. Bush', *The New York Times Magazine*, 17 October 2004, p. 51.

42. Karen Hughes, 'Address,' Roy and Margaret Shilling Lectureship, South-western University, Georgetown, TX., 6 February 2003.

Chapter Five

Drinking the Kool Aid

Conquest as Liberation

The invasion of Iraq was a failure, but first it was a stunning success. It achieved, albeit temporarily, the spiritual triumph that the Bush Administration sought, reconsecrating America as divinely commissioned to spread the blessings of freedom around the world.

When Baghdad fell, an American tank pulled down the gigantic statue of Saddam that stood in Firdos Square, producing an icon vaguely reminiscent—in reverse—of the famous flag-raising at Iwo Jima. The media images insisted that American soldiers had not performed this feat: they kept the tank invisible off-camera, and featured Iraqis slapping the face of the statue with their shoes. This fantasy was re-affirmed in the official chronology that was prepared for President Bush: 'April 9...Regime Fractured. Saddam statue toppled by people of Iraq.'[1]

This is not military conquest, said the pictures, but the drama of freedom triumphing over fear. An inborn passion for American democracy had brought down the heathen idol under which Iraqis had been enslaved. The scene was screened over and over, exorcising remembered images of the falling twin towers, even though alert viewers could easily pick out the cable that had actually done the job, high above the heads of the surrounding Iraqis.

The predominant strategic goal of the invasion had become the capture of Baghdad, 'regime removal' replacing 'regime change,' as though taking down Saddam would obviate the need for a long occupation to create a stable new regime, to say nothing of a democratic government.[2] This costly mistake was grounded on the

1. Michael R. Gordon and General Bernard E. Trainor, *Cobra II: The Inside Story of the Invasion and Occupation of Iraq* (New York: Pantheon Books, 2006), p. 553.

2. Thomas E. Ricks, *Fiasco: The American Military Adventure in Iraq* (New York: Penguin Press, 2006), pp. 134-35.

belief that the Iraqis' innate love of American-style freedom would transform Iraq automatically, once the evil oppressor had been destroyed.

The triumph was celebrated on the flight deck of the carrier Lincoln, under the great banner proclaiming MISSION ACCOMPLISHED. It is now commonplace to ridicule this scene; but in an important sense, the words on the banner were true. 'The mission,' Maj. Michael Eisenstadt observed, now redefined as 'getting rid of the regime, had indeed been accomplished.'[3] Like any hallucinogen, this dose of ecstasy soon wore off; and the work of establishing civil order in Iraq remained undone. 'What Bush did,' remarked the military analyst Thomas Ricks 'was to tear down the goalposts at halftime.'[4]

The fantasies dramatized in these moments of vainglory were a good deal worse than useless; they impaired the continuing U.S. mission. The goal of spreading democracy remained in force; but it now turned out to be a separate task. Not only would democracy fail to appear by magic after the 'evil' was abolished, the tactics that had been adopted to abolish evil would place that goal in jeopardy.

* * *

Thomas Ricks observes that the administration pursued 'two contradictory delusions' in the run-up to the invasion. For public consumption they insisted on a 'worst case' regarding Iraq's possession of chemical, biological and nuclear weapons. In their councils, however, they adopted a 'best case' on post-invasion issues, assuming that an enthusiastic welcome would greet U.S. forces and quickly translate into a stable democratic government.[5]

These delusions were soon contradicted by the realities they concealed, but they did not contradict each other. They merge seamlessly in the governing fantasy, that of America's military power smashing evil and bringing freedom. The Iraqi people have distinctive political and religious traditions, quite remote from the Protestant and Enlightenment traditions of American democracy,

3. Ricks, *Fiasco*, p. 135.
4. Ricks, *Fiasco*, p. 145.
5. Ricks, *Fiasco*, pp. 58-59.

to say nothing of free-market capitalism. But this was not taken into account by the White House visionaries. Nor did they recognize that Iraqis who hated Saddam would resent the national humiliation inflicted by the invasion, and seek to command the sequel on distinctively Iraqi terms.

General Buzz Moseley, who directed the air war from his command post near Riyadh, was momentarily aware of the split between the official fantasy and the real-world conditions soon to be confronted. He was exhilarated to watch Iraqis rejoicing at the fall of Saddam, but he also had qualms.

> "I've got mixed emotions about this," he confided to an aide. "We've conquered a country today and for the first time we started it." The aide quickly corrected the general: Iraq had been "liberated." "You're right," Moseley added. "That's a better way to describe it."[6]

This uneasy exchange raises core issues. How will Americans live with having carried out an unprovoked invasion? How will the American military incorporate this dishonorable action into its traditions? How will the Iraqis react, over time, to a conqueror who 'started it?' How long would the anti-Saddam celebration last? And what would replace it?

The aide swiftly quashes such questions, sensing the unwelcome conclusions to which they might lead, and the general himself dismisses them, bravely re-affirming the faith that 'One day...Iraq would become the jewel of the region.'[7] It would become an exemplary outpost of freedom and democracy, America's city on a hill in the Middle East.

The invasion itself was marked by surprises that revealed discrepancies between the guiding illusions and the conditions that the troops were compelled to face.

To U.S. planners, an insurgency was hardly imaginable. They expected — as military forces moved swiftly forward — that the obvious virtue of the invasion would inspire Iraqi fighting men to join the American cause, in numbers much larger than the usual handful of battlefield desertions. 'Entire units...with their equipment and structure intact,' would seek service under U.S. command. Iraqi officers would sign Articles of Capitulation that

6. Gordon and Trainor, *Cobra II*, p. 433.
7. Gordon and Trainor, *Cobra II*, p. 433.

had been drawn up in advance by military lawyers to formalize the mass defections.[8] Not a single Iraqi officer did so.

Major General Jim 'Tamer' Amos, a Marine air wing commander, was shocked and enraged when the anticipated welcome did not take place. After a brutal battle in the southern city of An Nasiriyah had demonstrated American superiority, Amos believed that Iraqis would begin to join the American effort. But he came under persistent attack as he brought his forces northward.

> When the Saddam Fedayeen came down and they were picking up our Marines, they became in my mind cannibals. My whole perspective of how we were going to fight this war changed. I decided that...I was going to personally kill every single Iraqi soldier that fought back...We went after the Iraqi army for vengeance after that.[9]

More was at stake now than subduing a weaker enemy. The 'cannibals' had administered an affront to the American soul, holding the blessings of freedom in contempt, and showing no gratitude for the American sacrifice on their behalf. Amos sought to regain his self-regard by administering 'vengeance.'

Amos's remarks blur together regular Iraqi units with the Saddam Fedayeen, fighters who were indistinguishable from civilians, until they unlimbered their weapons. On the second day of fighting, an American sergeant waved at a group of Iraqis on the invasion route north of Nasiriyah, expecting a friendly reply. 'Instead of waving back,' Thomas Ricks remarks, 'they began attacking with AK-47 rifles, rocket-propelled grenades, and mortars, riding at the American tanks in pickup trucks.'[10]

The vengeful anger inspired by such surprises prompted Americans to lash out in ways that assisted the developing insurgency, and there were American officers who understood this. Army Major Jim Gavrilis made progress quelling the insurgency in Ar Rutbah because he could see that 'the people were ultimately the center of gravity.' Gavrilis decided to 'focus on the people and build positive relationships with them...We showed that we cared more about the people of Ar Rutbah than did the Saddam Fedayeen.'[11] Major General David Petraeus, commenting on

8. Gordon and Trainor, *Cobra II*, p. 105.
9. Gordon and Trainor, *Cobra II*, p. 362.
10. Ricks, *Fiasco*, p. 118.
11. Ricks, *Fiasco*, p. 152.

comparable successes in Mosul, drew a distinction between an 'anti-insurgency' whose object is to kill the enemy, and a 'counter-insurgency' that aims to 'undercut support for the enemy.'[12]

Petraeus did not blindfold detainees once he realized it would insult the dignity of Iraqis. He stopped the practice of breaking into homes at night to look for insurgents and incriminating material, out of consideration for Iraqi feelings about household privacy. Of every mission, Petraeus asked 'will this operation produce more bad guys than it takes off the streets?'[13]

Petraeus, a close student of insurgencies, whose PhD thesis at Princeton had discussed the lessons of Vietnam, was put in command of military operations across Iraq in February of 2007, after years of conflict between strategies based on abolishing evil, and strategies based on an attentive reading of local realities.

The core problem was simple enough. The more you conceive yourself as a champion of goodness, and conceive your antagonists as fit only for divine vengeance, the more you will deal out brutalities on the very population whose allegiance you must win. As your self-righteous blindness drives the population into the arms of the insurgency, the more ground you lose.

Officials in Washington stood by their delusions, however, as conditions on the ground contradicted them. 'I don't think anybody could have predicted,' and 'I don't think anybody anticipated' became a mantra of the administration's response, when in fact the development of an insurgency amid post-invasion chaos had been foreseen by many observers.[14] 'I don't think anyone anticipated that the riches of Iraq would be looted by the Iraqi people,' said one such true believer, defending America's failure to safeguard the National Museum in Baghdad, despite the well-documented record of comparable thievery during the Gulf War.[15] Conceived as liberating the Iraqis from evil, the invasion freed Iraqi criminals from the restraints of Iraqi law.

The presumption that America acts with god-like power and goodness is evident in Donald Rumsfeld's response to the museum disaster.

12. Ricks, *Fiasco*, p. 229.

13. Ricks, *Fiasco*, p. 231.

14. See Frank Rich, *The Greatest Story Ever Sold: The Decline and Fall of Truth From 9/11 to Katrina* (New York: Penguin Press, 2006), pp. 42, 66, 85-86, 177.

15. Ricks, *Fiasco*, p. 85.

It's a fundamental misunderstanding to see those images...of some boy walking out with a vase and say, "Oh, my goodness, you didn't have a plan." That's nonsense...Freedom's untidy, and free people are free to make mistakes and commit crimes and do bad things. They're also free to live their lives and do wonderful things, and that's what's going to happen.[16]

Rumsfeld's comment echoes the classic Christian doctrine of God-given free will, which no political regime can grant or take away. In this self-excusing fantasy, America occupies the place of God, looking down upon 'some boy' who was not free to pursue a virtuous life—seeking the good and sometimes making mistakes—until the American invasion made him free.

For Rumsfeld's Pentagon, it was not America's responsibility to replace the infrastructure America had destroyed, or to supply the systems of governance that are necessary to protect decent citizens from criminal assaults. Participants in conversations about the early reconstruction efforts were staggered when Larry DiRita, Rumsfeld's special assistant, 'slammed his fist on a heavy oak table, and said, 'We don't owe the Iraqi's anything! We're giving them their freedom. That's all we should give them. We don't owe them any other benefit.'[17]

Under the delusion of granting freedom, the invasion replaced one form of agonizing bondage with a worse one, in which people leading ordinary lives are beset by unpredictable eruptions of violence: a trip to the market must be weighed against the danger of being blown to pieces by a car bomb, or being robbed on the street by 'some boy.'

Saddam as Hitler

Washington officials remained firmly entrenched in their determination to foster freedom by abolishing evil, and formulated plans to that effect, which L. Paul Bremer III had in hand when he arrived in Baghdad on 12 May 2003 to assume control of the Coalition Provisional Authority (CPA). The CPA was charged with building America's subsidiary 'city on a hill,' which would be erected,

---

16. Ricks, *Fiasco*, p. 136.
17. Bob Woodward, *State of Denial: [Bush at War, Part III]* (New York: Simon & Schuster, 2006b), p. 161.

according to officials in Washington, on the ruins of an evil empire that the invasion had broken, but not eradicated.

Before Bremer departed from Washington, the Pentagon had prepared an order for the 'De-Baathification of Iraqi Society,' that would 'wipe the country clean of the Baath party ideology.' Douglas Feith, who had developed the policy, wanted to issue the order immediately, but Bremer insisted it should be announced and implemented under his direct authority, once he arrived in Baghdad. Still, the Pentagon leadership wanted to make sure Bremer would not temporize: Feith underscored Rumsfeld's insistence that the decree must be issued as soon as possible, 'even if implementing it causes administrative inconvenience.'[18]

'We are determined to eradicate Saddamism,' Bremer announced when he arrived in Iraq, and forthwith dismissed from government office every member of the Baath Party.

> I thought it was absolutely essential to make it clear that the Baathist ideology, which had been responsible for so many of the human rights abuses and mistreatment of the people...had to be extirpated finally and completely from society, much as the American government decided to extirpate Nazism from Germany at the end of the Second World War.[19]

Bremer recognized that this action could prove 'a lot more than inconvenient. Senior Baathists had formed the leadership of every Iraqi ministry and military organization'.[20] But he swiftly followed up with the dissolution of the Iraqi armed forces, on exactly the same theory, that of clearing away the agents of evil, the better to establish the city of American virtue. Never have pious delusions prompted a more self-defeating blunder. Their livelihoods terminated, the civilian and military officials now formed 'a vast pool of humiliated, antagonized, and politicized men,' observed a senior fellow at the U.S. Institute of Peace.[21]

These newly created malcontents were accustomed to exercising authority, were practiced in public administration, were better informed than most Iraqis about the operation of the civil and

---

18. L. Paul Bremer and Malcolm McConnell, *My Year in Iraq: The Struggle to Build a Future of Hope* (New York: Simon & Schuster, 2006), p. 39.

19. Ricks, *Fiasco*, p. 160.

20. Bremer and McConnell, *My Year in Iraq*, p. 40.

21. Ricks, *Fiasco*, p. 162.

military infrastructure, and they knew where vast stockpiles of weapons were located. The Pentagon plan was a fantasy of social and political purification, expunging the evils of Baathism and Saddamism; it awarded an immense gift of talent, expertise and operational resources to the insurgency.

Bremer confirmed the moral vision informing this action by making a pilgrimage to Al-Hillah, where he viewed a mass grave of Shiite Iraqis who had been slaughtered by Saddam Hussein, during an uprising in 1991 that followed American victory in the Gulf War. The U.S. government was implicated in this atrocity, because President George H. W. Bush had encouraged the uprising, and then failed to provide support for it, leaving the Shia at Saddam's mercy. Memories of this betrayal contributed to the mistrust that Bremer and other American officials encountered in post-invasion Iraq.

But Bremer's vision of radical evil exculpated America. To him, Al-Hillah was a monument to Saddam's evil, pure and simple, and once again he brought to bear the memory of Nazism. 'It's like the Einsatzgruppen during the Holocaust', he said to a young Marine. 'Hitler's mobile killing squads, army, and police massacred over a million people at isolated places like this…Jews, Gypsies, prisoners of war, Catholic clergy.' Al-Hillah had become a holocaust museum for Bremer, in which he discerned the essence of the monstrous evil he had come to obliterate. 'That killing field was the face of the old regime, which our military had defeated in three weeks.'[22] His job was to complete the mission, to clear away the remnants of evil, and transfer leadership to the pure in heart.

Bremer followed this doctrine in hiring people at the CPA to restore the shattered Iraqi infrastructure, where candidates were judged on their moral rectitude, as shown by their stand on the issues of private conduct—abortion, homosexuality, stem-cell research—that were embraced by Bush's constituents on the Christian Right. Applicants' commitment could readily be proven by participation in Bush campaigns stateside, while competence for the tasks at hand counted for little.

Once again, policy followed theological prescription. What mattered was God's protection and blessing on the enterprise, and this could be secured by making sure that it was carried out by

22. Bremer and McConnell, *My Year in Iraq*, p. 51.

people who obeyed God's law. God had 'permitted' the attacks of 9/11 because of rampant immorality — so the theocons taught — and it was critical this should not happen in the Coalition Provisional Authority.

Youthful and 'ideologically minded Republicans, whose only professional experience was working on election campaigns,' staffed ministries responsible for supplying water and electricity, maintaining transportation systems, replacing the police and military capability, and reconstructing hospitals and restoring a system of medical care. Thomas Ricks notes that one such official 'who worked on the budget for security forces, reported that his favorite job before that was "my time as an ice cream truck driver"'.[23]

Bremer's loyalty to the ruling fantasy thus drew a motley of increasingly disoriented Bush loyalists into the administration of post-invasion Iraq, while driving highly competent and fiercely motivated persons into a violent and shrewdly managed opposition.

On 19 August the UN Headquarters in Baghdad was destroyed by a bomb that killed Ambassador Sergio Viera de Mello, whereupon the UN reduced its staff from 800 to 15. The World Bank, the International Monetary Fund, Oxfam, and the UK agency Save the Children departed in the following weeks. The result was to strip the American occupation of the atmosphere of international legitimacy these institutions had imparted. 'That was a brilliant campaign,' remarked Col T.X. Hammes, a Marine counterinsurgency expert. 'They hit the UN, the Red Cross, the Jordanian embassy, and the Iraqi police'.[24]

The capture of Saddam Hussein on 13 December interrupted the general deterioration and was greeted as a harbinger of success. 'We've really got to run with this,' Bremer told an aide. 'It just might be the tipping point.' When he visited Saddam in prison, the guiding imagery sprang into his mind: 'I suddenly thought of Hitler in his bunker in April of 1945.' Surely, once the monster was dead, the evil he had spawned would soon follow. There were enthusiastic celebrations among Shia and Kurds, and Bremer also hoped 'the moderate Sunnis will realize that Baathism is finally dead'.[25]

23. Ricks, *Fiasco*, p. 203.
24. Ricks, *Fiasco*, p. 214.
25. Bremer and McConnell, *My Year in Iraq*, pp. 259-60.

Bremer explained to Iraqis what the event meant to them:

> This is a great day in your history…For decades, hundreds of thousands of you suffered at the hands of this cruel man. For decades, Saddam Hussein divided you citizens (*sic*) against each other…Those days are over forever. Now it is time to look to the future, to your future of hope, to a future of reconciliation.[26]

For a time insurgent attacks did indeed slacken, but then they resumed and reached greater intensity than before.

The insurgency was not a system of cells coordinated by Saddam, as his solitary spider-hole hideout made obvious. It was sustained by increasing numbers of Iraqis who were alienated by the invasion, and by American high-handedness thereafter. They were not centrally controlled, but congregated in loose alliances around ethnic, familial, religious, and political persuasions in a multitude of local settings. Removing Saddam may actually have emboldened Iraqis who had stayed away from the insurgency because of their hatred of Saddam, but now had greater freedom to act on their dislike for the occupation. '"We are not fighting for Saddam,"' said a student from Fallujah, '"We are fighting for our country, for our honor, for Islam. We are not doing this for Saddam."'[27]

As he struggled with the deteriorating security situation, and the difficulties of assembling a representative government, Bremer decided that the mentality of the Iraqi people posed a major problem. American-trained Iraqi forces proved unwilling to go into battle against fellow Iraqis in support of the CPA, and representatives of the rival Sunnis, Shia and Kurds were extremely difficult to mobilize into a working collaboration. Bremer's vision of Saddam as Hitler didn't ring true for Iraqis, and the freedom-loving instincts liberated by his downfall did not make them loyal to American objectives.

Bremer was defeated by Iraqi opposition when he sought to privatize state-owned businesses. Sharing the blessings of American market freedom was the express purpose of a three-year plan of privatization that Bremer announced soon after his arrival in Baghdad. 'Markets allocate resources much more efficiently than politicians,' Bremer explained, as he launched a plan for 're-allocating people and resources from state enterprises to more productive

26. Bremer and McConnell, *My Year in Iraq*, p. 254.
27. Ricks, *Fiasco*, p. 264.

private firms.' The opening phase of this program would offer a range of companies to American investors, including 'cement companies, fertilizer operations...sulfur mining and extraction businesses, and the airline and automobile tire makers.' Such investors would have no obligation to invest the profits from these companies in Iraq, but would be free to transfer them out of the country. This plan aroused fierce resistance in the Iraqi Ministry of Industry, as Pratap Chatterjee explains, and was halted in February of 2004 when the Iraqi Governing Council emphatically rejected it.[28]

It is not difficult to understand the national pride that prevented the Iraqis from entering into Bremer's enthusiasm for the plan. They had no reason to share the vainglorious fantasy that increasing American wealth would count as a victory for freedom, and thus strengthen the cause of freedom worldwide. But Bremer did not see Iraqi skepticism in these terms. To him, the Iraqis were psychologically damaged, not culturally different; and the damage had been inflicted by Saddam Hussein.

When President Bush visited Iraq in June of 2003 Bremer explained to him that

> it's hard for us to understand how psychologically shattered the Iraqi people are...Saddam held power almost three times as long as Hitler. Most Iraqis have had no experience with free thought. They vaguely understand the concept of freedom, but still want us to tell them what to do.[29]

The President realized that this might pose a problem. 'Will they be able to run a free country?' he asked.[30]

When Bremer prepared to depart the country a year later, he returned to this theme: 'The regime's most devastating impact was on the psychological infrastructure of the Iraqi people.' As though the Iraqis would have readily embraced the American plans for them, except for their long incarceration by Saddam, Bremer explained that Iraqis had lived for decades 'in that dark room where they had been taught to trust no one. Given the numbing brutality of day-to-day life...building a society of trust will be a huge undertaking.'[31]

28. Pratap Chatterjee, *Iraq, Inc.: A Profitable Occupation* (New York: Seven Stories Press, 2004), pp. 174, 180, 182.
29. Bremer and McConnell, *My Year in Iraq*, p.29.
30. Bremer and McConnell, *My Year in Iraq*, p. 71.
31. Bremer and McConnell, *My Year in Iraq*, p. 393.

Bremer labored tirelessly to construct a governmental apparatus that could plausibly be called representative, sturdily resisting efforts to install a sham regime that would in essence be autocratic. He succeeded in holding an election, at which large numbers of Iraqis voted their preferences. But this effort took place in the midst of a collapsing security situation, as American troops were withdrawn from the scene, and too many of those remaining failed to understand the requirements of an effective counter-insurgency. The horrors at Abu Ghraib were only the most spectacular example of the recurrent self-defeating exercises in vindictive cruelty, deployed to create an illusion of increased security while producing greater peril.

Bremer constructed a government that was unable to govern. A semblance of civil order was maintained by the U.S. military, but that was insufficient to forestall assassination attempts on Bremer, on visiting Pentagon dignitaries, and on Iraqi officials, to say nothing of allowing ordinary Iraqis to go about their lives unthreatened by explosions in the streets and markets, and by kidnappings and assassinations. In the end Bremer himself was a virtual prisoner of the CPA offices in the Green Zone, and an elaborate ruse was required to get him out of the country alive.

Unreal Cities

Troops and lower-level officials struggling with daily realities in Iraq used slang expressions that allude to cities created by delusion, and comment with eerie pertinence on the failed dream of establishing an exemplary outpost of American democracy. Jim Jones's Jonestown was a real-world nightmare, while the Emerald City—ruled over by the Wizard of Oz—was an elaborate fantasy land ostensibly dreamed up by a little girl. Both provide parables of misplaced faith undergoing collapse.

In an appalling parody of the Puritan 'city on a hill,' the Reverend Jim Jones determined that the corruptions of American society made it necessary for him to lead his followers—members of a cult he had founded in Los Angeles—to establish a home in the wilderness where they could live as God intended. Jones took more than a thousand true believers to Guyana in 1978, where they formed a jungle community he called 'Jonestown.' Jones considered himself the reincarnation of Christ, demanded absolute faith and rigorous obedience from his followers, and arranged for community-wide Kool Aid drinking events, to prepare for the day when they would all journey together to paradise. As the real world closed in, in the form of a congressional inquiry, Jones finally laced the Kool Aid with cyanide, as promised, and 913 of his followers perished.[32]

To 'drink the Kool Aid,' means to embrace suicidal delusions, specifically religious delusions: it evokes a spooky irrational world in which fantasies have replaced the perception of reality.

Jay Garner led the first efforts to provide order in post-invasion Iraq, and foresaw most of the disasters that befell Bremer. When he learned about Bremer's de-Baathification orders, he made a frantic unavailing effort to dissuade him. But when he returned to Washington, Garner couldn't bring himself to lay before President Bush the 'tragic mistakes' that would eventually wreck the effort. Long after the debacle was plain for all to see, Garner gave an interview to Bob Woodward in which he recalled his exit interview in the Oval Office. Administration fantasies had already been punctured by multiple sharp reverses, including the increasing pace of the insurgency after the capture of Saddam Hussein, which made a mockery of the administration's claim that it consisted only of die-hards and dead-enders.

Garner tried to explain to Woodward how it seemed impossible to bring up unwelcome truths in the Oval Office: 'I think if I had [described the deteriorating situation] to the president in front of Cheney and Condoleezza Rice and Rumsfeld in there, the president would have looked at them and they would have rolled their eyes back.' Garner paused for a moment, and then continued: 'They didn't see it coming…As the troops said, they drank the Kool Aid.'[33]

Administration true believers were able to screen disconcerting information from awareness in part because subordinates quickly realized that criticism would be rejected on grounds of being criticism. Making no secret of their absolute faith in their own rightness, they created an atmosphere in which expressing doubt became tantamount to siding with the terrorists. Expressing unshakable faith, by contrast, was the mark of a team player. In Paul Wolfowitz's office at the Pentagon—a major source of

---

32. See Mary McCormick Maaga, *Hearing the Voices of Jonestown* (Syracuse, NY: Syracuse University Press, 1998).

33. Woodward, *State of Denial: [Bush at War, Part III]*, p. 226.

pre-invasion planning—'the phrase "drinking the Kool Aid" was regarded as a badge of loyalty,' as in Jim Jones community of devoted souls in Guyana.[34]

The Wizard of Oz is another source of slang expressions that became current in the early days of the debacle in Iraq. Centered on a gleaming magical city, this story provided a way to express on-the-ground perceptions that White House fantasy had been sold to the American public in a dazzling media blitz.

The Wizard of Oz was quickly recognized, after its publication in 1900, as a comment on the startling power of national media in America's emerging mass culture. An instant classic, Frank Baum's seemingly innocent story became a staple for editorial cartoonists condemning the irresponsible 'yellow journalism' then in its early heyday. The Bush Administration's successful propaganda campaign for the invasion of Iraq echoes William Randolph Hearst's famous exploit, when he used the power of his media outlets to stir up war against the Spanish in Cuba in the 1890s.

Hearst was told by his illustrator Frederick Remington that there would be no war: from his standpoint in Havana, Remington could see no signs of imminent hostilities. Hearst is said to have replied 'You furnish the pictures, and I'll furnish the war.' Hearst mounted a massive campaign of inflammatory misrepresentations, including a Remington picture of Spanish officials strip-searching American women on intercepted American vessels. A 1906 political cartoon depicted Hearst as 'the wizard of Ooze,' as his political fortunes declined postwar.[35]

The Wizard is famous for stupendous magical powers; he occupies the Emerald City, where his awe-inspiring voice echoes from a gigantic throne room. 'Everything is all right,' he proclaims to his jittery subjects. 'The great and powerful Oz has got things well in hand. So you can all go home and there's nothing to worry about.'[36] Dorothy and her companions, believing that their hearts' desires

34. Rajiv Chandrasekaran, *Imperial Life in The Emerald City: Inside Iraq's Green Zone* (New York: Alfred A. Knopf, 2006), p. 294.

35. L. Frank Baum, W. W. Denslow and Michael Patrick Hearn, *The Annotated Wizard of Oz: The Wonderful Wizard of Oz* (New York: Norton, 2000), p. 262.

36. In Judy Garland, Frank Morgan, Ray Bolger, Bert Lahr, Jack Haley, Noel Langley, Florence Ryerson *et al.*, *The Wizard of Oz* (Warner Bros. Family Entertainment. [S.l.]: Turner Entertainment Co., 1999), Adaptation by Noel Langley from the book by L. Frank Baum.

can be fulfilled by the great magician, make a pilgrimage to the city, and discover that the Wizard is a staged illusion. The giant voice, the huge talking head, the bursts of flame, and the rolling smoke are all generated by a hidden mechanism in the throne room that is operated by a frightened little man.

Observers of the Iraq debacle have found many occasions for invoking this legend, with leading policymakers as contrivers of the grandiloquent humbug. Eleanor Clift's 'Wizard of Oz Letter,' discusses a request from President Bush that Vice-President Cheney accompany him to a congressional committee meeting that was scheduled to take his testimony, because the President evidently feared that he would be unable to explain his war policy all by himself. It was a moment when the mask of wizardry slipped, revealing the intimidated little man behind it.[37]

Another Oz scenario applied to Iraq takes place when the Wicked Witch of the West dissolves after Dorothy throws water on her and the Witch's warriors burst into exclamations of joy. 'It was assumed that the dramatic ouster of Saddam would create a Wizard of Oz moment,' noted General Carl Strock. 'After the wicked dictator was deposed, throngs of cheering Iraqis would hail their liberators and go back to work under the tutelage of postwar organization.'[38] As to the post-invasion debacle, Col. Alan King observed, 'We were like the Wizard of Oz…[the Iraqis] expected miracles of us, in terms of living standards.'[39]

The Coalition Provisional Authority, from which this miracle was to emerge, was hard pressed to maintain its own living standards, as the chaos of the streets mounted, together with the danger of insurgent attacks penetrating the offices themselves. These functions were eventually secured in the seven-square-mile sector that Saddam had set aside for his Republican Palace, called the 'Green Zone' because of its lovely lawns and gardens. At an entrance to the palace stands a mural of the twin towers, on which is emblazoned a declaration of the misplaced faith: THANK GOD FOR THE COALITION FORCES & FREEDOM FIGHTERS AT HOME AND ABROAD.[40]

37. Eleanor Clift, 'Wizard of Oz Letter,' *Newsweek*, 2 April 2004.
38. Gordon and Trainor, *Cobra II*, p. 463.
39. Ricks, *Fiasco*, p. 327.
40. Chandrasekaran, *Imperial Life in The Emerald City*, p. 10.

The Green Zone, and the happy life it would generate for ordinary Iraqis, was supposed to work like West Berlin, a showcase of democracy contrasting with the dismal sameness of the Communist-dominated Eastern sector. But the Green Zone was also to serve as a dynamic, expansive force, not just a bulwark against aggression. The initiatives adopted and administered in the Green Zone were to reach outward to transform the Iraqi wilderness, to build there a whole society as beautiful and productive as what lay within the walls.

Rajiv Chandrasekaran describes what developed in fact, an insular bureaucracy where American decision-makers worked to reshape a society they misunderstood from the start, and hardly ever saw first-hand. For those safe inside the Green Zone,

> the real Baghdad—the checkpoints, the bombed-out buildings, the paralyzing traffic jams—could have been a world away. The horns, the gunshots, the muezzin's call to prayer, never drifted over the walls. The fear on the faces of American troops was rarely seen by the denizens of the palace.[41]

The insurgency made it too dangerous outside the Zone, so that the wizards and panjandrums of American policy could not expose their fantasies to conversations with ordinary Iraqi citizens. Chandrasekaran entitles his book *Imperial Life in the Emerald City: Inside Iraq's Green Zone*, consummate emblem of the Wizard of Oz reality in which the American effort was enmeshed.

The Emerald City is what became of Ronald Reagan's 'shining city on a hill,' in the administration of George W. Bush. As the inheritor and spokesman of a debased tradition, in which Puritan warnings against spiritual arrogance are erased from an inspiring vision of American possibility, President Bush is a relatively minor figure in bringing on the disasters that followed from the orders he signed. 'Only the illusions churned out by public relations apparatchiks and perpetuated by celebrity-worshipping journalists,' remarks Andrew Bacevich, 'prevent us from seeing that those inhabiting the inner sanctum of the West Wing are agents more than independent actors.'[42]

---

41. Chandrasekaran, *Imperial Life in The Emerald City*, p. 19.
42. A. J. Bacevich, *The New American Militarism: How Americans are Seduced by War* (New York: Oxford University Press, 2005), p. xii.

American citizens, including American leaders, remain hapless puppets following the routines prescribed by flawed traditions so long as we fail to confront those traditions directly, and choose our pathway forward, instead of having it chosen for us. Faith in America as a beacon of freedom embraces many possible meanings, not only the delusional meanings dramatized in Iraq.

The remaining chapters of this book examine a conception of sacred heroism that is inseparable from the traditions of continental expansion that inform America's imperial ambitions. The story of catastrophic success in Iraq remains incomplete, until we recognize that the Bush Administration cast itself in the role of frontier hero, deploying the hero's distinctive methods and exulting in the conventional scenarios of his triumph.

When these grandiose fantasies collided with real-world conditions, the administration succumbed to the resultant vexations, and fell victim to a spiritual depravity that came to center stage as the shouts of victory rang hollow.

Chapter Six

AVENGING ANGEL

Saint George

The plane was a lone figure against the vast westward expanse of ocean and sky, as it brought the Commander-in-Chief from the American mainland to the flight deck of the USS Lincoln. After two fly-bys, the plane swooped down and made a perfect tailhook landing. Then the cockpit opened and the President emerged, his lean muscular body moving easily in the snug flight suit.

His words were few, suiting the casual potency of his gestures: 'Thank you,' he said, 'preciate it.' 'Yes, I flew it,' he said. 'Yeah, of course, I liked it. I miss flying, I can tell you that.'[1]

This brilliantly orchestrated political theatre counteracted the disgrace inflicted by the 9/11 terrorist attacks. The Navy S-3b jet, emblazoned 'Navy One' for the occasion, awakened visual memories of the lawless hateful planes of 9/11. The great tower of the warship, standing erect and proud with its 'MISSION ACCOMPLISHED' banner, recalled the stricken and falling World Trade Center. The scene summoned up fragmentary visions of the nightmare, and banished them in a festival of triumph.

'The tyrant is fallen and Iraq is free,' Bush declared tersely in the speech that followed his landing, but that was not the core meaning of the pageant. American freedom was the driving force in the drama staging Bush as a military hero, not concern for the ravaged people of Iraq. 'I have conquered,' was the hero's message; 'America is free.'

Americans had yearned for liberation from the fear that God had ceased to bless America, allowing evil to pierce the shield that He had erected to protect His chosen. Triumph in Iraq now

---

1. See Frank Rich, *The Greatest Story Ever Sold: The Decline and Fall of Truth from 9/11 to Katrina* (New York: Penguin, 2006), p. 89 and Elizabeth Bumiller, 'Keepers of Bush Image Lift Stagecraft to New Heights', *The New York Times*, 15 May 2003.

demonstrated that the true target of divine wrath was not the United States.

The tempest of destruction had been 'carried out with a combination of precision and speed and boldness,' the President explained, inflicting a retribution that fit the crime: 'The terrorists and their supporters declared war on the United States. And war is what they got.' The death of American soldiers had served the cause of divine justice. 'Their final act on this Earth was to fight a great evil and bring liberty to others.' Having 'taken up the highest calling of history,' the American military fulfilled the biblical promise of divine deliverance: 'To the captives "come out," — and to those in darkness, "be free."'[2]

In his warrior costume, the President symbolized the stupendous military technology under his command. But powerful religious and cultural traditions were also implicit here. Long before he made his approach in the Navy S-3B Viking, virtuous lone warriors have appeared against an empty horizon—Alan Ladd, John Wayne, Clint Eastwood have played the part—approaching on horseback to bring deliverance to a fearful and stricken community.

'Western' heroes play a key role in the myth of America as God's people, as they move westward into the wilderness to claim their divine birthright and subdue peoples already living there. The zone of interaction between chosen and not-chosen is the 'frontier,' and the frontier hero—this savior on horseback—embodies the sacred collective mission, and exemplifies the deadly force required to achieve it. This mythology likewise defines the American 'freedom' that President Bush invoked: the freedom of unencumbered access to the resources claimed by the chosen, against figures of evil who contest their claim.[3]

The American myth of the redemptive gunman, however, belongs within a religious tradition that transcends American concerns. The Western hero is an American version of St. George, the Christian knight of the Crusades, in whom the core issues of legitimate deadly

2. 'President Bush Announces Major Combat Operations in Iraq have Ended', www.whitehouse.gov/news/releases/2003/05/20030501-15.html

3. For a discussion of this figure in the context of other superhero myths, see John Shelton Lawrence and Robert Jewett, *The Myth of the American Superhero* (Grand Rapids, MI: W.B. Eerdmans, 2002) and Robert Jewett and John Shelton Lawrence, *Captain America and the Crusade Against Evil: the Dilemma of Zealous Nationalism* (Grand Rapids, MI: W.B. Eerdmans, 2003).

force are at stake. St. George is venerated by Eastern and Russian orthodox communions, as well as by Roman Catholicism, and serves as the patron saint of numerous cities and nations: Moscow, Beirut, Ferrara, England, Greece, Germany, the Netherlands. 'God for Harry! England and St. George!' shouts Shakespeare's King Henry the Fifth, as he leads a victorious charge against the French.[4]

In the classic icon, St. George appears on horseback, wielding a spear that slays the dragon of evil. He symbolizes the conflict between the sacred community and its demonic adversaries: heathens in the Holy Land, godless nations next door, or impious insurgents within the state. St. George bestows divine blessing on the deadly force that is necessary for the maintenance of sovereignty, whether city-wide, national, or imperial. National churches across Europe, integrated into state governance and supported by taxes, enshrine St. George as a signal that Christianity authorizes the military power that sustains the state. No established church is permitted to exist in America, but the need for such sacred legitimacy is nonetheless compelling.

As a rule the solitary gunman of the mythic west is not decked out in explicitly Christian symbolism, because the religious meanings of this figure conflict with a Christian version of warrior heroism that centers on Christ-like suffering. Mainline denominations embrace a tradition in which Christ is not an agent of state-sponsored deadly force, but its victim: the meaning of his death directly contradicts the triumphant violence of St. George. Before exploring the emergent religious vision that fuses Christian wrath with frontier heroism, we must sketch the tradition of Christlike suffering that it displaced.

Christlike Sacrifice

The American Civil War prompted Christian Americans to seek spiritual resources to cope with the national crisis, and with the hardship and loss it occasioned for hundreds of thousands of

---

4. See 'St George' in Alban Butler and Kathleen Jones, *Butler's Lives of the Saints* (Tunbridge Wells, Kent: Burns & Oates, 1999), vol. 4 [April], pp. 162–64. William Shakespeare, 'The Life of Henry the Fifth' (III.2.35), in Stephen Greenblatt *et al. The Norton Shakespeare: Based on the Oxford Edition* (W. W. Norton & Co, Inc., 1997), p. 1477.

individuals. Abraham Lincoln noted that soldiers on both sides prayed to the same God for victory; and this paradox gave rise to skepticism about Christian belief, as though war itself refuted the faith. Stephen Crane's *The Red Badge of Courage*, the most compelling novel of the Civil War, includes a savage parody of Christian doctrine. But Crane wrote two decades after the war had ended and, despite the uncanny power with which he captured battlefield experiences, he had never himself seen combat.

Julia Ward Howe, by contrast, wrote 'The Battle Hymn of the Republic' under the immediate stress of wartime. The lines of verse came to her before dawn, in December 1861, following a long day spent near Washington at a review of Federal troops who were bound for a conflict whose outcome was gravely in doubt. The Southern states had seceded one after another in a procession that began in January of 1861, with the attack on Fort Sumpter taking place in April and disaster befalling Union troops at Bull Run in July. The battle at Gettysburg would provide a harbinger of Union victory, but that would take place in July of 1863, many agonizing months in the future.

Howe set her poem to the tune of 'John Brown's Body,' which the Union troops had adopted as a marching song. Howe joined in singing the rousing anthem with the soldiers as they departed from the review, and her poem incorporated the theme of death and resurrection that had become central to the legend of John Brown's execution. 'John Brown's body lies a'mouldering in the grave,' goes the opening verse of the song, 'but his soul goes marching on.' In Howe's 'Battle Hymn,' likewise, the death and resurrection of Jesus illuminates the fate of soldiers who are killed in battle.[5]

At the center of Christian piety stands the figure of a dying man, and the many conflicting versions of Christian teaching are unanimous in holding that he did not deserve to die, but died that others might live. The salvation available through the death and resurrection of Jesus bears an immediate application to the death of soldiers who go into danger on behalf of the community.[6]

5. See 'Julia Ward Howe' in Wesley T. Mott (ed.), *Dictionary of Literary Biography*, vol. 235, *The American Renaissance in New England* (Third Series; NP: The Gale Group, 2001), pp. 227–34.

6. See Drew Gilpin Faust, *This Republic of Suffering: Death and the American Civil War* (New York: Alfred A. Knopf, 2008), pp. 6, 17.

Lincoln's Gettysburg Address touches on this theme in describing the Union dead as men who gave their lives that America's great experiment in democracy 'shall not perish from the earth.' In his conclusion Lincoln visualizes a fulfillment in which the nation itself will be reborn. To make certain 'these dead shall not have died in vain' the living must dedicate themselves to realizing 'a new birth of freedom' for the nation as a whole. Keeping faith with the Union soldiers depends on achieving a collective transformation, toward a new and more just America.[7]

Julia Ward Howe likewise pictures the soldier's death as a life-giving sacrifice. Lincoln's muted allusion to Christ, to the Easter miracle, and to the spiritual transfiguration of ordinary mortals are all explicit here:

> In the beauty of the lilies Christ was born across the sea,
> With a glory in His bosom that transfigures you and me:
> As He died to make men holy, let us die to make men free.[8]

Civil War soldiers took courage from the death of Jesus because of the promise that resurrection awaits the believer who dies in battle. Gerald Linderman recounts the story of a gunner who was converted after losing two comrades at Chancellorsville, and had then survived the first two days at Gettysburg. He had written a letter home toward the end of the third day, rejoicing in having been spared. Then a shell struck nearby. '"There lay our noble comrade,"' wrote a friend, '"the top of the skull blown off and the brain actually fallen out upon the ground in two bloody, palpitating lobes."' But the friend voiced no shock, Linderman explains: in his eyes God's '"chariot and horses of fire had caught [the dead man] up into Heaven."'[9]

In due course such faith was disturbed, not confirmed, by the wholesale gore of the Civil War battlefield. As new weapons' technology brought an increased level of carnage, witnessing gross bodily mutilation became a commonplace experience for ordinary citizen soldiers. In the wars of the eighteenth century, soldiering was confined, for the most part, to a low-life rank and file, including

---

7. See Garry Wills, *Lincoln at Gettysburg: The Words that Remade America* (New York: Simon & Schuster, 1992), and Faust, *This Republic of Suffering*, p. 189.

8. 'Howe' in Mott (ed.), *Dictionary*, p. 230.

9. Gerald F. Linderman, *Embattled Courage: The Experience of Combat in the American Civil War* (New York: Free Press, 1987), p. 65.

mercenaries, with an officer class drawn from the gentry and aristocracy. But in the Civil War the horrors of battle came to public awareness with grievous intensity. Ambrose Bierce was among the first American writers to record the shock: the bitter clash between his battlefield experience and the reigning conventional piety formed a major theme of his writing life-long.[10] Fifteen years after the war ended, General Sherman provided the classic summary. War is not glory, he declared, not even divine glory: 'It is all hell.'[11]

Stephen Crane's *The Red Badge of Courage* stages a mock-crucifixion that dramatizes the impact of battlefield gore on faith in the soldier's Christ-like sacrifice. Henry Fleming, the novel's protagonist, encounters Jim Conklin, a Christ-figure with wounded hands and a wounded side who makes a strange 'rite-like' progress to a seemingly pre-ordained place of dying, where terminal convulsions set in. 'The tremor of his legs caused him to dance a sort of hideous hornpipe. His arms beat wildly about his head in expression of implike enthusiasm.' Conklin then falls to the ground, and Fleming could see 'that the side looked as if it had been chewed by wolves.' 'Hell,' says Henry Fleming, shaking his fist at the sky.[12]

Ernest Hemingway's *A Farewell to Arms* carries forward the claim that Christian notions of the soldier's redemptive sacrifice are themselves a desecration, a way of evading the brutal realities that men in battle face. Lofty pious language nauseates Hemingway's protagonist Frederick Henry (the name recalls Crane's Henry Fleming): 'Words such as glory, honor, courage or hallow were obscene,' only an idiom of shouted speeches and 'proclamations that were slapped up by billposters over other proclamations.' He 'had seen nothing sacred and the things that were glorious had no glory and the sacrifices were like the stockyards at Chicago if nothing was done with the meat except bury it.'[13]

10. Faust, *This Republic of Suffering*, pp. 196–200.

11. Charles Royster, *The Destructive War: William Tecumseh Sherman, Stonewall Jackson, and the Americans* (New York: Knopf, 1991), p. 253.

12. Stephen Crane and Sculley Bradley, *The Red Badge of Courage: An Authoritative Text: Backgrounds and Sources: Criticism*, A Norton Critical Edition (New York: Norton, 1976), p. 50.

13. Ernest Hemingway, *A Farewell to Arms* (New York: Scribner, 1969), pp. 184–85.

The Wrath of the Lamb

The Bush Administration made little use of sacrificial Christian imagery in promoting the war in Iraq, and indeed downplayed the sacrifices actually taking place. Pat Tillman, the handsome professional football player who gave up a lucrative contract in order to join the military, was portrayed as having made a noble sacrifice after he was killed in Afghanistan. But this story became one of the administration's early public relations disasters when it became known that Tillman had been killed by friendly fire, and that his superiors subsequently concealed the fact from the public, and from his family, in order to maintain the inspiring fiction. The story of Christ-like sacrifice requires that the hero perish in virtuous combat, not through a horrible accident.

Many soldiers were killed in Afghanistan and Iraq, who have indeed been sacrificed. But the concept of sacred warmaking that has animated the Bush Administration takes little interest in soldiers' vulnerability to suffering and death. On the contrary, the administration has a firm policy against public ceremonies to greet coffins when they arrive in the United States, and the television and print media are forbidden to record the arrivals.

The image of the fighting man preferred by the administration is George W. Bush on the flight deck of the USS Lincoln, a man in excellent health, invincible and triumphant, who exults in a victory achieved not through blood and agony, but through the power of a fabulous technology, here eloquently represented by the great carrier with its attendant warplanes and missile launchers.

Dead soldiers coming home have been treated as an embarrassment because, for the administration's favored narrative, they are an embarrassment. They are a reminder that soldiers are mortal men and women, not unstoppable angels of death. And the same is true of living soldiers and their ordinary needs.

It became notorious early in the conflict that soldiers' families had to spend their own money to purchase urgently needed equipment. 'I can honestly say that half the gear I wear I bought myself,' remarks Jason Hartley: 'most of us paid for our own gear (pistol belt, suspenders, ammo pouches, canteens and covers etc)... The Army is getting a well-outfitted infantryman on the cheap.'[14]

14. Jason Christopher Hartley, *Just Another Soldier: A Year on the Ground in Iraq* (New York: HarperCollins, 2005), p. 38.

In the early years of the war, soldiers scavenged dumps for sheet metal and plywood that could be used to reinforce the sides of HumVees, and sometimes packed them with sandbags.

Couple this with the multiplying 'stop-loss' orders, which force soldiers into extended combat tours, and add the 'almost palpable disdain' for treating wounded veterans that was demonstrated by their shabby treatment at Walter Reed Army Medical Center, and you have a predictable outcome of the Bush Administration's tacit but powerful investment in a Christian vision of warmaking in which soldiers are not suffering mortal men but invulnerable agents of God's wrath.[15]

Julia Ward Howe's 'Battle Hymn' supplies the classic language here as well, derived from biblical passages in Isaiah and Revelation that envision the end of the world as a battle, when Christ will destroy the assembled forces of evil with an omnipotent assault. Hence the opening lines of the Battle Hymn:

> Mine eyes have seen the glory of the coming of the Lord;
> He has trampled out the vintage where the grapes of wrath are stored;
> He has loosed the fateful lightning of his terrible swift sword.[16]

This apocalyptic vision draws imaginative power and spiritual authority from the horror of the battlefield. Howe's trampled vintage alludes to a famous passage in *Revelation* that pictures 'the great winepress of the wrath of God,' pouring forth an ocean of blood 'even unto the horse bridles, by the space of a thousand and six hundred furlongs.'[17]

Bestselling contemporary revivals of bloodthirsty Christian apocalypse have been noticed by the literary media mostly as subliterary trash. But Tim LaHaye's 'Left Behind' books have sold millions of copies to readers who find in them a confirmation for the religious reality of their world.

15. For a fuller discussion see Joseph E. Stiglitz and Linda Bilmes, *The Three Trillion Dollar War: The True Cost of the Iraq Conflict* (New York: W.W. Norton, 2008), pp. 61–90. See p. 68, for the expression 'almost palpable disdain' which comes from Defense Secretary Robert Gates, who replaced Donald Rumsfeld.

16. Jewett and Lawrence in *Captain America*, p. 62 discuss Howe's conflation of these seemingly contradictory themes.

17. *Revelation* 14:19–20 in *The Holy Bible Containing the Old and New Testaments and the Apocrypha: Translated out of the Original Tongues with the Former Translations Diligently Compared and Revised, by His Majesty's Special Command* (New York: Cambridge University Press: nd).

As Chris Hedges has shown, Christian communities are rapidly taking form outside mainstream denominations, which are giving religious expression to the urgent anxieties and resentments that have come to afflict middle-class families. The increasing economic polarization of America into a super-rich elite and a prostrate underclass has left the middle range of formerly secure and self-respecting families scrambling to maintain themselves, as they face rapidly escalating costs for housing, transportation, medical care, and education.[18] These anxieties are certain to increase, amid the severe recession that was triggered off by the financial crisis that began in 2008.

Drawing its membership largely from citizens who struggle against multiplying threats to their self-respect, the religious right wing offers them ecstatic dramas of triumph over the morally undeserving. Media intellectuals correctly point out that this movement actually serves the political interests of the newly dominant economic elite, but such empirical analysis is crushed by the force of true belief. Sociologists demonstrate that capital punishment and gun ownership have no beneficial effect, but to the faithful they provide a symbolic empowerment that strengthens the heart, offering a vision of effective action against a sea of troubles.

Sarah Palin became an instant celebrity for the Republican right wing because she embodied this appeal. Not contaminated by association with the sophisticated urban Northeast, and blessedly free of book-learning about foreign relations, she is native to the wilderness where God sheds his grace on the self-reliant. She knows how to field-dress the moose that falls to her .30–30, and is a faithful member of the Wasilla Assembly of God.

To Christian culture-warriors the social order appears to have fallen mysteriously under the influence of a pervasive evil, and their rage at their own undeserved distress is projected against figures who embody that evil. The 'lifestyle' issues of abortion, euthanasia and homosexuality appear as markers of a corruption afflicting society as a whole, the nation fallen away from God. Focusing on issues of 'personal' morality, such believers join the ranks of a culture-wide moral conflict involving evil powers beyond their control, but not, they believe, beyond God's control. They avidly

18. Chris Hedges, *American Fascists: The Christian Right and the War on America* (New York: Free Press, 2006).

consume depictions of a magical transformation of reality, which will culminate when all of God's enemies are arrayed against Him.

> Warships, tanks, personnel carriers, bombs, rockets, launchers, and all manner of battle paraphernalia from tents to food and medical supplies had been arriving at Holy Land ports daily for months, vast encampments growing around the entire expanded city of Jerusalem.[19]

So LaHaye introduces the final confrontation in *Kingdom Come*, his novel of the ultimate showdown.

Satan commands this fighting force, against which stands the lone figure of Jesus, with the whole world watching, mostly on television. 'The cosmic battle of the ages between the forces of good and evil, light and darkness, life and death, was about to commence.' When Satan orders the attack, Jesus quietly repeats the words that God first spoke to Moses, 'I AM WHO I AM,' and Satan's forces are devoured by fire from heaven. 'The clouds rolled back and the heavens opened, and orange and yellow and red mountains of white-hot, roiling flames burst forth. Satan's entire throng—men, women, weapons, everything—was vaporized in an instant'.[20]

Christopher Bodley, chaplain to a battalion of Marines in Iraq, invokes this conception of Christ as he leads divine services on the eve of battle. '"They nickname you Devil Dogs," he tells his flock,'—alluding to a Marine tradition—'"But Jesus was the original Devil Dog. He faced evil, and he beat it. Jesus is the Devil Dog you will want on your side going into battle."'[21] However bizarre this theology may seem, it is firmly rooted in New Testament texts foretelling the unquenchable fire that will consume the enemies of God when Christ returns in judgment, and it has strong precursors in the Puritan teaching brought to bear on war with the tribes. For believers today, as in the past, Christ's victory at Armageddon provides a model to believers, showing how they should contend with the 'evil' they encounter in the world around them, namely through implacable hostility aimed at total destruction.

Thus Rod Parsley exhorted his faithful followers to Christian revolution in 2006:

19. Tim F. LaHaye and Jerry B. Jenkins, *Kingdom Come: the Final Victory*, Left Behind Series (Carol Stream, IL: Tyndale House Publishers, 2007), p. 344.

20. LaHaye and Jenkins, *Kingdom Come*, pp. 346–47.

21. Evan Wright, *Generation Kill: Devil Dogs, Iceman, Captain America, and the New Face of American War* (New York: Berkeley Caliber, 2004), p. 47.

Man your battle stations! Ready your weapons!...I came to incite a riot.
I came to effect a divine disturbance in the heart and soul of the church.
Man your battle stations. Ready your weapons. Lock and load![22]

Informed mutual respect across disparate religious traditions is abhorrent to this sensibility, as is reasoned debate grounded in empirical evidence. Doubt and disagreement are symptoms of a fatal and contagious disease, that of acquiescence in Satan's plans. Whether they are dupes or conscious infidels, Satan's followers in America today must be destroyed if they can't be converted, and the leaders of this movement have fashioned a rhetoric of fangs-bared ferocity. 'Sometimes I wish God would give me a Holy Ghost machine gun. I'd blow your head off,' shouted the faith healer Benny Hinn in responding to his critics. 'To hell with you! Get out of my life! Get out of my way!' snarled Paul Crouch. 'Quit blocking God's bridges or God's going to shoot you—if I don't. I don't even want to talk to you or hear you! I don't want to see your ugly face'.[23]

For Chris Hedges, this movement of 'American Fascists' seeks ultimately to destroy democracy in America, eliminating debate and popular sovereignty from our political order, and replacing it with authoritarian Christianity. The bitterness and resentment underlying the fascist impulse is widespread, Hedges notes, perhaps enough to fuel an explicit movement toward dictatorship, should a major crisis raise public anxieties to an intolerable height. But in the meantime, outbursts of fanatical frenzy are generally kept within the family, as the movement seeks power by infiltrating democratic processes.

Damon Linker describes the rhetorical strategies that enabled the Christian right wing to gain predominant authority in the Republican Party, with George W. Bush as their champion. Conservative Roman Catholics—Michael Novak, Richard John Neuhaus and George Weigel—have provided the intellectual leadership of this effort, enabling them to create a 'Theocon' coalition with Protestant biblical literalists and Pentecostals. These latter groups were formerly at odds with each other and with Catholicism. But they are drawn together by a shared hatred of the 'tyranny' of secular liberalism, and by their posture of ardent submission to institutionally formalized religious authority. Submission to the

22. Hedges, *American Fascists*, p. 30.
23. Hedges, *American Fascists*, pp. 172–73.

Roman hierarchy, submission to literalist interpreters of the Bible, and submission to those who arouse and administer the action of the Holy Spirit has become a source of unity, instead of an occasion for conflict.[24]

Linker explains that this coalition has attained political power by suppressing reference to the members' actual (and quite disparate) religious experiences and convictions, in order to forge what Neuhaus termed a 'public language of moral purpose' that would define and advocate issues in palatable terms. Despite the sacrifice of intellect required for unquestioning obedience to religious authority, these partisans learned to make 'sophisticated intellectually respectable arguments about American society and history, democracy and justice, culture and the law'.[25]

The Theocons' stealth campaign gave its leaders access to the inner counsels of the Bush Administration, conferring a Christian blessing on the attitudes that animated the top decision-makers. Theocon leadership also delivered a solid block of political supporters who were repaid by policies that conformed to their views on stem-cell research, abortion, gay rights, contraception, and the teaching of evolution. They were also promised funding for 'faith-based' social service organizations that would provide opportunities for proselytizing.

The administration's adherence to the militarism of the Christian Right was not coupled with the public promotion and celebration of their principles. Yet, the double-coding of presidential speeches, as Bruce Lincoln has demonstrated, frequently signaled his commitment to the self-righteous ferocity lying at the heart of their spirituality. Bush's declaration that 'the terrorists may burrow deeper into caves,' Lincoln observes, covertly alludes to a passage in Revelation foretelling that the enemies of God will hide 'in caves and among the rocks of the mountains,' in an unavailing effort to find shelter from 'the wrath of the Lamb.' The effect of these allusions, for Christians who have taken to heart the requisite passages, is to 'associate American bomb runs with the wrath of the Lord.'[26]

24. Damon Linker, *The Theocons: Secular America Under Siege* (New York: Doubleday, 2006), p. 63.

25. Linker, *The Theocons*, p. 51.

26. Bruce Lincoln, *Holy Terrors: Thinking About Religion After September 11* (Chicago, IL: University of Chicago Press, 2006), pp. 30–31.

Sergeant David Bellavia evokes the spiritual power he found in this vision of Christ amid the fierce combat that followed the attack on Fallujah. 'A thousand thoughts tumble through my mind. They get jammed up, piling on top of each other so all I get are unintelligible fragments. My palms are slick with sweat.' Momentarily paralyzed by the emotional storm, Bellavia finds release as an incantation comes unbidden to his mind: 'The power of Christ compels you.' It is a line from *The Exorcist*, spoken as Christ and Satan battle for dominion in an afflicted soul.[27]

Bellavia notes that an AC 130 — ground-support aircraft with appalling anti-personnel firepower — 'is the closest man has come in imitation of the fist of God'.[28] But as he goes deeper into intimate combat, Bellavia finds the supernatural power of destruction within himself. He is close enough to the enemy to hear them praying softly 'Allahu Akbar [God is great],' and finds himself praying too:

> I will be completely fearless, and if I say I believe in You, then fuck it. I believe in You..."The power of Christ compels you."...I seize those words. I embrace them. They become a lifeline. I stake everything on the strength they evoke. I utter them again, louder. I have my own mantra now. It is my talisman, my testament of faith. THE POWER OF CHRIST COMPELS YOU!...In one sudden rush, I carry the fight to the enemy.[29]

The devout passion felt by Sgt. Bellavia was aroused by battlefield stress, but its essential contours were not invented in battle. Bellavia absorbed them from doctrines of Christian combat with demonic forces of hell that were part of his early Roman Catholic training. Such burning candid intensity, to say nothing of its parochial ring, makes such confessions unsuited to seeking political power in a multicultural democracy.

So the Christian right pursued its political ambitions covertly, and the President marked its triumph covertly, because the underlying religious temperament sounds weird and exotic to Americans not familiar with them, and are marked as irrational fantasies by many who are. Yet this temperament can represent

27. David Bellavia and John R. Bruning, *House to House: An Epic Memoir of War* (New York: Free Press, 2007), p. 214.

28. Bellavia and Bruning, *House to House*, p. 80.

29. Bellavia and Bruning, *House to House*, p. 240.

itself plausibly as the revival of a more broadly shared vision of America as God's authorized empire, and it makes a powerful appeal to troubled souls for whom the heart has compelling reasons that transcend the sophisticated reasonings of a morally suspect elite.

Even when the confluence of Catholic, Fundamentalist and Pentecostal militarism remains tacit, however, unwelcome consequences flow from viewing American military might as the agent of God's apocalyptic power to destroy evil. The realities of war itself are then presumed to resemble the cosmic drama, with its quick and decisive victory. In addition, when war is envisioned as God's prime instrument for resolving political conflict, it becomes the ultimate arbiter of human reality.

War is then hailed as a center of value for the society as a whole, a foundation of national policy rather than its instrument. James Carroll and Andrew Bacevich have discussed the historic re-emergence of 'militarism' in the second half of the twentieth century, and have shown that the Bush Administration incorporated the resultant mindset. It is a mentality, Bacevich notes, characterized by 'a tendency to see military power as the truest measure of national greatness.'[30] The invasion of Iraq demonstrated ways in which this misplaced faith ensnared those who acted on it.

The political theater featuring George W. Bush's landing on the flight deck of the USS Lincoln invoked powerful themes of Western-style heroism into which Christian militarism had been incorporated. The virtuous lone hero wielding god-like deadly force against figures of evil has had much broader play in American novels and movie-houses than in mainstream churches. Yet, the Western mythology has a religious force in itself, as a key component of America's sacred mission as God's city on a hill.

Referring to the 'cowboy' mentality of the Bush Administration is commonplace, and it is well known that the administration has deliberately invoked 'Western' themes. But we must recognize that this vision of the cowboy has little to do with actual cowboys or with life on the western frontier. It was instead a creation of

30. A. J. Bacevich, *The New American Militarism: How Americans are Seduced by War* (New York: Oxford University Press, 2005), p. 2. See James Carroll, *House of War: The Pentagon and the Disastrous Rise of American Power* (Boston, MA: Houghton Mifflin Co., 2006).

America's urban culture, and served the spiritual needs that became urgent as manhood itself was cheapened amid the bureaucratic impersonality of life in a mass society. These stresses have been strengthened in our own time as the American middle-class loses the economic self-determination that supports its self-respect.

To understand the media success of the administration's play-acted heroism, and to grasp the logic through which this vainglory led to depravity, it is necessary to recognize that, for all his apparent liberation from social conventions, the 'cowboy' plays out the most predictable of stereotypes, defined by a longstanding tradition that awards him the role of divine avenger.

Chapter Seven

SIX-GUN SAVIORS

Make-Believe Cowboys

E.C. 'Teddy Blue' Abbott was a working cowboy. Born in Nebraska in 1860, he ran away from his tyrannical father to join a trail-driving team at the of age 15, and at 29 had the exceptional good fortune to get 'a start in life.'[1] He fell in love with an honest, capable woman, stopped drinking in order to marry her, and was able to purchase a ranch in Montana and raise a family. Reflecting on this experience many years later, Abbott emphasized 'how damn hard it was to start out poor and get anywheres.'[2] As a rule, cowboys were rural working-class men who spent their money as fast as they made it and died in destitution, usually quite young.

The cowboys of American fantasy are not modeled on Teddy Blue Abbott, but on a famous showman named William F. 'Buffalo Bill' Cody, who elaborated the role and starred as its exemplar. Abbott himself knew Cody, and was amused by his capers. After Cody was rich and famous, he showed up with a wagon load of whiskey at a roundup where Abbott was working. All the work stopped, as Cody organized horse races and sharp-shooting contests, and offered $100 to the first man to rope a jack rabbit. The owners of the outfit, waiting for the herd to be delivered in Ogallala, came down to see what was holding things up, and ran Cody off.

'He was a good fellow,' Abbott concludes, 'and while he was no great shakes as a scout, as he made the eastern people believe, still we all liked him, and we had to hand it to him because he was the only one that had brains enough to make that Wild West stuff pay money. I remember one time he came into a saloon in North Platte,

---

1. E. C. Abbott ('Teddy Blue') and Helena Huntington Smith, *We Pointed Them North; Recollections of a Cowpuncher* (Norman, OK: University of Oklahoma Press, 1955), p. 205.

2. Abbott & Huntington Smith, *We Pointed Them North*, p. 208.

and he took off his hat, and that long hair of his that he had rolled up under his hat fell down on his shoulders. It always bothered him, so he rolled it up and stuck it back under his hat again, and Brady, the saloon man, says: "Say, Bill, why the hell don't you cut the damn stuff off?" And Cody says: "If I did, I'd starve to death."[3]

As he pioneered the myth of the make-believe cowboy, Cody wove together themes of American identity into a powerful narrative that became, for most Americans, the true story of the West and a symbol for the national destiny. Looking into Cody's triumph will permit us to set forth the distinctive characteristics of the mythic figure he embodied, to understand how it was implanted in the culture of the Eastern seaboard as America became a mass society in the late nineteenth century, and how it has maintained its dominant position into our own time.

After a series of odd jobs — farming, trapping, riding for the Pony Express — Cody began to work regularly as a scout for gentlemen game-hunters and adventure-seekers who traveled west from eastern cities on the transcontinental railroad. Urbanites who couldn't afford the trip joined the adventure by reading dime novels, and Cody first achieved national recognition in the lively market for this literature that soon sprang up. He published a Ned Buntline novel in 1869, portraying himself as 'Western Hero,' and as this character ballooned in popularity, Cody organized a stage melodrama in 1871, performing before live audiences as a dauntless frontiersman and Indian fighter.[4]

As Richard Slotkin explains, theatrical stardom in the East and scouting out West soon blended into each other. In 1876, as Cody was performing in Delaware, he received a request from Wyoming to scout for the 5th Cavalry, who had been ordered into battle against the Sioux and Northern Cheyenne. Cody then announced from the stage that he must temporarily suspend his 'play-acting' to take part in 'the real thing.'[5]

Custer's defeat at Little Big Horn followed Cody's arrival in Wyoming, and as the word spread eastward, Cody seized the occasion for theatrical self-promotion. He put on his stage costume —

---

3. Abbott & Huntington Smith, *We Pointed Them North*, pp. 51–52.

4. Richard Slotkin, *Gunfighter Nation: The Myth of the Frontier in Twentieth-century America* (Norman, OK: University of Oklahoma Press, 1998), pp. 63–87.

5. Slotkin, *Gunfighter Nation*, p. 71.

'black velvet slashed with scarlet and trimmed with silver buttons and lace' — and rode out in search of hostile warriors. He soon encountered one, shot him dead, scalped him, and waved the scalp aloft, subsequently proclaiming in print and from the stage that he had taken 'the first scalp for Custer.'[6]

The parallel with Bush aboard the USS Lincoln could hardly be clearer, the two heroes avenging an attack on American interests that conveys an affront to American pride, the shock of an outright Sioux victory in 1876 foreshadowing the shock of 9/11. Both heroes act with meticulous attention to public expectations, providing a drama that is meant to serve as a talisman and vindication of America's rightful place in the world. Bush's triumph still seems flawed because Osama Bin Laden remains alive, as Sitting Bull remained alive when Cody scalped the warrior. But Cody's public believed his spurious claim that the warrior he scalped was among the leaders at Little Big Horn, much as a majority of Americans today still believe that the slain Saddam Hussein had a hand in 9/11.

Political theater in both instances trumped reality on the ground, which testifies to the social force of the drama. This cowboy figure may seem vaguely comical, the stuff of comic books and movies, but he takes part in a ritual of legitimacy of the sort indispensable to successful warmaking. America the 'chosen people' claims the 'promised land,' and battles the not-chosen along a line of conflict known as the 'frontier.' The 'frontier hero' enters that sacred arena as a complement to the original story of America-the-chosen, and a hero of the folk version that succeeded it. He is a representative of God's civilized order, but possesses 'savage' traits and skills that allow him to prevail against those deemed actual savages, as Cody demonstrates in scalping the warrior.

Cody's insight into the meaning of his performance took the form of a circus that toured the United States and then in Europe from 1883 to 1916. 'Buffalo Bill's Wild West' made Cody an international celebrity, who mingled with American leaders and European royalty, and not as a mere entertainer. The true purpose of the show was educational, said the official program: 'to PICTURE TO THE EYE, by the aid of historical characters and living animals, a series of animated scenes and episodes, which had their existence

6. Slotkin, *Gunfighter Nation*, pp. 72–73.

in fact, in the wonderful pioneer and frontier life of the Wild West of America.'[7]

This pageant was grounded in a nineteenth century version of the scenario that was inaugurated at Massachusetts Bay: American expansion across the continent portrayed as Christian civilization progressively triumphing over heathen savagery. An opening scene represented the 'primeval' situation, populated exclusively by Indians and wild animals, which was followed by Indians (Squanto, Pocahontas) greeting whites on the eastern seaboard. Then the scene switched to the West, with skits representing life on a cattle ranch, a buffalo hunt, and Indian attacks both on frontier cabins and the stagecoach.

The program emphasized that 'Buffalo Bill' plays the key role, as the frontier hero 'to whose sagacity, skill, energy, and courage...the settlers of the West owe so much for the reclamation of the prairie from the savage Indian and wild animals, who so long opposed the march of civilization.'[8]

The crucial religious claim is made quietly here, but distinctly. Buffalo Bill and the settlers did not conquer the wilderness, they 'reclaimed' it from those who had wrongfully presumed a right to the lives they led before the children of promise arrived, including the right to occupy the land that supported those lives. White society owned this territory *de novo*, in virtue of God's promise, not by forcing the natives to relinquish it. This claim underlies the classic gestures performed by Cody and George Bush. Waving the scalp and celebrating Saddam's fall on the flight deck of the USS Lincoln were both moments of divine justice triumphant. Not celebrations of conquest, they were gestures of a violated innocence striking back at an invasive and defiling evil.

At moments, Cody's make-believe became comical, even farcical. When Federal forces in Wyoming were making ready to arrest Sitting Bull in 1890, Cody showed up, having obtained an order from General Nelson A. Miles that gave Cody personal responsibility for bringing in the great warrior. The soldiers on the ground were appalled by the chaos they were certain would ensue, and kept Cody drunk for several days, as they sought countermanding orders

---

7. Slotkin, *Gunfighter Nation*, p. 67.
8. Slotkin, *Gunfighter Nation*, p. 68.

from President Harrison, and eventually succeeded in blocking the plan.[9]

Such escapades did nothing to impair the cultural authority of the myth Cody embodied, because that myth was not founded on how men on the frontier—like Teddy Blue Abbott—actually lived their lives. Cody became a superstar because of trouble in the souls of Eastern urbanites, as their lives were transformed by profound social changes in the late nineteenth century, the emergence of a mass society increasingly dominated by great corporations who fought each other for monopoly control. Make-believe cowboys held a mystical fascination for ordinary folk caught up in these changes, and the market for novels of Western heroism expanded rapidly. An enduring new tradition in American political life also emerged, in which aspirants for national office portrayed themselves as Western heroes, Ronald Reagan and George W. Bush serving as the most recent exemplars of this well-established pattern.

* * *

Theodore Roosevelt was the first national figure to translate Buffalo Bill heroism into political power. As an ambitious young politician in New York, Roosevelt was handicapped by family wealth, a Harvard education, an aristocratic Dutch-patroon name, and a fondness for stylish dress. Political enemies sneered at him as 'the exquisite Mr. Roosevelt,' as a 'Punkin-Lily.' One inspired opponent claimed that Teddy was 'given to sucking on the knob of an ivory cane.'[10]

Roosevelt traveled West to dabble in cowboy life, like many men of his class, and in 1883 purchased a ranch in North Dakota. Teddy Blue recounts meeting Roosevelt during this time, commenting that 'rich men's sons from the East were nothing new.' The range 'was as full of them as a dog's hair of fleas.'[11] After the death of his wife,

9. See Robert Marshall Utley, *The Last Days of the Sioux Nation* (New Haven, CT: London: Yale University Press, 2004), pp. 123–26 and Robert Marshall Utley, *The Lance and the Shield: the Life and Times of Sitting Bull* (New York: Henry Holt, 1993), pp. 294–95.

10. Gail Bederman, *Manliness & Civilization: A Cultural History of Gender and Race in the United States, 1880–1917*, Women in Culture and Society (Chicago, IL: University of Chicago Press, 1995), p. 170.

11. Abbott & Huntington Smith, *We Pointed Them North*, p. 191.

Western living became an obsession for Roosevelt, and through it he found not only a way to grieve, but also to reconstruct his public image. He cast off his reputation as a dandy and emerged as an exemplar of strenuous frontier living.

Roosevelt had always found outdoor rambles salutary, and now plunged into a life of hunting, ranching, and publishing books about it. He quickly issued *Hunting Trips of a Ranchman*, followed by *Ranch Life and the Hunting Trail*, and went to work on *The Winning of the West*, a four-volume history retelling the story enshrined in Buffalo Bill's Wild West, the advancement of civilization led by frontier heroes. In 1886 Roosevelt returned to New York City politics, ran successfully for Mayor as the 'Cowboy of the Dakotas,' and versions of this charismatic new selfhood sustained his political triumphs lifelong.[12]

Arduous western endeavors extended the frontiers of civilization, Roosevelt proclaimed, but they also rescued the civilized man from boredom and impotence. Ranching gave Roosevelt a chance to live a 'vigorous, primitive' life, 'having little in common with the humdrum, workaday business world of the nineteenth century.' Life as a 'western' rancher was revitalizing; it awakened a masculine energy not otherwise available to 'a sleek city merchant or tradesman.'[13] Roosevelt hailed the Spanish-American and Philippine-American wars — late nineteenth century exercises in imperialist expansion — as salutary for an America gone soft. 'I should welcome almost any war,' he remarked, 'for I think this country needs one.'[14]

The burgeoning Eastern market for Buffalo Bill's circus, like TR's political popularity, rested on a fascination with the West that was rooted in the social transformation of the urban Northeast. It didn't matter that Buffalo Bill was not much of a scout, or that TR was a rich New Yorker who only played at being a cowboy, or that George W. Bush (also a scion of old Northeastern wealth) bought his ranch in Crawford just prior to running for President. So long as the charade is performed credibly, it will activate the presiding mythology, conferring moral authority on the performer and

---

12. Bederman, *Manliness & Civilization*, pp. 170–215.

13. Bederman, *Manliness & Civilization*, p. 176.

14. Kristin L. Hoganson, *Fighting for American Manhood: How Gender Politics Provoked the Spanish-American and Philippine-American Wars* (New Haven, CT: Yale University Press, 1998), p. 39.

strengthening his claim on political power. This magical self-deception still works, better than a century after it entered American public life.

The 'savage' is the designated enemy in the drama of frontier heroism, as it took form in the late nineteenth century, but not the only enemy. The hero also struggles against the desolating proprieties and complexities of civilized life, which TR called 'workaday,' 'humdrum,' and 'sleek.'

The yearning to recapture primordial energies, argues historian Jackson Lears, arose because of economic conditions that bore in on middle-class urbanites in Gilded Age America, amid the emerging corporate capitalism. Earlier phases of capitalist development placed the independent entrepreneur at the forefront of action, pursuing self-directed initiatives in a sharply competitive local or regional marketplace. As nationwide corporations came to dominate transportation and communication systems, however, a national market came into existence, served by large retail firms that created schedules of work and systems of management that aimed at efficiency through standardization.

Industrial firms prior to this era depended on the skills of local managers and shop foremen, who could speed up or slow down the pace of work, depending on the needs of the regional market. But now such processes were controlled from the top, in national offices that governed the efforts of workers in far flung locales. The result for most working men was a life of relative material comfort, gained not through competitive success, but through obedience to the bureaucratic systems by which large corporations were managed. Affluent denizens of corporate society were vulnerable, moreover, to fluctuations in the national economic order they were in no position to understand.[15]

The spiritual result was a vague but pervasive unease, of enervating comfort at risk from unpredictable and vaguely perceived threats. Men felt cut off from the sources of 'real life' in a hypercivilized world that offered seductive comforts. This 'weightlessness,' Lears argues, brought with it a hunger for vehement masculine excitements. A new male subculture subscribed to magazines like *The Police Gazette*, where readers could thrill to

---

15. T. J. Jackson Lears, *No Place of Grace: Antimodernism and the Transformation of American Culture, 1880–1920* (New York: Pantheon Books, 1981).

the primordial violence of John L. Sullivan and other bare-knuckle heavyweights. The novels of Sir Walter Scott returned to popularity, celebrating the exploits of chivalric men-at-arms, and Edgar Rice Burroughs's *Tarzan* offered the African jungle as a setting for the life of manly adventure.

The adulation of 'real men' — including self-styled Western heroes — has become more intense in our own time, to compensate for the relative insecurity and powerlessness that now afflicts formerly self-confident middle-class Americans in the wake of economic globalization and a political order benefiting the rich. The financial crisis that exploded in the summer of 2008 harshly dramatized this vulnerability, increased the number of Americans in danger of losing middle-class status, and deepened the attendant anxieties. The character of the cultural response to this development will depend in part on the duration and extent of the subsequent hard times, but the appeal of violent hypermasculinity is unlikely to diminish, and spokesmen for its religious and political versions can be counted on to compete for an enlarged following.

Public enthusiasm for the swagger of the Bush Administration flourished in a media culture devoted to dramas of violent domination. Nature programs are now monopolized by depictions of carnivores attacking their prey; the make-believe brutality of professional wrestling has given way to caged men battering each other into submission; moralistic bullies like Dr. Phil, Judge Judy and Donald Trump are embraced as oracles of wisdom. The Christian Right found a congenial home in the world of sanctimonious infotainment, from the 'fair and balanced' sarcasms of Fox News, to the raucous dueling monologues that are staged as political discussion, to professional trash-talkers like Rush Limbaugh and Ann Coulter. A public appetite for cruelty, arising from the economic anxieties of an embattled middle class, eagerly consumed the attack-dog rhetoric of the neocon/theocons; it found gratification in White House propaganda advocating the invasion of Iraq, and found much to feed on in the images of destruction and horror that soon filled the media.

Yet even the most powerful American men are galled by the entanglements of bureaucratic routine. Donald Rumsfeld called a meeting at the Pentagon on 10 September 2001, to describe an 'adversary that poses a threat, a serious threat, to the security of the United States of America.' This enemy imposes 'its demands across time zones, continents, oceans and beyond. With brutal consistency, it stifles free thought and crushes new ideas.' No foreign dictator, however wicked and resourceful, Rumsfeld declared, 'can match the strength and size of this adversary. The adversary is closer to home. It's the Pentagon bureaucracy.'[16] Oblivious to the attack scheduled to strike the Pentagon on the following day, Rumsfeld was preoccupied with assailing the noxious bureaucratic rigamaroles that trip up the initiatives of real men.

Messiahs on Horseback

Zane Grey's *The Riders of the Purple Sage* (1912) is a classic of 'Western' writing in which the struggle between conventional Christianity and the emerging ideal of primordial virility is played out. There are no Indians in this novel; the evil to be destroyed is a Mormon hierarchy that controls the Utah town of Cottonwoods. Mormon ecclesiastics and public officials make up a corrupt power structure that threatens the novel's virtuous protagonists. The emasculating power of a bureaucratized social order lies at the heart of the parable, in which a feminized Christianity falls victim to political and economic tyranny.

Near Cottonwoods stands Withersteen House, at the center of a splendid ranch that Jane Withersteen inherited from her father. The head of the Mormon church, Bishop Dyer, is also Judge Dyer, a sign of the interlocked institutional authority that controls the community. Bishop/Judge Dyer has determined that Jane shall marry Tull, a believer in good standing, so as to bring the Withersteen wealth firmly under Mormon control. But Jane is headstrong as well as rich; she embraces a gentler Christianity, and annoys the church leadership through her generosity to poverty-stricken Gentile families. Worse yet, she is attracted to a Gentile ranch hand named Venters.

The novel opens as Tull appears at Withersteen House with a gang of men to drive Venters away, roughly brushing aside Jane's protests. When Venters also defies them, the Mormons prepare to administer a ferocious beating. Jane is dazed by this revelation of her helplessness, and unconsciously begins to pray. She yearns for

---

16. Michael R. Gordon and Bernard E. Trainor, *Cobra II: The Inside Story of the Invasion and Occupation of Iraq* (New York: Pantheon Books, 2006), p. 9.

the advent of 'a fearless man, neither creed-bound or creed-mad, who would hold up a restraining hand in the face of her ruthless people.'[17]

Then she sees 'a horseman, silhouetted against the western sky...in the golden glare of the sun,' and immediately recognizes 'an answer to her prayer.' The god-like horseman dismounts with quick uncanny smoothness of motion; he wears 'black leather' and 'two black-butted guns.' The lethal menace radiating from his presence halts Tull and his men. The stranger glances at them only a moment, makes no reply to their greeting, then speaks with quiet courtesy to Jane: 'Evenin' ma'am'.[18] The hero's name is Lassiter, a messiah on horseback appearing solitary against an empty horizon.

The balance of the novel pursues a debate about Lassiter's guns, as Jane is increasingly trapped by the legal, moral and religious apparatus controlled by the Mormons. Herds of cattle are stolen under the eyes of Mormon cowboys posted to guard them, while her Mormon house-servants spy on her and report to Bishop Dyer her involvement with Lassiter, with whom — forgetting Venters — she falls passionately in love.

Jane believes she has a Christian duty to win Lassiter away from his career as a gunfighter, and begs him to give up his guns, even as Lassiter's lethal virility awakens her desire. Leaning against Lassiter in a moonlit grove, 'Jane slipped her hands down to the swinging gunsheaths...locked her fingers around the huge, cold handles of the guns...[and] trembled as with a chilling ripple over all her body. "May I take your guns?"'[19]

Jane tries to seduce Lassiter, so she believes, not out of carnal lust, but in order to awaken him to the redemptive power of Christian love. She hopes to play the role of an altruistic self-sacrificing wife, who redeems her husband from the moral injuries he sustains amid the combat of a wicked world. Knowing that Lassiter intends to kill Bishop Dyer, she claims that her blandishments are intended to 'save human life,' a principle transcending the moral tyranny of Mormon doctrine: 'that's God's law, divine, universal for all Christians,' she exclaims.[20]

17. Zane Grey, *Riders of the Purple Sage* (New York: Bantam Books, 1990), p. 6.
18. Grey, *Riders of the Purple Sage*, p. 6.
19. Grey, *Riders of the Purple Sage*, p. 123.
20. Grey, *Riders of the Purple Sage*, p. 131.

The debate between them moves past social proprieties and tender sentiment to the plane of elemental natural forces, however, where her womanly sexuality responds to his primordial masculinity. Lassiter thus speaks with an authority grounded on 'nature,' not social obligation, as he declares the creed of the six-gun savior. 'Gun-packin' in the West since the Civil War has growed into a kind of moral law...Your Bishop has shot half a dozen men, an' it wasn't through prayers of his that they recovered. An' today he'd have shot me if he'd been quick enough on the draw. Could I walk or ride down to Cottonwoods without my guns?'[21]

A man without a gun, Lassiter insists, is 'not a man,' no matter how virtuous he may be, while a virtuous gunfighter establishes a law that would mean nothing without the enforcement he provides. The six-gun savior does not obey human codes of law; he acts with divine authority. Lassiter's communion with natural forces makes him an agent of God's judgment, as is dramatized when he shoots Judge Dyer in his own courtroom.

The messiah on horseback is a transcendant figure; he does not belong to the social order that surrounds him, and the carnage he inflicts has little to do with actual gunfights between actual men, no matter how accurate their marksmanship may be. Lassiter appears as though by magic in the courtroom, where Dyer has posted eight bodyguards, five of whom immediately jump out the window. The other three go for their guns, and Lassiter kills all three 'quicker than eyesight,' but not with the 'big black guns.'[22] For these lesser malefactors, he uses a third revolver, which he now replaces in his belt, then reaches down to the holsters on his legs to draw forth the instruments of apocalyptic vengeance.

Jane Withersteen's Christianity does not envision a God who tortures people. But Lassiter — the answer to her prayer — now inflicts on Dyer the torments of the damned. Instead of killing the judge with a single shot, Lassiter waits for him to draw with his right hand, and shoots the gun away, along with a piece of the hand. As Dyer reaches to retrieve the gun, Lassiter fires another 'thunderin' shot' that virtually tears off Dyer's arm. The left arm comes off next. Then Lassiter 'turns the black guns loose' and fires into Dyer's body, some nine shots in all. Still conscious, Judge Dyer goes down

21. Grey, *Riders of the Purple Sage*, p. 132.
22. Grey, *Riders of the Purple Sage*, p. 243.

on his knees. 'You'd better call quick on the God who reveals Hisself to you on earth,' Lassiter declares, 'because He won't be visitin' the place you're going to.'

Dyer now receives a divine revelation: he sees for himself the God whose justice demands the eternal torture of evildoers, and sees that his own dying torment is only a foretaste of what lies ahead. 'He stared horrible at somethin' thet wasn't Lassiter, nor anyone there, nor the room...Whatever he seen, it was with the look of a man who <u>discovers</u> somethin' too late...An' with a horrible <u>understandin'</u> cry he slid forrard on his face.'[23]

The apocalyptic authority of the lawless lawman remains a powerful theme in the movieland versions of this mythology, an authority typically played against the impotence of Christian self-sacrifice. Instead of facing the ultimate realities of human conflict, such feminized piety is typical of a social order that is helpless in the face of savage assault. Ethan Edwards, the John Wayne protagonist in *The Searchers* (1956), stands in contrast to the Reverend Samuel Jackson Clayton, captain of the local militia. Edwards knows the ways of Indians; Clayton does not. Edwards withstands the direct encounter with violent rape and murder; Clayton is shielded from such horrors. Clayton represents Christianity as an appurtenance of civilized order; Edwards represents the power to establish that order, destroying its savage enemies by savage means.[24]

The ethos of the Bush Administration arises from a marriage of these seeming opposites, in which Christ and the six-gun savior become one flesh. Yet, President Bush and his colleagues did not invent this amplified form of the mythology; it is explored with great acuity in the films of Clint Eastwood.

* * *

Eastwood has played lawless lawmen in many guises, with deepening insight into the complexities of the figure. Dirty Harry portrays the righteous avenger in the costume of a hard-boiled city cop; disgusted by the noxious maze of municipal regulations that

23. Grey, *Riders of the Purple Sage,* p. 244.

24. John Ford, Max Steiner, Frank S. Nugent, John Wayne, Jeffrey Hunter, Vera Miles, Ward Bond, Natalie Wood, and Alan Le May, *The Searchers* (Burbank, CA: Warner Bros. Entertainment, 2006).

restrains mayors and police chiefs, he takes the law into his own hands. Like Lassiter, Dirty Harry tortures and kills the wicked.

Eastwood has also explored the sordid mischances to which such a hero is prone. The protagonist in 'Mystic River' (directed by Eastwood) is maddened by the brutal murder of his daughter, and persuades himself that he knows the guilty party. As is typical in such a scenario, he becomes impatient with the slow pace of the official investigation, seizes upon misleading 'evidences' of guilt, and murders the presumptive culprit just as it becomes clear he is innocent.

Eastwood underscores the central place of revenge in the career of the 'western' hero. Both Lassiter and Ethan Edwards are men set apart, obsessed by a mission to avenge the suffering of the innocent, especially helpless women. The atrocity that spurs the revenge quest is a stock incident in the narrative of the western hero, typically when a rancher crosses a ridge to see his home a smoking ruin, his wife ravished and children kidnapped. It is at once an image of male disempowerment and the archetypal demonic assault, first depicted in Rowlandson's captivity narrative. The 'real man' as divine avenger rises to meet the occasion.

We have noted that movieland narratives often stage the hero's ferocity against Christian teachings of love and forgiveness. But Eastwood anchors his character on the newly emerging bedrock: the gunfighter's explosive violence delivers the wrath of the Lamb. His masterpiece of this fusion is *Pale Rider*, a film that foretells the conviction that took form in the Bush White House immediately after 9/11, that the law must be set aside if divine justice is to be executed.[25]

Like Zane Grey's Lassiter, the 'Rider' is invoked by the prayers of a woman reckoning with her own helplessness in the face of a corrupt public order. Megan Wheeler lives beside a creek in a small encampment of California gold-miners, whose existence is threatened by a large mining operation owned by the perfidious Coy Lahood, who controls the local bank, controls the sheriff, and has political connections in Sacramento.

The narrative begins as a gang of LaHood's toughs ride through the camp to lay it waste, jerking down tents and clotheslines, pulling

25. Clint Eastwood, Michael Butler, Dennis Shryack, Michael Moriarty, Carrie Snodgrass, Christopher Penn, Richard Dysart, Sydney Penny, and Richard Kiel, *Pale Rider*, Clint Eastwood Collection (Burbank, CA: Warner Home Video, 2000).

over board huts, scattering livestock, and wrecking the mining emplacements. They also trample Megan's dog, and she utters a prayer over its grave that rejects pious consolation and calls for divine intervention:

> The Lord is my shepherd, I shall not want.
> BUT I *DO* WANT.
> Yea though I walk through the valley of the shadow of death I will fear no evil.
> BUT I *AM* AFRAID
> Thy rod and thy staff they comfort me
> WE NEED A MIRACLE

Here the camera looks upward to the hills, as Jane Witherspoon had looked upward, and the heaven-sent lone rider appears, on a grey horse.

The rider next appears in town as Lahood's toughs, armed with axe handles, are beating Hull Barrett, a virtuous miner who shares the household with Megan and her mother. The rider picks up an axe handle and, with a bravura demonstration of supernatural violence, leaves the thugs groaning on the ground.

He then accompanies Barrett to his household in the encampment, arriving as Megan reads aloud from the Book of Revelation: 'And when he had opened the fourth seal, I heard the voice of the fourth seal say "Come and see"'—here the camera follows her gaze out the window, and Eastwood appears on his grey—'And behold a pale horse and his name who sat on him was Death. And Hell followed with him.'

The rider soon dons a clerical collar and accepts the nickname 'Preacher,' confirming that he wields hellfire to execute the judgments of the Christian god. The community of miners feels a tension between the rider's talent for violence and his Christian calling. They suspect he's not really a clergyman, and the narrative itself temporarily separates the hero's piety from his deadly menace, then unites them with startling force.

The ultimate showdown develops when Lahood hires a gang of gunslingers headed by Marshall Stockman, who 'upholds whatever law pays the most.' Stockman and Lahood are figures of an amoral social order, in which the law and its enforcement have nothing to do with right and wrong. Stockman is puzzled because he recognizes the rider, but remembers him—incomprehensibly—as a man he knows to be dead. He is also startled to learn that the Rider knows his name. We've already been shown that the Rider bears a circle of six large scars from bullet wounds in his upper back, and the camera lingers over these scars, so that the point is unmistakable. No man suffering such wounds could survive.

These scars are stigmata, says the implied backstory. Pale Rider is a Christ-figure, bearing emblems of his unjust death at the hands of Stockman and his gang, but now risen from the dead to inflict vengeance on the evil-doers. The scripted retribution quickly follows. The Rider wipes out the hired gunmen, Barret kills Lahood, and the Rider faces off against the demonic Stockman along the dusty main street. As he administers apocalyptic vengeance with his sixgun, Pale Rider rids the town of evil. Absent the deadly force wielded by this figure of righteousness, so the narrative says, the world is governed by corrupt economic and political power enforced by legalized murder.

Movieland narratives of the righteous revenger typically include a moment of crucifixion, when the hero falls victim to the powers of evil. The avatars of Rambo and the Terminator, like those of the hard-boiled cop and the western hero, arrive at the triumph of redemptive violence only after a collapse into seeming defeat, usually the result of severe punishment dealt out by the bad guy. After losing his life as a vulnerable mortal, he rises again as a supernatural avenger. In *High Plains Drifter*, as in *Pale Rider*, the Christ figure literally returns from the dead.

In *Dirty Harry* the hero's death is symbolic. A vicious kidnapper leads Harry Callahan on a wild goose chase through San Francisco, which ends at the foot of a towering cross. The kidnapper forces Harry, hands lifted, to stand directly against the cross and then inflicts a savage beating. As Harry struggles to rouse himself from his semi-conscious daze, he collapses spreadeagled on his back and the camera looks up at the gigantic cross looming over him, marking his defeat as a crucifixion.

The resurrected Harry soon traps his quarry in Kezar Stadium, and when the kidnapper insists on his rights and demands a lawyer, Harry tortures him to find out where the kidnap victim is hidden. There follows a confrontation with the District Attorney in which we learn that the kidnapper must go free because of Harry's illegal violence. 'That man had rights,' says the DA. But Harry is a divine avenger, entitled to inflict the torments of the damned on evildoers. His status as the slain and risen Christ is marked again at the final confrontation. After the kidnapper takes hostage a busload of school children, the agent of wrath magically appears, a lone figure against a desert background. The evildoer's shock of recognition is registered in a single breathless word: 'Jesus.'[26]

Six-gun Saviors in the White House

St. George did not provide an immediate role model for George W. Bush, but his American avatar did so—our Christian six-gun savior propelled into a career of revenge by the atrocity of 9/11. Like many another American, the President had absorbed uncountable rehearsals of this role in movies and folk legends of the Wild West. Bush and his cohorts spurned the idea that the 9/11 attack should be treated as a crime, its perpetrators to be tried before an international court. To them, supernatural evil had shattered man-made systems of legal restraint, making way for the primordial sacred drama. It was a time, in Vice-President Cheney's words, to unleash 'the full wrath of the United States of America.'[27] Divine violence—executed by 'real men'—was now required.

Bush and Cheney immediately determined that a 'War on Terror' was the appropriate response. As with the 'War on Poverty' and the 'War on Drugs,' this demonstrated a misplaced faith in war. Within the prevailing mythology, 'war' means the repudiation of hesitant, half-committed efforts, in the belief that an all-out attack will lead promptly to the unconditional surrender of the enemy. Yet with 'Terror,' as with 'Poverty' and 'Drugs,' there is no enemy capable of surrendering. The militarist fantasy prescribes that these age-long scourges of human society will be driven from the field in defeat, never again to trouble the nation's life. The result in Iraq, not surprisingly, was self-defeat; yet this became apparent only slowly, as the fog of religious euphoria faded in the next several years.

The American public immediately accepted the announcement of a 'War on Terror,' and other nations followed suit. Yet, at the moment of inception, Vice-President Cheney may have felt some misgivings. 'One of the interesting things here,' he said to Tim

26. Clint Eastwood, *Dirty Harry* (New York: Warner Home Video, 1971).
27. Stephen F. Hayes, *Cheney: The Untold Story of America's Most Powerful and Controversial Vice President* (New York: HarperCollins, 2007), p. 353.

Russert on 'Meet the Press' five days after 9/11, 'is the way in which people have rallied around the notion that, in fact, this is war.'[28]

The 'fact' of a 'War on Terror' is now so deeply implanted in political rhetoric as to seem intuitively obvious, but to decision-makers at the time this was not apparent. Looking back on that period, Condoleeza Rice commented that Cheney's 'biggest impact [was]...just the intellectual contribution to the conceptualization of the war on terror.' Inherent to this concept was that legal obstructions to the work of the six-gun savior would have to be cleared away.

At a White House meeting on the morning following 9/11, President Bush made clear the limitless authorization he now demanded, and was prepared to confer on his team. 'Nothing else matters. Everything is available for the pursuit of this war. Any barriers in your way, they're gone.' Donald Rumsfeld found himself cast in the unwelcome role of defending legal niceties before the enraged frontier hero. He pointed out that international law did not permit the use of military force for revenge, Richard Clarke recalled, but only to prevent subsequent attacks, whereupon 'Bush nearly bit his head off. "No," the President yelled...I don't care what the international lawyers say, we are going to kick some ass.'[29] The President's anti-genteel language here, as he sets aside legal obligations, marks the transition into a zone of frontier confrontation, where social requirements are transcended and natural god-like powers must be invoked.

Yet, ass-kicking performed explicitly in defiance of the law would be explicitly criminal, with unwelcome political consequences, so it became necessary to construct a system through which the hero's lawless warmaking could masquerade as lawful. Vice-President Cheney assumed major responsibility for this, and brought to the task a temperament well seasoned in the traditions of Western heroism, especially as they collide with the legalistic punctilio of government functionaries in the East.

Richard Cheney grew up in Nebraska and then Wyoming, in a family proud of its part in the nineteenth-century westward expansion. But his father did not live the dream of self-directed

28. Hayes, *Cheney*, p. 355.

29. Richard A. Clarke, *Against All Enemies: Inside America's War on Terror* (New York: Free Press, 2004), p. 24.

success as a rancher or oilman. He was a government bureaucrat, with the Soil Conservation Service. It is plausible to suppose that Cheney's boyhood love of hunting and fishing, which extended far into his Washington career, carries for him a note of liberation from humdrum routine; many western men find themselves living out the western myth, especially when they become enmeshed in the complex world of the urban East. Cheney's western inheritance is hard to read because of its most obvious trait, the curt and unhurried manner of speaking that serves his penchant for secrecy. 'Am I the evil genius in the corner that nobody ever sees come out of his hole?' Cheney said in 2004 amid fierce criticism of his inscrutable role in the Bush Administration. 'It's a nice way to operate, actually.'[30]

Long before 9/11, Cheney was dedicated to claiming the entitlements of the cowboy myth as inherent powers of the presidency. Believing that executive authority had been fatally weakened in the wake of Vietnam and Watergate, he took part in the Senate hearings that investigated the White House role in an illegal sale of arms to Iran, whose proceeds were conveyed secretly to the Contras in Nicaragua. Clearly undertaken in defiance of the law, these actions disturbed Cheney, but his final judgment on the affair criticized the Senate committee itself for seeking to usurp the power of the presidency in matters of foreign policy. The 'Congressional vacillation and uncertainty about our policies' and 'a Congressional track record of leaks' are ample evidence, Cheney declared, that the Congress is unfit to take part in the leadership that the Constitution assigns the President.[31]

After 9/11 Cheney established a legal 'War Council' — composed of John Yoo, Jim Haynes, Timothy Flanigan, David Addington and Alberto Gonzales — to clear away legal requirements that might impede the President's will. A major showdown had arrived, after all, and the six-gun savior had leapt into the saddle. He must now be given the freedom to act on his recognition of what must be done, despite the qualms of lesser souls. The White House lawyers were not asked whether the President's plans were legal, but provided quasi-legal reasoning that would allow him to do

30. Hayes, *Cheney*, pp. 3, 11, 24.
31. Hayes, *Cheney*, p. 199.

whatever he judged best.[32] The result, as Jane Mayer observes, was that 'this insular, unelected, self-reinforcing group' circumvented the legal apparatus that had authority in areas where the President wanted to act.[33]

Jacob Weisburg summarizes the sweeping authorization Bush was provided, to order activities held criminal under existing law:

> 1) the ability to detain anyone, citizen or not, at any time, indefinitely, in secret and without recourse to the courts; 2) the insistence that military personnel and intelligence officers were not fettered by the Geneva Conventions, or other national and international laws governing human rights; 3) the power to use extreme interrogation methods, amounting to torture, to extract information; and 4) the right to monitor communications of all sorts without legal warrant.[34]

Under Cheney's guidance, the 'War Council' devised a strategy for coping with violations of the law. They wrote legal opinions that claimed for the President an inherent right to act as he chose, and kept these self-exculpatory legal analyses secret—even from the agencies whose activities they governed. Lawyers for the National Security Agency, for example, became fearful the NSA wiretapping program was illegal, but were rebuffed when they asked to see the legal basis for the orders they'd been given.[35] Jack Goldsmith observed this process first-hand, and summed it up: when the War Council found laws they didn't like 'they blew through them in secret based on flimsy legal opinions that they guarded closely so no one could question the legal basis for the operation.'[36]

Secretary of State Colin Powell lost a key battle within the White House to uphold the Geneva Conventions, which prohibit torture. He concluded, writes Jane Mayer,

> that Bush was not stupid but was easily manipulated. A confidant said that Powell thought it was easy to play on Bush's wish to be seen as doing the tough thing and making the "hard" choice. "He has these cowboy characteristics, and when you know where to rub him, you

32. Meticulous discussions of this enterprise are provided by Philippe Sands, *Torture Team: Rumsfeld's Memo and the Betrayal of American Values* (New York: Palgrave Macmillan, 2008) and by Jane Mayer, *Dark Side: The Inside Story of How the War on Terror Turned into a War on American Ideals* (New York: Doubleday, 2008).

33. Mayer, *Dark Side*, p. 66.

34. Jacob Weisberg, *The Bush Tragedy* (New York: Random House, 2008), p. 176.

35. Mayer, *Dark Side*, p. 268.

36. Mayer, *Dark Side*, p. 70.

can really get him to do some dumb things. You have to play on these
swaggering bits of his self-image. Cheney knew exactly how to push
all his buttons."[37]

Animated by the national traditions of the make-believe cowboy,
and serving the public's ardent desire for a god-like militant
America, the President and Vice-President established a functioning
Presidential despotism in pursuing the war on terror. Deliberately
circumventing the constitutionally mandated system that places legal
limits on Presidential action, Bush and Cheney became formidable
domestic enemies of the Constitution they had sworn to defend.

Yet they garnered substantial public support, and Congressional
support, because the frontier heroism they invoked has deep roots
in America's soul, despite its conflict with abiding commitments to
democratic governance. For the frontier hero, courts and lawyers
maintain civilized order, but tough smart men using deadly force
create that order when the savages attack, and the law must be
swept aside. Debating Senator Mathias, a fellow Republican in 1983,
Cheney summed it up: 'To keep coming back to the notion that
every set of circumstances in which military force might be used
lends itself to consultation and legal arguments is nice, but the world
doesn't work that way.'[38]

Behind Cheney's strong silent presence, and Bush's public
performances, stands a conviction about how the world works. It
is at heart a religious conviction, having ultimate authority, and
not to be judged by any standard beyond itself. The world works
this way: trans-legal God-sent deadly force is the final arbiter of
human affairs, determining whose version of order will prevail,
and whose will not.

37. Mayer, *Dark Side*, p. 125.
38. Hayes, *Cheney*, p. 177.

Chapter Eight

MORAL CLARITY AND MORAL COLLAPSE

Shock and Awe

The men who planned the war in Iraq relied on a theory of warmaking suited to the god-like role the Bush Administration intended to play. It was outlined in an essay entitled 'Shock and Awe' by Harlan Ullman and James Wade, from the National Defense University. With its heavy dependence on sophisticated weapons and communications systems, this doctrine appealed to Pentagon officials who wished to serve the interests of defense industries that produce such devices.

But 'Shock and Awe' had a religious appeal as well, since it describes military action approximating that of an angry god, 'achieving rapid dominance' through soul-crushing assault. The objective is 'so to overload an adversary's perceptions and understanding of events that the enemy would be...rendered totally impotent.' It is not enough to destroy military capabilities until the enemy perceives that resistance is futile; he must be thunderstruck. 'The goal,' say the writers, 'is to use our power with such compellance that even the strongest wills will be awed.'[1]

Fantasies of omnipresence amplify this vision of omnipotence. The assault must gain the 'control and management of everything that is significant to the operations bearing on the particular Area of Interest (AOI). And we mean everything! Control of the environment is far broader than only the objective of achieving dominant battlefield awareness.'[2]

1. Harlan Ullman and James P. Wade, *Shock and Awe: Achieving Rapid Dominance* (Philadelphia, PA: Pavilion Press, 1996), pp. 15, 17.
2. Ullman and Wade, *Shock and Awe*, p. 32.

Omnipresence is achieved through

> an interconnected and interoperable grid of netted intelligence, surveillance, reconnaissance, communications systems, data analysis and real-time deliverable actionable information to the shooter... whether the shooter is a tank division, an individual tank, an artillery battery, an individual rifleman, a naval battle group, an individual ship, and air wing/squadron, or an aircraft in flight.[3]

Critical to omnipresence is a pace of action that moves ahead of the adversary's capacity to observe his situation, orient himself, decide upon a response, and act. This OODA loop, or 'decision cycle' is generic to all combat; disrupting it confers victory; completely destroying it produces shock and awe, and this requires combat to be 'unrelenting and omnipresent at times, places, and tempo of choosing.' As Wade and Ullman bring their heady exposition to a climax, omnipresence becomes omnipotence through omniscience: 'absolute knowledge and understanding of self, adversary and environment.'[4]

It's worth taking a moment to consider this.

Who has achieved absolute self-understanding? Socrates's injunction 'Know yourself' inaugurated a philosophical quest that now engages every thoughtful person. St. Paul spoke for honest souls across a worldwide range of spiritual traditions when he remarked that we see ourselves and the world imperfectly, 'through a glass darkly.' For Paul, absolute knowledge can come only after death, when 'I shall know, even as I am known';[5] for Buddhists, self-knowledge is the unattainable goal of a life-long meditative quest.

Claiming absolute knowledge of the 'adversary' is comparably exorbitant, indeed ludicrous, when measured against the ignorance of Iraqi culture and politics that confounded American efforts. Absolute knowledge of the 'environment' equally lies beyond the reach of mortals.

3. Ullman and Wade, *Shock and Awe*, p. 62.

4. Ullman and Wade, *Shock and Awe*, p. 64.

5. *I Corinthians* 13:12. *The Holy Bible Containing the Old and New Testaments and the Apocrypha: Translated out of the Original Tongues with the Former Translations Diligently Compared and Revised, by His Majesty's Special Command* (New York: Cambridge University Press, nd).

Exponents of Shock and Awe think their cosmic boast doesn't mean what it says. What's on their mind is Global Positioning Satellite surveillance combined with instant communications systems and computerized video representation that will allow commanders to see every detail of the battlespace on their computer screens: 'total control and signature management of the entire operational environment.' The hapless adversary, entangled in the broken coils of his OODA loops, is blinded and then annihilated by coordinated whirlwinds of deadly fire. But amid such breathless rhetoric, the cosmic boast remains, promising that the U.S. military will enjoy god-like power over evildoers cowering in darkness.

Donald Rumsfeld was fascinated by Wade and Ullmann's 'Shock and Awe,' and recommended the essay to his subordinates.[6] The doctrine had a seductive appeal for U.S. officials setting out to abolish evil by seizing the role of God in a fanciful apocalyptic drama, and it cast its enchantment over the early stages of the war. Andrew Bacevich notes that Victor Davis, the military historian, saw 'transcendence at work,' not just 'soldiers in battle,' as he contemplated the rapid advance on Baghdad in March of 2003.[7] But the dazzling invasion turned out to be a pathway toward chaos and political disaster, as clear-headed observers warned that it would.

The glamor of 'Shock and Awe' warfare beguiled the administration and its advocates into perverting a doctrine called 'moral clarity' that they derived from the work of Natan Sharansky. Sharansky had endured a lengthy imprisonment under the Soviet Union, and had served for nine years as an Israeli politician, when he wrote *The Case for Democracy: The Power of Freedom to Overcome Tyranny and Terror*, where he argued that a realistic on-the-ground pursuit of democracy for the Palestinians was the answer to terror. The Bush Administration broadcast its embrace of Sharansky's principles; but the White House envisioned the Israeli/Palestinian conflict as an apocalyptic collision of good and evil, and when Bush's 'Road Map' for peace in Israel/Palestine imposed this distortion of 'moral clarity,' Sharansky was much dismayed.[8]

6. Andrew Cockburn, *Rumsfeld: His Rise, Fall, and Catastrophic Legacy* (New York: Scribner, 2007), pp. 159–60.

7. A. J. Bacevich, *The New American Militarism: How Americans are Seduced by War* (New York: Oxford University Press, 2005), p. 24.

8. Natan Sharansky, *The Case for Democracy: The Power of Freedom to Overcome Tyranny and Terror* (Green Forest, AR: Balfour Books, 2005), pp. 242–57.

The claims of democracy take a derivative place in the meaning that the administration gave to 'moral clarity.' Rather than principled debate, mortal combat itself becomes the model of ethical interchange, the only basis on which moral distinctions can be grounded. 'Once the bullets start to fly,' observed Paul Rieckhoff, 'there are only two kinds of people: warriors and victims,'[9] and this situation is converted into a moral dichotomy when warfare itself is accorded divine status, providing the source and structure of moral authority.

For the holy warriors in the Bush Administration the combat of absolute good and absolute evil is present in every conflict, including intellectual and moral disagreements about policy. Philippe Sands, the distinguished Professor of International Law at University College London, interviewed Douglas Feith about decisions taken early in the war, when Feith served as Under Secretary of Defense for Policy at the Pentagon. Sands asked whether certain decisions may have led to a loss of moral authority. 'The problem with moral authority,' Feith replied, 'was people who should know better, like yourself, siding with the assholes.'[10]

Neoconservative champions of White House policy have perfected this style of moral reasoning, Andrew Bacevich observes. It is 'fiercely combative' rhetoric that emphasizes

> not balance (viewed as an evidence of timidity), or the careful sifting of evidence (suggesting scholasticism) but the ruthless demolition of any point of view inconsistent with the neoconservative version of truth, typically portrayed as self-evident and beyond dispute...A willingness to compromise suggest(s) a lack of conviction. Fervor, certainty, and contempt for the other side, meanwhile, become marks of honor.[11]

Warnings against self-righteous delusion are themselves marked as evil, as appeals to relativistic 'nuance' that only obscure self-evident moral truth.

As the dismaying results of the 'Shock and Awe' campaign became apparent, the leaders in Washington took comfort in this

---

9. Paul Rieckhoff, *Chasing Ghosts: A Soldier's Fight for America From Baghdad to Washington* (New York: NAL Caliber, 2006), p. 97.

10. Philippe Sands, *Torture Team: Rumsfeld's Memo and the Betrayal of American Values* (New York: Palgrave Macmillan, 2008).

11. Bacevich, *The New American Militarism*, p. 72.

program of intellectual and moral evasion, and they rebuffed those who brought information not sufficiently pre-digested to support their illusions. But this moral luxury, indulged by the Bush leadership, was not so readily available to men in the field.

Moral Clarity in Battle

Individual soldiers in Iraq at times brooded uneasily over the seductions of possessing god-like power: 'I'm a thirty-year-old infantryman who will soon be given the ultimate authority of killing anyone I adjudicate to be a threat,' commented Jason Hartley.

> There's a darkly intoxicating aspect to this kind of thing...I'm over-armed with my rifle and grenade launcher and the veritable ammunition dump that is the vest over my body armor. Because of this, my power over these [Iraqis] is near absolute. I can see how the bully feels, how one could grow fond of this darkly amusing massive imbalance of power.[12]

Hartley's restless musing gave way to horror when his unit visited an Iraqi household to thank a man who had helped them. U.S. soldiers brought shoes and clothing for the children, but the man's brother was also visiting the home, and was an insurgent. He flew into a rage and threw a hand grenade, whereupon the Americans opened fire, leaving both brothers dead, with the survivors—old men, women, and children—mourning clamorously over the shattered bodies.

'What do you say in a situation like this when you leave?' Hartley asks: '"Um, sorry about killing part of your family. We'll just leave the clothes and shoes right here. See ya later, I guess."'[13] The commonplace words of parting evoke the surreal reality that has taken command of Hartley's soul, as it took command of the moment when the imperatives of kill-or-be-killed locked home, making a moral nightmare of moral clarity.

A pathway of escape from Hartley's inner torment is sketched in his description of a briefing where his battalion commander 'starts telling us how we need to be sensitive to the Iraqis and the painful period the people of that country are going through.' In response,

---

12. Jason Christopher Hartley, *Just Another Soldier: A Year on the Ground in Iraq* (New York: HarperCollins, 2005), pp. 54, 86.

13. Hartley, *Just Another Soldier*, pp. 285–86.

the unit's sniper shouts, 'SIR, GIVE ME AN M24...AND PLENTY OF AMMO, AND EVERYTHING WILL BE ALL RIGHT!' Hartley wishes he too could expel his distress by exulting in the intoxications of American firepower. 'God,' he writes, 'I wish I had that kind of clarity.'[14]

Jack Coughlin, a top-ranked Marine sniper, jauntily describes his M40A1 rifle as 'my long arm of justice.'[15] Yet Coughlin knows that justice and killing are not the same, and a chronic moral distress shows up in his sarcastic invocation of biblical teaching.

> Through the powerful telescope on my rifle, I see the expressions on the faces of my victims at the moment I quench that spark of life in their eyes. You don't dwell on that point, because you are just doing your job, and the sniper's one true commandment is "Thou Shalt Kill."[16]

Coughlin is both troubled and gleeful over his role as the arbiter of life and death: he returns again and again to the experience of deciding who will live and who will die.

> [My target] was calmly walking around as if he, instead of me, were the king of the world, and in his right hand he carried an AK-47 that looked almost new. Then he turned around, and that was his death notice.[17]

Like fear, the compassion aroused in combat can produce hesitation, which can mean death, not only for yourself but also for comrades. Soldiers learn to respond to compassion as though it were enemy fire, yet feel the threat to their own humanity that this entails. 'I maintained a stable mental plateau,' Coughlin remarks, 'by being totally convinced that I had done the right thing.'[18] But he discovers that taking refuge in the logic of moral clarity poses problems of its own.

'We did not intend to kill civilians,' Coughlin says, 'but we did, and we would just have to live with it.'[19] The engagement took place outside an embattled town, as his unit was approached by

---

14. Hartley, *Just Another Soldier*, p. 28.
15. Jack Coughlin, Casey Kuhlman, and Don Davis, *Shooter: The Autobiography of the Top-ranked Marine Sniper* (New York: St. Martin's Press, 2005), p. 63.
16. Coughlin, Kuhlman, and Davis, *Shooter*, p. 25.
17. Coughlin, Kuhlman, and Davis, *Shooter*, p. 208.
18. Coughlin, Kuhlman, and Davis, *Shooter*, p. 292.
19. Coughlin, Kuhlman, and Davis, *Shooter*, p. 225.

Iraqi military vehicles and civilian vehicles carrying Iraqi fighters, but also by cars in which innocent families were fleeing. It was impossible to be certain whether people in civilian clothes were armed or not, until the vehicles were torn apart by gunfire.

'I was stuck right in the front row with a huge spyglass,' Coughlin recalls, 'not only watching the butchery in magnified detail but also participating in it.' Walking away after the firing ended, Coughlin realizes that he had snapped psychologically. Needing to believe he had 'done the right thing,' he had faced a situation where the only option entailed butchery. 'I was consumed in the totally unfamiliar world of a waking nightmare, and my only thought was a faith-shaken prayer. *Oh, my God, what have we done?*'[20]

Coughlin realizes that he has received a wound that would remain with him lifelong:

> Such incidents always happen in war, and they weigh heavily upon the warrior, for although he has done nothing wrong, he will carry the guilt and replay those images in his head for the rest of his life. And the legacy of not being able to talk about such terrible things has been passed down through generations...So it sucks at your soul like some private leech.[21]

Beyond Coughlin's stoicism lies the agony of soldiers who are trapped into self-loathing by the 'good guy vs bad guy' moral logic. Colby Buzzell recounts an occasion on which he was ordered to stop refugees from passing a checkpoint, 'people [who] were completely miserable. Old people, women, children. Some people who looked like they could barely walk.'[22]

Before the order to stop them, Buzzell had been searching the meagre baggage they carried, and then letting them through. As the afternoon wore on, however, the chance to flee had attracted increasing numbers, eventually amounting to a very large crowd, and Buzzell was given the order to stop them. The refugees couldn't believe it: instead of turning around, they pushed forward begging and pleading and growing angry, until Buzzell swung his M4 around on them. 'They all understood what that meant, and without any protest they all slowly turned around and walked away.'

20. Coughlin, Kuhlman, and Davis, *Shooter*, p. 232.
21. Coughlin, Kuhlman, and Davis, *Shooter*, pp. 232–33.
22. Colby Buzzell, *My War: Killing Time in Iraq* (New York: Berkley Caliber, 2005), p. 304.

'I felt like the biggest fucking asshole on the planet,' Buzzell writes. 'In fact I felt like a Nazi, and for the first time ever, I felt like I was the bad guy.'[23]

Buzzell placed a JPEG of Picasso's *Guernica* on the website where he posted his blogs, further marking the devastation of Iraq as the work of Nazi 'bad guys.' Guernica was an undefended Basque town subjected to terrorist bombing by fascists during the Spanish Civil War. When word of the atrocity reached Paris, Picasso immediately set to work creating a huge masterpiece in black and white that evokes the obscene cruelty and chaos of the attack.

> The women with outstretched arms, Buzzell writes, 'with that look on their faces that says "Why?" reminded me of the house raids we were doing, the scared crying Iraqi women in the corner, holding their babies, who were also crying, while we searched the house...And the fallen soldier with a broken sword stirred up a bunch of emotion as well. Of course if you look by the fallen soldier's hand, you see a little flower growing, which means hope comes out of destruction. Which hopefully is the case with Iraq.'[24]

Buzzell seeks comfort in a very different kind of victory, not the work of an invincible righteous army crushing evil, but a redemption as vulnerable as a flower growing in the battle zone, amid weeping women and children.

* * *

White House leadership also suffered disconcerting anxieties, from 9/11 forward, which they sought to fend off through obsessively repeated certainties, and soon enough, moral clarity led to moral collapse. In the end, it's a familiar sad story, however new the details of its current enactment may be.

Those who play God, taking the role of divine avenger, encounter experiences showing they're not God, which sets up a strain between their self-righteous self-image and the 'bad guys' they are covertly aware of becoming. This spiritual dilemma is an ingredient to the age-long logic of the revenger's tragedy, in which the revenger becomes the evil that he hates.

23. Buzzell, *My War*, p. 306.
24. Buzzell, *My War*, p. 116.

The snare of idolatry is not sprung by some jealous god looking down from on high; it works through the soul of the idolater himself, the hubris that consigns its victims to degradation in the course of destroying them. The experience of helplessness arouses anxieties in those who deem themselves omnipotent, and they seek solace for these anxieties by further acts of vainglory, which they believe to be obedience to a Truth that cannot, must not, be questioned.

Men enmeshed in the rhetoric of sacred war look with yearning toward the only deliverance available, the promise of a victory that will retroactively cancel questions about the grounds for initiating the war, and about the way it was waged. History is written by the winners, runs the truism, so that justifications will be found post-facto if victory is attained, and condemnations drowned in choruses of celebration.

Such hopes gain force from the recognition that political sovereignties rise and fall on their capacity to defend themselves militarily from rival powers. Defeat in war—real full-scale defeat, not costly embarrassments like Vietnam or Iraq—brings havoc to every area of the nation's life. Defenders of American wars typically complain that their critics would not be able to make their criticisms, absent the political system that the war at least ostensibly seeks to preserve. Success in war thus becomes the linchpin for all other values; religious or ethical commitments must serve the effort to achieve victory.

The film *Patton* presents the famous general as a devoted student of warfare, and places him on a stage from which he declares that history is at heart the history of warmaking. Patton's army is on the move in the Italian campaign during World War II, crossing a vast mountain landscape. Vehicles climb from a broad valley on a long curving road, as the general's jeep dashes into the foreground and he stops to gaze at the panorama. 'Look at that column,' he says, 'Compared to war, all other forms of human endeavor shrink to insignificance.'[25]

Such is the logic of moral clarity writ large for commanders: defeat or victory takes the place of kill or be killed. Those who

25. Franklin J. Schaffner, George C. Scott, Karl Malden, Ladislas Farago, and Omar Nelson Bradley, *Patton* (Beverly Hills, CA: 20th Century Fox Home Entertainment, 1998).

worship war become its prisoners: they blindly pursue victory because self-doubt will open the floodgates of moral awareness and confound them with nightmares of self-defeat.

Dead Certainty

Counselors to President Bush became accustomed to the phobic anger with which he responded to the doubts and misgivings inseparable from waging war, as though the Commander in Chief should be exempted from hearing about them. General Richard B. Myers, the Chairman of the Joint Chiefs of Staff, told Bob Woodward that:

> when any doubt started to creep into the small, windowless Situation Room, the President almost stomped it out. Whether it was alarming casualties, bad news...or just a whiff of one of the uncertainties that accompany war, the President would try to set them all straight.
>
> "Hold it," Bush said once, "we know we're doing the right thing. We're on the right track here. We're doing the right things for ourselves, for our own interest and for the world. And don't forget it. Come on, guys."[26]

Bush voices his certainty in tense repetitive phrases, obsessively repeating what he cannot afford to doubt. 'I know it is hard for you to believe', he said to Woodward, 'but I have not doubted what we're doing. I have not doubted what we're doing...There is no doubt in my mind we're doing the right thing.' Bush explained that the operation under his command depended for its effectiveness on the faith that flowed from his own soul, so it was imperative this faith should be unshakeable. 'A President has to be the calcium in the backbone,' he explained to Woodward. 'If I weaken, the whole team weakens. If I'm doubtful, I can assure you there will be a lot of doubt...It will send ripples throughout the whole organization.'[27]

George Weigel, the Roman Catholic theocon who enjoyed frequent access to the Bush White House, explains that 'the political powers-that-be' possess a God-given power to make the right choices, to which others must defer. In the initiation and conduct of war,

---

26. Bob Woodward, *State of Denial: [Bush at War, Part III]* (New York: Simon & Schuster, 2006), p. 371.

27. Woodward, *State of Denial: [Bush at War, Part III]*, p. 371.

statesmen exercise a 'charism of political discernment,' a gift of the Holy Spirit belonging to their office and 'not shared by bishops, stated clerks, rabbis, imams, or ecumenical and interreligious agencies.'[28] This unique spiritual autonomy gives the President, so the theory runs, the right to claim unquestionable authority, and to view dissent from that authority as a blasphemous defiance of God's will.

Bush was deeply invested in his faith during the critical early stages of the fiasco in Iraq. Prince Bandar of Saudi Arabia, a longstanding intimate of the Bush family, recounts conversations in 2004 when the President's 'deep religious convictions came up time and time again, as he talked about his faith and his relationship with God. The President made it clear that he felt no doubt that a higher authority was looking after him and guiding him.' Bush explained that he had 'asked for and received such guidance,' and 'relied on his faith to carry him through.'[29]

Religious souls in many traditions practice prayer and meditation to find the strength that is needed to sustain unresolved, and indeed unresolvable, doubts and uncertainties. Sustaining the ambiguities and anxieties endemic to mortal experience requires spiritual courage that can be amplified through communion with great teachers, sacred texts, religious art and music, or through devotions addressing a G*d whose mystery always remains beyond comprehension.

There is a marked difference between such a living faith, however, and the calcified certainty that Bush sought to bolster through prayer. Bush's version of Christianity holds no monopoly on the provision of delusionary certainty, and many evangelical Christians derive spiritual courage and wisdom within the tradition that Bush has used as a substitute for them. Religious communities worldwide offer means of sustenance for devout and morally competent souls, and guidance toward the attainment of spiritual maturity. But authoritarian religiosity, in whatever tradition, masks inner fears that authentic faith addresses directly.

As adverse circumstances arouse such fears, authoritarian believers cling all the more rigidly to the ideology that maintaining their self-confidence requires. The result is often a cascade effect,

28. Damon Linker, *The Theocons: Secular America Under Siege* (New York: Doubleday, 2006), pp. 131–32.

29. Woodward, *State of Denial: [Bush at War, Part III]*, p. 334.

poor decisions producing additional poor decisions because the decider lacks the spiritual courage to question them. It's better for a person bearing responsibility to lack 'religious faith,' if 'faith' is an evasion of the responsibility to examine the context of policy with care, and to correct policy as developing circumstances indicate.

When appeals to the guidance of 'a higher authority' are linked with heedless inflexibility, a leader indeed sends out 'ripples,' but they undermine the competence of the organization he leads, and inspire doubts in its wisest members. Public observers have long recognized that Bush's tireless reaffirmations of his resolute optimism are an example of protesting too much, an effort to keep himself persuaded. Loyal associates with frequent access have likewise been shaken by his effort to appear unshakable.

Colin Powell and Richard Armitage were intimates of the administration who urgently wanted Bush to succeed. They were alike worried about his inability to tolerate doubt, and talked about it often. Powell and Armitage 'always had self-doubt,' writes Woodward in summarizing these conversations.

> They lived on it, mainlined it. "If you didn't," Powell said, "if you didn't get up in the morning wondering if you're doing a good enough job...you're not worth much."
>
> "Not worth shit," Armitage said.
>
> Bush and Cheney, the two agreed, dread being swamped by paralyzing uncertainty if they let the slightest doubt seep in. They cannot have any doubt about the correctness of the policy because it opens too many questions in their minds.[30]

The war became self-perpetuating through an analogous logic, of which Powell and Armitage were also aware, when battlefield deaths raised the stakes. 'The cause, sanctified by the dead,' notes Chris Hedges, 'cannot be questioned without dishonoring those that gave up their lives.'[31] The leadership thus derives a propaganda advantage from the needless deaths for which they are answerable. Powell and Armitage put their finger on exactly this process, as the failure of the war policy could no longer be kept from public awareness, and media expressions of doubt began to multiply. Public support could be secured by exploiting the frantic desire of

30. Woodward, *State of Denial: [Bush at War, Part III]*, p. 325.

31. Chris Hedges, *War Is a Force that Gives Us Meaning* (New York: Anchor Books, 2002), p. 145.

those who had lost husbands, wives and children, to believe their loved ones did not die for a mistake.

> What the President says in effect is we've got to press on in honor of the memory of those who have fallen. Another way to say that is we've got to have more men fall to honor the memories of those who have fallen.[32]

Because the experience of doubt was felt by the President as a threat to the entire operation in Iraq, those who raised questions were perceived as enemies, virtually as allies of Al Qaeda. Some such response may make sense for soldiers on the battlefield, where a moment of hesitation can spell disaster, and George W. Bush without experience of combat may have felt justified by a fantasy version of those necessities. But the central counsels of war are in certain respects insulated for good reason from battlefield pressures. Such intolerance among the leadership does not come from external necessities, but arises within the men themselves.

The result was a series of startling insults dealt out to persons who gave President Bush news he did not want to hear. In the days before the Iraqi elections of 30 January 2005, the CIA brought reports that were skeptical about U.S. support for the venture. 'Is this Baghdad Bob?' asked the President after one such briefing, likening the advisor to a propagandist in Saddam's regime whose broadcasts were intended to weaken American resolve.[33]

Like President Bush, Donald Rumsfeld adopted a defensive bullying mentality when faced with disconcerting news. Frank Miller had served for two decades in sensitive positions connecting the Pentagon with the civilian leadership, but now found himself — along with trusted colleagues on the staff of the National Security Council — treated by Rumsfeld 'like [a] third-class citizen of dubious loyalty.' Jay Garner, the official first charged with managing the post-invasion administration of Iraq, came to a disagreement with Rumsfeld, whereupon Rumsfeld snapped: 'It doesn't seem like you're on our team.'[34]

---

32. Woodward, *State of Denial: [Bush at War, Part III]*, p. 325.
33. Woodward, *State of Denial: [Bush at War, Part III]*, p. 382.
34. Woodward, *State of Denial: [Bush at War, Part III]*, p. 109.

Shaken Souls

The anxieties driving the Bush White House to cling to ideology were augmented by reports from the battlefield in Iraq, but did not originate there. They flared into life on 9/11.

Cheney was lifted bodily and carried downstairs to the White House basement; Rumsfeld heard and felt the explosion as the airliner crashed into the Pentagon; President Bush—at Cheney's direction—took refuge at Offutt Airbase, only venturing back to Washington when it seemed safe. Fighter aircraft patrolled the skies, and Cheney had ordered them to shoot down commercial airliners—killing the American citizens aboard—if those airliners refused to land at the nearest airport when commanded by the fighter pilots. American soldiers in Iraq were tormented by the guilt of killing Iraqi civilians under military necessity. Had the passengers on United Flight 93 not mobilized to battle the hijackers, Cheney would have borne a burden exponentially more intense.

It is hard to imagine that Bush, Cheney and Rumsfeld passed through September 11, 2001 without subliminal queasiness about their failure to prevent the disaster. Marines on the ground in Iraq did not have to contemplate responsibility for the scenes in New York and Washington, more than three thousand citizens slaughtered under a cloudless blue sky as they started the day's work. The failure of the White House to heed advance warnings, fully revealed, could have ignited a political firestorm. If there was guilt amid the emotional distress that Bush, Cheney and Rumsfeld were schooled to expel from consciousness, there was also fear.

It is now well established that CIA Director George Tenet briefed Condoleeza Rice on 10 July 2001 about the danger that Al Qaeda was planning a terrorist attack inside the United States, and subsequently gave the same briefing to Rumsfeld, and Attorney General John Ashcroft. As the evidence of an imminent attack mounted in the following weeks, the CIA felt their warnings had not been taken seriously, and their increasingly fervent efforts culminated in the President's Daily Brief for 6 August which was given a title meant to set off alarms: 'Bin Laden Determined to Strike in US.' Tenet told Richard Clarke, the National Security Council's counterterrorism director, 'It is my sixth sense, but I feel it coming. This is going to be the big one.'[35]

35. Woodward, *State of Denial: [Bush at War, Part III]*, p. 50.

The President was vacationing in Texas during August, so CIA officers were dispatched to drive home the message. Noting their desperate urgency, the President scoffed, 'All right. You've covered your ass.'[36]

The CIA possessed information that Al Qaeda operatives were in the United States, attending aviation schools where they learned to fly passenger aircraft. But the agency was officially enjoined from sharing such information with the FBI, who had the power to make arrests.[37] The FBI likewise had critical information they declined to share with criminal prosecutors. A vigorous response from one of the senior officials who had been briefed about the threat might well have broken through the walls separating these bureaucratic compartments, and have prevented the attacks.

When an independent bipartisan commission was proposed to investigate 'preparedness for and the immediate response to' the 9/11 attacks, there was a chance this aspect of the story might become part of the official record. The White House responded as if they had something to hide. As Daniel Froomkin wrote in *The Washington Post*, the administration fought the establishment of the commission, and the President himself 'refused to face the panel alone, or in public, insisting instead on a private, unrecorded interview with Vice-President Cheney at his side.'[38] The Executive Director of the commission, Philip Zelikow, had close ties to the White House, and maintained telephone contact with Rice and Karl Rove during the commission's work.[39]

An investigator for the commission discovered an NSC archive filled with emails and memos sent by Richard Clarke to Condoleeza Rice during the summer of 2001, culminating in a desperate appeal September 4, which asked the senior officials to 'imagine themselves on a future day when...hundreds of Americans lay dead in several countries, including the U.S.'[40] How would decision makers feel,

36. Ron Suskind, *The One Percent Doctrine: Deep Inside America's Pursuit of its Enemies Since 9/11* (New York: Simon & Schuster, 2006), p. 2.

37. Lawrence Wright, *The Looming Tower: Al-Qaeda and the Road to 9/11* (New York: Knopf, 2007), p. 342.

38. Dan Froomkin, 'The White House Mole', White House Watch, *Washington Post*, 4 February 2008. www.washingtonpost.com/wp-dyn/content/blog/2008/02/04/BL2008020401554.html. Philip Shenon, *The Commission: The Uncensored History of the 9/11 Investigation* (New York: Twelve, 2008), pp. 340–45.

39. Shenon, *The Commission*, pp. 106–108, 168, 172–74.

40. Shenon, *The Commission*, p. 148.

looking back on decisions that had led to this? But Zelikow effectively blocked the commission from pursuing the line of study Clarke's writings would open up.

Yet, Clarke's challenge stands: what indeed did they feel, these high officials who had spurned so many warnings, once the tragedy was plain for all to see?

Three days after 9/11 the senior members of the administration's national security team met at Camp David, in an atmosphere Condoleeza Rice found unique. 'They'd seen a lot together before,' she commented. But 'this was different, and it was palpable in the room...I could sense there was — I'm trying to find the right word — tension isn't the right word, but anxiety. Anxiety.'[41]

Amid the wash of anxiety and guilt, the leadership took refuge in a fantasy of god-like empowerment, trusting this would meet their own emotional needs, and those of a traumatized public. As they dreamed of the 'Shock and Awe' assault they unleashed upon Iraq twenty months later, the leaders were in a disorderly flight from themselves, and from the larger foreign policy challenges confronting the nation. Their decisions increased the threat that had exploded in our midst, and set the administration on a course of spiritual and political degradation.

These initial anxieties were sharpened after the illusory triumph of 'Mission Accomplished' faded away. It became apparent that Saddam Hussein and his military leaders had prepared themselves for the 'shock and awe' assault, and had ordered the army officers to resist strongly for only two weeks. They were then to engage in a campaign of vandalism and pillage that would wreck the administrative infrastructure that Americans would need in order to manage an occupation. It seems that the Iraqi leadership had also stockpiled large numbers of weapons, and laid aside billions of dollars in currency, in order to mount the insurgency that took Bush, Cheney and Rumsfeld by surprise.[42] The result was the highly effective guerilla campaign, which deepened the sense of frustration and helplessness besieging White House officials.

41. Stephen F. Hayes, *Cheney: The Untold Story of America's Most Powerful and Controversial Vice President* (New York: HarperCollins, 2007), p. 351.

42. Scott Johnson and Evan Thomas, 'Still Fighting Saddam: The attacks keep coming, and the war doesn't seem over to the soldiers on the ground. With his money and his diehards, Saddam casts a long shadow — and a guerilla war may have been his strategy all along,' *Newsweek*, 21 July 2003, pp. 22–25.

Programs of illicit intelligence gathering had been established immediately after 9/11, including harsh methods of interrogation that were applied to captives taken in Afghanistan and held at Bagram Air Base and Guantanamo. Yet as the Iraq insurgency gathered force, the results were found to be inadequate. Donald Rumsfeld exploded with rage, banged on the table, and declared that the intelligence being gathered in Iraq was 'shit,' compared to the yield at Guantanamo. He then ordered that the Guantanamo commander, General Geoffrey Miller, be sent to Iraq, to 'Gitmo-ize' procedures at Abu Ghraib.[43] Among other qualifications, as we shall see, General Miller appreciated the Christian underpinnings of the 'Gitmo' approach.

43. Cockburn, *Rumsfeld*, p. 193.

Chapter Nine

A Theology of Torture

Advertising the Dark Side

Five days after 9/11, Vice-President Cheney appeared on 'Meet the Press' with Tim Russert, and made a point of mentioning certain measures that he couldn't talk about openly.

> I'm going to be careful here, Tim.... We also have to work, though, sort of the dark side. We've got to spend time in the shadows in the intelligence world. A lot of what needs to be done here will have to be done quietly, without any discussion...You need to have on the payroll some very unsavory characters, if, in fact, you're going to be able to learn all that needs to be learned in order to forestall these kinds of activities. It is a mean, nasty, dangerous dirty business.[1]

Cheney's meaning could hardly have been clearer: the administration had adopted a torture policy. It was part of a secret program whose details were being worked out at the CIA as Cheney spoke, to which President Bush affixed his signature the next day.[2] Yet, Cheney disavowed what he was saying in the act of saying it.

Cheney's double-talk is a clue to the complicated impulses that were summoned to life within the White House leadership, and the public at large, by the humiliation 9/11 inflicted. To the end of the Bush Administration the torture program remained an official secret, yet its existence and much of its character was common knowledge. This paradox is sharpened by the fact that the Vice-President, with his famous penchant for secrecy, announced it at the inception. The nation and the world must know that torture would be inflicted on terrorists, yet the administration must disavow it.

1. Richard Cheney and Tim Russert, 'The Vice President Appears on Meet the Press with Tim Russert', The White House News and Policies, 16 September 2001. www.whitehouse.gov.vicepresident/news-speeches/speeches/vp20010916.html.

2. Jane Mayer, *Dark Side: The Inside Story of How the War on Terror Turned into a War on American Ideals* (New York: Doubleday, 2008), pp. 38–41.

The paradox of American torture as a public/secret enterprise is rooted in a longstanding conflict of religious values. For many centuries torture was a standard practice in Christian nations, in keeping with a theology that has recently been revived on the Religious Right, in conflict with more commonplace understandings of Christian belief. But the religious dispute at the core of Cheney's paradox is complicated and obscured by the commonly accepted justifications for torture.

Cheney invoked a modern fictionalized notion of torture that has come to seem like common sense. It's the 'ticking bomb' theory, which claims that torture is capable of extracting crucial information quickly, answering the need 'to learn all that needs to be learned in order to forestall these kinds of activities.' Darius Rejali's encyclopedic study of modern torture traces this fantasy to its origin in Jean Larteguy's 1960 novel, *Les Centurions*, about the French struggle against insurgents in Algeria. Larteguy's fiction—famously dramatized in the film *The Battle of Algiers*—swiftly displaced factual accounts of the struggle, because torture exerts an appeal not connected to its usefulness in gaining information.[3]

No advantage would follow from Cheney's advertising the project, if gathering intelligence were the governing purpose. It is noteworthy that he made no comparable announcement of other such projects, for example the surveillance of the personal and business communications of American citizens. In addition, Cheney's words increased the danger that the odium attached to torture, and the laws that prohibit torture, would create severe problems for the administration, as indeed they did.

The American people got Cheney's message. When the pictures of abuse at Abu Ghraib were made public, London's *Daily Mirror* ran an illustrated article claiming that British soldiers were guilty of degrading Iraqis, whereupon a storm of protest challenged the *Mirror*'s claim. Americans felt no such incredulity: 'We believed the Abu Ghraib images without question,' writes David Levi Strauss; 'they only confirmed what we already knew.'[4] The protracted indifference of the American public can be traced to the same source.

3. Darius M. Rejali, *Torture and Democracy* (Princeton, NJ: Princeton University Press, 2007), p. 545.

4. David Levi Strauss, 'Breakdown in the Grey Room: Recent Turns in the Image War', in Meron Benvenisti *Abu Ghraib: The Politics of Torture* (The Terra Nova Series; Berkeley, CA: North Atlantic Books, 2004), p. 93.

Not wanting to face the grisly particulars, the public tacitly accepted the policy in general terms, even though the administration never produced support for its repeated claim that torture is necessary to forestall terrorist attacks.

As late as March 2008, Jane Mayer reports, President Bush faced the prospect of legislation that would forbid CIA operatives to use 'enhanced' techniques of interrogation, limiting them to the methods practiced by the Army, which conform to the Geneva Conventions and the requirements of American law. Senator Jay Rockefeller, with access to information kept secret from the public at large, issued a summary of the evidence:

> As Chairman of the Senate Intelligence Committee, I have heard nothing to suggest that information obtained from enhanced interrogation techniques has prevented an imminent terrorist attack. And I have heard nothing that makes me think the information obtained from these techniques could not have been obtained through traditional interrogation methods used by military and law enforcement interrogators. On the other hand, I do know that coercive interrogations can lead detainees to provide false information in order to make the interrogation stop.[5]

Rockefeller concluded that 'the CIA's program damages our national security by weakening our legal and moral authority, and by providing al Qaeda and other terrorist groups a recruiting and motivational tool'.[6] Yet despite Rockefeller's efforts, seconded by a growing community of well-informed protest, the legislation failed, and the CIA continued unchecked.

Torture sometimes extracts accurate information, Darius Rejali notes, but not reliably and not quickly. It is 'even clumsier in some cases than flipping a coin or shooting randomly into crowds'.[7] Rejali massively documents Rockefeller's view, that torture brings a host of disadvantages, shaming the cause in which it is enlisted, inspiring deepened resistance in adversaries, and flooding the intelligence-gathering apparatus with the misinformation that victims provide in the hope of ending their agonies.

The military has firm rules forbidding torture on commonsense grounds, which include preventing an adversary from justifying

---

5. Mayer, *Dark Side*, p. 330.
6. Mayer, *Dark Side*, p. 330.
7. Rejali, *Torture and Democracy*, p. 478.

the torture of American prisoners by the example of America's own practices. 'Use of torture and other illegal methods,' states the U.S. Army Field Manual, 'is a poor technique that yields unreliable results, may damage subsequent collection efforts, and induce the source to say what the interrogator wants to hear.'[8] Even so, the specious claims of the Bush Administration carried the day with the American public.

* * *

The motivation for torture is not rational. The fact that torture is counterproductive has not led governments, including democratic governments, to repudiate its use in times of public outrage. Within a week after 9/11, members of the British intelligence service flew to Washington and cautioned against repeating mistakes the British committed in their torture campaign against the IRA. '"Watch out,"' warned a top official. '"It's dangerous. It makes you the bad guys. And when it gets to court—and in your society, just like ours, it will—every one of these guys will get off."'[9] Such arguments had no effect amid the humiliation and rage that 9/11 inspired.

Getting information is not the reason for torture. The 'ticking bomb' theory is the modern pretext for an ancient barbarity, which allows a terrorized and humiliated community to collect a blood debt from captives held answerable for the affront. 'The terrorist's suffering is uniquely satisfying,' Rejali comments,

> regardless of whether he reveals any information. Beneath the urbane, civilized appeal to torture for information lurks a deeper impulse, born from fear and satisfied by pain. When a public official is prepared to spill the blood of a detained, helpless individual, breaking bonds of law and morality, this appears to satisfy a debt incurred by the violence of the terrorist.[10]

Official torture is employed more frequently by despotisms than by democracies, Rejali points out, and this is commonly cited as an evidence of the political degradation to which tyrannies are subject. Their fragile hold on legitimacy leads to systemic anxieties, as in

8. Amnesty International, USA Blog, 'Denounce Torture: Torture Ineffective', http://blogs.amnestyusa.org/denounce-torture/archive/2006/06/10/614w0igmvst.htm

9. Mayer, *Dark Side*, p. 30.

10. Rejali, *Torture and Democracy*, p. 534.

Nazi Germany, the Soviet Union, and Saddam Hussein's Iraq. But in democracies as well, torture has the effect of 'purging the wounded community's furious emotions.'[11] Cheney's evocation of 'unsavory characters' carrying out a 'mean, nasty, dangerous, dirty business' on the bodies of terrorists would assuage the humiliation inflicted by 9/11. America's adversaries gained propaganda benefits and material aid from the White House torture program. The Abu Ghraib photographs became a major turning point in the destruction of U.S. legitimacy. 'The image of the United States,' commented Senator Jack Reed (D-RI), became 'an American soldier dragging a prostrate, naked Iraqi across the floor on a leash.' Far from 'saving American lives' the torture program inspired foreign jihadis to join the insurgency. According to Matthew Alexander, these dedicated fighters accounted for 'at least half of American losses.' An interrogator who employed non-abusive methods in Iraq, Alexander estimates that American lives lost as a result of torture approaches the number killed on 9/11.[12] Yet before these predictable real-world costs came due, the White House torture program was tacitly accepted, because of the spiritual satisfactions it offered. 'The larger problem here,' remarked an active CIA officer, 'is that this kind of stuff just makes people feel better.'[13]

Such costly gratification was very appealing to the general public. The television series '24' premiered twenty-five days after 9/11, and enjoyed five years of tremendous popularity. Episode after episode depicted 'ticking bomb' scenarios in which catastrophe is forestalled. Suspects were 'beaten, suffocated, electrocuted, drugged, assaulted with knives, or more exotically abused,' noted Jane Mayer, and 'almost without fail, these suspects divulge critical secrets.'[14] Arguments against torture were placed in the mouths of the timorous and weakminded, and failures of torture were virtually never dramatized. Scenes of torture in television

11. Rejali, *Torture and Democracy*, p. 535.

12. Andrew Cockburn, *Rumsfeld: His Rise, Fall, and Catastrophic Legacy* (New York: Scribner, 2007), p. 197. Matthew Alexander, 'I'm Still Tortured by What I Saw in Iraq,' *The Washington Post*, 30 November 2008. http.www.washingtonpost.com/wp-dyn/content/article/2008/11/28. See also Matthew Alexander and John Bruning, *How to Break a Terrorist: The U.S. Interrogators Who Used Brains, not Brutality, to Take Down the Deadliest Man in Iraq* (New York: Free Press, 2008.)

13. Rejali, *Torture and Democracy*, p. 535.

14. Jane Mayer, 'Whatever It Takes', *New Yorker*, 19 & 26 February 2007, 19 February, p. 66.

programming multiplied twenty-five fold during this period, and were significantly recast. Torturers in earlier programming were vicious scoundrels; now they became patriotic heroes.

In November of 2006 the Dean of the U.S. Military Academy at West Point, General Patrick Finnegan, obtained a meeting with the writers for '24', and brought along experts with long experience in interrogation for the FBI and the U.S. military. The popularity of '24' made it difficult, they explained to the writers, to persuade West Point cadets that torture is counterproductive, abhorrent to American ideals, with gravely adverse psychological effects on those who inflict it. 'They should do a show where torture backfires,' General Finnegan stated.[15]

But the show's representatives had little interest in what the military men had to say. Effective techniques of interrogation require building rapport with potential informants, the experts argued, and this process is incompatible with tormenting them. But such techniques do not provide the emotional satisfaction of witnessing what a '24' writer called 'improvisations in sadism.' Joel Surnow, the executive producer of the program, recognized that his product served a strong public appetite, speaking to 'what people's fears are—their paranoia that we're going to be attacked.'[16]

During its five-year vogue, '24' provided tacit support for the torture program. Military officers at Guantanamo were encouraged by the Pentagon to develop new techniques, and watched '24' looking for ideas. This also calmed misgivings about the legality and morality of the enterprise.[17] If the public was behind it, and the TV show said it works, and the White House sponsored it, how could torture be wrong?

The core paradox of the policy was recapitulated through this public/secret phenomenon, a television program offering guidance and moral support to those secretly developing and executing the program, and also to millions of viewers who both did and did not know that abuses like those they witnessed were taking place under White House auspices.

* * *

15. Mayer, 'Whatever It Takes', p. 72.

16. Mayer, 'Whatever It Takes', pp. 68, 71.

17. Philippe Sands, *Torture Team: Rumsfeld's Memo and the Betrayal of American Values* (New York: Palgrave Macmillan, 2008), pp. 61–62.

Torture is a retail version of 'Shock and Awe,' fulfilling fantasies of god-like empowerment for shaken souls. It aims at 'breaking' a detainee, so that humiliating involuntary responses take over: s/he voids bladder and bowels, convulses uncontrollably, screams and sobs, begs for mercy, goes into catatonic stupor, answers questions with frantic eagerness, and this continues for hours on end, day after day, week after week. The torturer achieves, or seems to achieve, absolute domination, derived from the absolute degradation of the adversary.

Such degradation has social meanings, as John Conroy observes. It is inflicted on members of a 'torturable class,'[18] a condition that has been shared by ghetto blacks in Chicago, especially when they shoot policemen, by Palestinians who use force against the government of Israel, by Irish militants who fought the British, and by Jews who were murdered by Nazi Christians in Germany. In the American South, 'niggers' formed a torturable class, abused and murdered on spurious claims of assault against white women, when whites detected gestures of defiance against white oppression.

Torture delivers the emotional satisfaction that comes from allaying the anxiety that is aroused when upstarts threaten to redefine the social landscape. Punishing a subject population that refuses to accept the terms of their subordination, especially when they resort to violent retaliation, provides gratification to those whose privileges are placed at risk.

Cheney's announcement of the torture policy, in his interview with Tim Russert, indicated that the war on terror would include the establishment of a new torturable class, those who had delivered an intolerable affront to American pre-eminence on the world stage. It was ostensibly composed of malefactors who had supported the 9/11 terrorists, but soon expanded to include hapless souls swept up indiscriminately and bundled into the torture centers at Bagram Airbase in Afghanistan, at Abu Graib and other prisons in Iraq, and at Guantanamo Bay, as well as those sent for torture to 'Black Sites' in nations prepared to cooperate with the American project.

General Geoffrey Miller, the commander at Guantanamo, who assisted in transferring these techniques to Abu Ghraib, recognized that they would assert a social message, Americans inflicting

18. John Conroy, *Unspeakable Acts, Ordinary People: The Dynamics of Torture* (Berkeley, CA: University of California Press, 2000), p. 27.

humiliations that would bespeak absolute dominion over subhuman adversaries. 'If you allow them to believe at any point that they are more than a dog then you've lost control of them,' he said, and this objective came increasingly to govern the torture program.[19] A drama of social place is unmistakably etched in the Abu Ghraib images: American soldiers are triumphantly in control. Iraqis are subservient dogs, and worse.

Torturable classes always tend to expand, John Conroy notes, in part because torture so enrages the subject population that increasing numbers are propelled into violent resistance; but it is also true because of the impact of torture on torturers. Torture programs do not recruit sadists, but 'well integrated, productive and secure personalities,'[20] with perhaps a greater-than-average impulse to obey authority. But inflicting torture is a powerfully absorbing experience, sucking perpetrators into a vortex of self-fuelling degradation.

Torturers are themselves humiliated and degraded as they humiliate and degrade their victims. Professional restraints collapse, institutional discipline breaks down, and the torture operation becomes self-enclosed, virtually an end in itself. At Abu Ghraib, MP's staged 'contests to see how quickly a prisoner could be brought to tears.'[21] Merle Pribbenow, with twenty-seven years' experience with the CIA's clandestine Directorate of Operations, recounts that interrogators sometimes missed information because they 'got so involved that they didn't even bother to ask questions.'[22]

The torture program Cheney announced five days after 9/11 carried the nation deeper into the 'dark side' than Cheney could have foreseen, and broadcast it worldwide, with notorious violations of deeply held American values, in particular the human rights that are enshrined in American law and in the long-standing policies of the U.S. military. The torture program was officially disavowed in good measure because the administration recognized it could hardly survive an outright declaration of the intent to violate these principles. But an alternative set of values also informed the instincts of the American leadership, a theology of torture that justifies the use of cruelty against evil men.

19. Cockburn, *Rumsfeld*, p. 194.
20. Conroy, *Unspeakable Acts*, p. 89.
21. Rejali, *Torture and Democracy*, p. 509.
22. Rejali, *Torture and Democracy*, p. 502.

A Theology of Torture

The spiritual allure of torture — the seduction that leads to the addiction — is expressed in the myth of the six-gun savior, and in the theological traditions that define it. The god-likeness of the mythical cowboy is grounded on a distinctive version of the Christian God. When Lassiter tortures Judge Dyer with bullets from his great black guns, Dyer involuntarily acknowledges a truth that justifies the cruelty dealt out to him. The judge receives a vision of the religious reality that he has violated and Lassiter has enforced.

This is a stereotyped sequence in the narrative of the divine avenger — whether as make-believe cowboy or as hardboiled cop — torture forcing a confession of the 'truth' that the torturer wants to hear. A 'bad guy' with critical information rebuffs a 'good guy' who demands the information, whereupon the 'good guy' escalates the force. Before 9/11 the abuse dealt out to the malefactor usually fell short of torture, the sudden onset of violence signaling an overpowering coercive force that need only be hinted at. The result is as predictable as the gesture itself: the desired information spills out.

Overt emblems of divine presence are usually absent from these scenes, which are presented despite their fanciful character as the grittiest realism. Even so, the power at work in such moments evokes the vision of God that has recently gained currency on the Christian Right, supplanting more conventional versions of Christianity to which torture is anathema. Charles Graner, who abused prisoners at Abu Graib in order to 'set the conditions' for torture, invoked the gentler Christian teaching when he said, 'The Christian in me knows it's wrong, but the corrections officer in me can't help but love to make a grown man piss himself.'[23] Graner didn't realize that a Christian warrant had become available to justify tormenting suspected terrorists.

* * *

Two distinct Christian traditions are at stake here: one claims that human beings possess God-given rights; the other embraces a

---

23. Philip Gourevitch and Errol Morris, *Standard Operating Procedure* (New York: Penguin Press, 2008), p. 127.

doctrine of original sin that holds we are innately disposed to rebel against the divine majesty. God is filled with vengeful wrath against the human race, so the doctrine teaches, because He is affronted by our chronic defiance of His law, and vindicates His dignity by tormenting us in this life and beyond. Given our inborn stubbornness, we obey God only after applications of divine vengeance have broken our self-will.

Before the late eighteenth century, this notion of original sin justified the practice of torture in Christian nations. As belief in human rights gained precedence, accordingly, torture became increasingly abhorrent, and was at length abandoned. Lynn Hunt's masterful treatment of this development notes that the standards asserted in the American 'Declaration of Independence' (1776) and the French 'Declaration of the Rights of Man and Citizen' (1789) arise from 'Greek ideas about the individual person,' and 'Roman notions of law and right,' as these were coalesced into 'Christian doctrines of the soul.' Belief in intrinsic human worth gathered force, Hunt observes, as spiritual self-awareness increased in the centuries following the Reformation and the Renaissance. Human personhood became a center of sacred dignity and freedom, and defenders of the old faith confronted new theologies that honored human rights.[24] This struggle of orthodox believers against more liberal Christianities convulsed religious communities in America during the early nineteenth century.

Yet, Elaine Pagels has shown that the earliest conceptions of Christian salvation provide support for the liberal tradition. Down to the time of Constantine, in the fourth century, Christians identified their salvation with liberation from oppression. They embraced 'freedom in its many forms, including free will, freedom from demonic powers, freedom from social and sexual obligations, freedom from tyrannical government and from fate.'[25]

Christians struggled during this early period to maintain their foothold amid a hostile Roman Empire. But when Constantine made Christianity the religion of the empire, the picture changed dramatically. 'Christian bishops, once targets for arrest, torture,

---

24. Lynn Avery Hunt, *Inventing Human Rights: A History* (New York: W.W. Norton & Co., 2007).

25. Elaine H. Pagels, *Adam, Eve, and the Serpent* (New York: Random House, 1988), p. xxv.

and execution, now received tax exemptions, gifts from the imperial treasury, prestige, and even influence at court.'[26] St. Augustine elaborated an alternative doctrine of salvation better suited to the new situation, arguing that salvation is forgiveness for indwelling sin, not liberation from external powers of coercion. Primordial rebellion against God's law, descending to every mortal from Adam's disobedience in the Garden of Eden, 'cost us our moral freedom, irreversibly corrupted our experience of sexuality...and made us incapable of genuine political freedom.'[27] Following Constantine, Christian doctrines justified state-sponsored cruelty, as required to curb the inherently rebellious and disorderly souls of men, and to manifest God's wrath against human sin.

In the late eighteenth century, Christian defenders of public torture battled advocates of human rights seeking to abolish it. Pierre-Francois Muyart de Vouglans derided reformers who saw a God-given dignity in every human heart. 'What experience taught was the need to control the unruly, not coddle their sensibilities,' Hunt summarizes. 'Only the awe-inspiring power of an avenging justice could rein in those tempers. The pageantry of pain at the scaffold was designed to instill terror in observers and in this way served as a deterrence.'[28]

Routines of public punishment in the American colonies were not as horrific as those in England and on the continent, but they were equally commonplace. As late as the second half of the eighteenth century, Hunt points out, 'one third of all the sentences in the Massachusetts Superior Court...called for public humiliations ranging from wearing signs to cutting off an ear, branding and whipping.'[29]

Jonathan Edwards, the most profound of Puritan theologians, held that cruelty dealt out to criminals dramatizes the justice of God. A person that 'enrages an arbitrary prince,' Edwards wrote in 1741, 'is liable to suffer the most extreme torments that human art can invent, or human power can inflict.' Far from disputing the legitimacy of state-sponsored torture, Edwards uses it to illustrate what God has in store for sinners, with the proviso that earthly

26. Pagels, *Adam, Eve*, p. xxv.
27. Pagels, *Adam, Eve*, p. xxvi.
28. Hunt, *Inventing Human Rights*, p. 93.
29. Hunt, *Inventing Human Rights*, p.77.

rulers, even when 'clothed in their greatest terrors,' can never inflict the agony that God visits upon those who defy Him.[30]

For this mindset there is no reason to keep torture secret. On the contrary, vindicating offended majesty requires a public spectacle. Jonathan Edwards anticipates the impulses that prompted Vice-President Cheney to advertise the torture policy, and the television show '24' to offer it for public consumption, as he pictures the awestruck veneration with which God's loyal servants will adore him, when they have witnessed the torments of the damned.

> When you shall be in this state of suffering, the glorious inhabitants of heaven shall go forth and look on the awful spectacle, that they may see what the wrath and fierceness of the Almighty is; and when they have seen it, they will fall down and adore that great power and majesty.[31]

The White House torture program was meant to dramatize the power and majesty of the United States of America, which is given the role of God in this drama of offended glory vindicated through extreme cruelty.

As belief in human dignity became an article of popular faith in nineteenth century America, and moved toward the center of American Protestantism, it collided with established doctrines of human sin and divine wrath. A powerful religious movement halted the whippings, brandings and other tortures that had long been dealt out by courts of law. The use of beatings to 'break the will' of children came under attack, as did their use for the 'correction' of wives by husbands. Flogging was outlawed in the U.S. Navy. Slavery became abhorrent because it depended on the use of torture.[32]

Yet, the authoritarian conception of God, which offers support and inspiration for authoritarian arrangements in religious and political life, did not die out. It has now found new champions on the Religious Right, and divine torture has gained strength as a theme of Christian spirituality. This development is illustrated by

30. Jonathan Edwards, 'Sinners in the Hands of an Angry God', in Jonathan Edwards and Ola Elizabeth Winslow, *Basic Writings* (New York: New American Library, 1966), p. 160.

31. Edwards, 'Sinners', p. 163.

32. For a discussion of these issues see Philip J. Greven, *Spare the Child: The Religious Roots of Punishment and the Psychological Impact of Physical Abuse* (New York: Vintage Books, 1990), and Richard H. Brodhead, 'Sparing the Rod: Discipline and Fiction in Antebellum America', *Representations* 21 (1988), pp. 67–96.

the reception of Mel Gibson's 'The Passion of the Christ.' Congregations of believers made pilgrimages to theatres in order to see the film together, and some were brought to tears, saying they never realized how much God loved them. Yet the love portrayed in Gibson's film makes sense only if God uses torture to vindicate His majesty against offenses that humankind necessarily commits.

* * *

Apologists for the Christian Right may not attack human rights as a matter of doctrine, but is noteworthy that Jerry Falwell blamed the American Civil Liberties Union for provoking God into permitting the attacks of 9/11. This anti-democratic religious movement, gaining momentum in the 1970s and 80s, has given Augustinian notions of sin and salvation a contemporary application. The writings of Andrew Murray, a South African Dutch Reformed clergyman (1828–1917), were republished during this period, and skillfully elaborate the key doctrines.

Sin expresses 'contempt of the authority of God' Murray explains, 'it seeks to rob God of His honor [and] it must awaken His Wrath.' Murray asserts that 'there is a day of judgment approaching when anger and wrath, tribulation and anguish shall be recompense to all disobedience and sin.'[33] An eternity of torture awaits every human being, except for those who believe in an alternative torture, God's wrath quenched in the blood of his son. 'God alone can point out the way of escape' Murray concludes, 'deliverance through the Blood of the Lamb.'[34]

Consider Murray's titles: *The Blood of the Cross* and *The Power of the Blood of Christ*. Consider those of contemporary writers in this movement — Maxwell Whyte, *The Power of the Blood* (1973, 2005); Rod Parsley's *The Backside of Calvary – Where Healing Stained the Cross* (1991); Benny Hinn's *The Blood: Its Power from Genesis to Jesus to You* (1993).[35]

---

33. Andrew Murray, *The Blood of the Cross* (Springdale, PA: Whitaker House, 1981), p. 92.

34. Murray, *The Blood*, p. 94.

35. Andrew Murray, *The Power of the Blood of Jesus* (Springdale, PA: Whitaker House, 1993); H.A. Maxwell Whyte, *The Power of the Blood* (New Kensington, PA: Whitaker House, 2005); Rod Parsley, *The Backside of Calvary – Where Healing Stained the Cross* (Tulsa, OK: Harrison House, 1991); Benny Hinn, *The Blood: Its Power from Genesis to Jesus to You* (Orlando, FL: Creation House, 1993).

They all evoke the tortures of Jesus and the spiritual power of his blood that is portrayed 'The Passion of the Christ,' Gibson's homage to what he calls 'the enormity of the blood sacrifice.' In Gibson's film we return following the crucifixion to the courtyard where the ghastly flogging took place, and there witness Mary and the Magdalen mopping up the sacred blood, with linen cloths provided by the wife of Pontius Pilate. A Roman Catholic legend merges here with Protestant Evangelical piety in a celebration of the redemption available through God-ordained torture.[36]

The piety of Christian blood sacrifice was given its classic theological elaboration by Anselm of Canterbury in the eleventh century. Anselm pointed out that the suffering of finite beings cannot satisfy the infinite affront to God's honor, so that God's justice cannot be 'satisfied' by the torture of sinful mortals in hell. Since all human beings are sinful, eternal damnation for everyone follows as an inevitable outcome. But God's love prompts Him to offer an exception, namely the crucifixion of his sinless son, Jesus Christ, which produces an infinite surplus of undeserved torture to which believers can lay claim. The blood of Christ provides an acceptable substitute for the punishment all humans deserve and supplies the satisfaction that God's offended dignity requires, for which our own suffering would not be sufficient. The overwhelming majority of the human race does not take part in this salvation, however, only those Christians who rely on the blood.

The torments God has in store for the rest of us are not confined to the afterlife. The commonplace troubles and miseries of daily life have an inner meaning: they are moments when divine wrath strikes at the disobedient, and for the faith-healers in this community it follows that Christ's blood can avert these injuries as well. 'Through the blood Jesus sacrificed on Calvary's tree, you can be cleansed of every physical sickness, discomfort and disease,' writes Rod Parsley, 'every form of mental anguish and torture.'[37]

This claim is preposterous on its face, and is refuted daily as believers sprain their ankles, catch colds, and worry over their medical bills. Yet, there is a grim plausibility in the underlying

---

36. For a full discussion see David Neff, 'The Passion of Mel Gibson,' *Christianity Today*, March, 2004. http://www.christianitytoday.com/movies/commentaries/passion-passionofmel.html.

37. Parsley, *The Backside of Calvary*, p. 72.

recognition that life is full of miseries crying out for explanation in religious terms. The theology of torture supplies that explanation, holding that God is enraged by the ingrained rebelliousness of human beings, and that human experience is a torture chamber, stocked with implements through which He inflicts a foretaste of the infinite torments that await us after death.

For unbelievers there is no escape from this fate, unless they are awakened by the terrors of God's wrath, repudiate their self-will, and accept the salvation available through Christ's blood. Thereupon, 'pleading the blood' provides an all-sufficient antidote for this-worldly afflictions. H.A. Maxwell Whyte chronicles his personal knowledge of misfortunes dispelled by pleading the blood: burns from boiling porridge, disease-bearing germs, a deadly auto accident, a 'spirit of suicide,' homosexual temptation, ptomaine poisoning.[38]

John Hagee, the prominent evangelist who played a major role in summoning political support for George W. Bush, fervently espouses this faith. He declares that 'every born-again believer who has been washed in the blood of Jesus Christ has a life insurance policy that no one can take away.' Hagee vividly illustrates the accompanying vision of life itself, in which unbelievers are subjected to manifold torments, meant to break their wills and produce abject surrender to God's majesty.[39]

> Remember, God plays hardball. He doesn't sit up in heaven saying, "Oh, my goodness, they're not obeying Me." He controls your breath. He controls your heartbeat. God says, "Hey, I can't get his attention." So He shuts off your business; He sees to it that your new car breaks down once a week...He puts you in the hospital in a full body cast with your feet and arms suspended in all four directions and you ask "I wonder if God is trying to speak to me?" Why yes, Bubba, He is.[40]

During the era in which our republic was founded, ancient strands of Christian theology came forward to reinforce belief in human rights, and to oppose torture. Powerful voices on the religious right now seek to reverse the process, defending the presumptive

38. Maxwell Whyte, *The Power*, pp. 71, 75, 78, 104, 150.

39. John Hagee, *Day of Deception*, in John Hagee, *Beginning of the End: Final Dawn over Jerusalem, Day of Deception* (Nashville, TN: Thomas Nelson Publishers, 2000), p. 110.

40. Hagee, *Day of Deception*, p. 103.

usefulness of cruelty and providing a theological expression of its primordial allure.

Not all evangelical Christians support torture, needless to say. On the contrary, the White House program has inspired the formation of 'Evangelicals for Human Rights' with a vigorous anti-torture agenda. Many devout souls consider themselves redeemed from sin by Jesus's sufferings, who do not take the crucifixion as an example of the torment that evil-doers deserve, but set their faces against such atrocities wherever they may appear. Historic figures of the evangelical tradition recognized that torture perpetuates evil rather than correcting it. 'Amazing Grace,' the great evangelical hymn of repentance, was written by John Newton, who had captained slave ships before his conversion, and speaks to his repudiation of slavery and its routines of torture.

Christians like Hagee and Parsley, however, believe that their tantrums of vindictive rage align them with the mind of Christ. From their stronghold in the company of the redeemed, they look out upon multitudes of the damned, those who remain subject to the righteous wrath of God. If those multitudes refuse to accept the reality of their sinful condition, resent and resist the enterprises of the chosen, and retaliate with terrorist tactics that threaten the American sanctuary of God's people, who can place a limit on the torments that can justly be inflicted upon them?

* * *

James Yee, a chaplain at Guantanamo Bay, became aware of the strategies of abuse adopted under General Geoffrey Miller and was alarmed to find that they exploited Muslim sensibilities. Detainees were mocked at prayer, copies of the Qur'an were thrown in the dirt, and pat-downs by female guards were 'exceptionally inappropriate.' More humiliating sexual offenses, so it was said, took place during interrogations.[41] Under Miller's command, Islam was used as 'a weapon against prisoners,' Yee observed, noting that Miller himself was 'a devout Christian and seemed to belong to the fundamentalist believers who are common in the Bush administration.' Miller told Chaplain Yee that he harbored '"deep

---

41. James Yee and Aimee Molloy, *For God and Country: Faith and Patriotism Under Fire* (New York: Public Affairs, 2005), pp. 110-13.

anger" toward "those Muslims" who attacked the World Trade Center,' which Yee took as 'a subtle warning,' since he is himself Muslim.[42]

Even so, Chaplain Yee—a West Point graduate dedicated to a military career—was stunned when Miller ordered his arrest on false charges of treason and sedition. Yee was kept in solitary confinement for seventy-six days, and likewise subjected to anti-Muslim humiliations.

Recalling that President Bush had proposed 'a crusade' in response to September 11, Yee recounted other evidences that his own faith was looked upon with contempt, recalling that Attorney General John Ashcroft said,

> "Islam is a religion in which God requires you to send your son to die for Him," while "Christianity is a faith in which God sends His son to die for you." Lieutenant General William Boykin, who routinely said in public that God, not the voters, chose George W. Bush, repeatedly insulted Islam. Dressed in full military uniform, he said Muslims worship "an idol," called the United States "a Christian nation" and said we can only beat our enemies if we "come against them in the name of Jesus." After issuing these statements, he was promoted to deputy undersecretary of defense.[43]

When General Miller was sent to Iraq, with instructions to upgrade the interrogation program at Abu Ghraib, General Boykin was dispatched by the Pentagon to brief Miller on his mission.[44]

The effort to destroy Chaplain Yee — the charges against him could have resulted in the death penalty had they been sustained — testifies to the abhorrence for torture that many Americans share. Officially tasked with providing 'religious support' to prisoners, Yee had dutifully reported the offenses against Muslim piety to which they were subjected. General Miller, and his superiors at the Pentagon, could easily foresee the public-relations disaster that would result if the insights of an on-the-scene witness found their way into the press. White House avowals of respect for Islam would have been discredited, avowals that were put forward precisely because a commitment to religious freedom, and respect for diverse religious traditions, enjoy significant support in the public at large. Better to

---

42. Yee and Molloy, *For God and Country*, p. 125.
43. Yee and Molloy, *For God and Country*, p. 125.
44. Cockburn, *Rumsfeld*, pp. 193–94.

pre-emptively silence and discredit Yee as a traitor than to cope with a political firestorm.

Many Americans take to heart the respect for human rights that is expressed in the Declaration of Independence and protected by the Constitution. These principles are also asserted in the Universal Declaration of Human Rights, and have the force of U.S. law as a treaty obligation under the Geneva Conventions, notably Convention Three, Article Three, which concerns prisoners of war and prohibits 'outrages upon personal dignity, in particular humiliating and degrading treatment.' Philippe Sands observes that no nation has 'done more to put [these provisions] in place or respect them than the United States.' Against this strong tradition of ethical sentiment and positive law, the Bush White House worked hard to promote the view that the protections of Geneva should not apply to captives taken in the War on Terror, and indeed declared them legally inapplicable until the Supreme Court ruled otherwise in June of 2004.[45]

President Bush and his White House collaborators did not overtly endorse torture, nor do Benny Hinn, Rod Parsley and John Hagee. But they eloquently evoked the depravity of terrorists, defined as 'unlawful combatants,' who were stripped of any claim to God-given rights. Vice-President Cheney sounded this theme when he addressed the graduates of West Point in the Spring of 2007. 'You will now face enemies who oppose and despise everything you know to be right, every notion of upright conduct and character, and every belief you consider worth fighting for. Capture one of these killers,' Cheney continued, 'and he'll be quick to demand the protections of the Geneva Convention and the Constitution of the United States.'[46]

Cheney's fantasy gains force from its context in Christianized popular myth. He imagines a terrorist captured by a West Point graduate who immediately begins to claim rights under the law. Wholly implausible as a real-world likelihood, this scenario tracks perfectly the Kezar Stadium scene in Dirty Harry. The evil-doer squalls hysterically about his legal rights, while Detective Callahan —

45. Sands, *Torture Team*, pp. 8, 173.

46. Richard Cheney, 'Vice President's Remarks at the United States Military Academy Commencement', The White House News and Policies, 26 May 2007. http://www.whitehouse.gov/news/releases/2007/05/print/20070526-1.html.

marked as an avenging Christ—tortures him to gain time-critical information. The mythology asserted here informs countless other such scenes from American popular culture in which torture is rendered not only legitimate but simple common sense, a 'no brainer,' as Cheney elsewhere confirmed.[47]

Looked at one way, it is deeply strange for a Vice-President to argue that America should abandon democratic rights because our enemies do so. But Cheney was driving at a deeper meaning behind the paradox: that the rights commonly deemed inalienable must give way when the agents of God's wrath confront radical evil.

UnAmerican Activities

When the initial cargo of prisoners arrived at Guantanamo in 2002, Donald Rumsfeld acted to render them legally powerless to resist their torturers, countering the efforts of Attorney General Ashcroft to construct a 'quasi legal' mechanism that might become useful if the prisoners ever appeared in a U.S. appeals court. To Rumsfeld, they were 'the worst of the worst',[48] and he persuaded President Bush to justify stripping them of their rights on exactly these terms: 'These are bad men, Mr. President, and I think we ought to let people know that,' Rumsfeld declared. '"Yeah, these are bad guys," said Bush...We need to get the communications machinery working, to get the word out.'[49]

The United States had been a world leader in defending universal human rights, and created elaborate guidelines through which to implement those standards in military practice. In *Torture Team*, Philippe Sands traces the secretive tactics through which the White House sought to dismantle this policy structure, and worked to circumvent the principled opposition of highly placed military leaders. General James T. Hill, Chief of the U.S. Southern Command, voiced the core issue in simple terms as he described his opposition to the abuses at Guantanamo. The military 'should treat everybody with a degree of respect irrespective of who they are.'[50] Alberto Mora, General Counsel to the U.S. Navy who sought to insist on

47. Tom Regan, 'Cheney Confirms Use of Waterboarding.' *Christian Science Monitor*, 26 October 2006. www.csmonitor.cm/2006/1026/dailyUpdate.html.

48. Sands, *Torture Team*, p. 68.

49. Cockburn, *Rumsfeld*, p. 135.

50. Sands, *Torture Team*, p. 86.

the primacy of the Geneva Conventions, was shocked by 'the President's sneering contempt for Common Article 3,' which outlaws 'outrages upon human dignity.'[51]

The President's ringing declaration on the evening of 9/11 is the watchword of the torture program: 'I don't care what the international lawyers say, we are going to kick some ass.'[52] In early February of 2002, President Bush formally asserted that the Geneva Conventions upholding human rights do not apply to the conflict with Al Qaeda, and the secretive White House 'War Council' produced legal sophistries defending this view that continued to serve his purposes over the next four years. Once the procedures based on the Geneva Conventions had been swept aside, Sands explains, the administration had no system by which to proceed, and the resultant improvisations yielded a sickening harvest of criminal abuse. When the Supreme Court ruled in June 2006 that the Geneva Conventions did indeed apply to detainees at Guantanamo, senior administration officials and their operatives on the ground were confronted with severe legal liabilities. Six months later, in a stunning display of legislative complicity and executive guilt, Bush signed into law the Military Commissions Act which retroactively immunizes government employees against prosecution for these offenses.[53]

Like other advocates and practitioners of torture, Bush, Cheney and Rumsfeld are not monsters or freaks, nor are the lawyers who concocted pretexts that gave their policies a specious color of legality, nor are the notorious guards at Abu Ghraib who 'conditioned' prisoners for interrogation under torture, nor are the nameless first-hand torturers with the CIA, and those working for private contractors, who inflicted torments sometimes ending in homicide.

They are our fellow-Americans, caught up in the commonplace addictive cycle that turns ordinary people into criminals and sadists, either as sponsors of the nightmare or as hands-on perpetrators. When the scandal over Abu Ghraib erupted, Rumsfeld succeeded in thrusting responsibility down the command chain, so that the soldiers depicted in the famous photographs were denounced as

---

51. Sands, *Torture Team*, pp. 8, 138.

52. Richard A. Clarke, *Against All Enemies: Inside America's War on Terror* (New York: Free Press, 2004), p. 24.

53. Sands, *Torture Team*, pp. 173, 208.

perverts who had violated American ideals, as distinct from their virtuous commanders in Washington.

The torture program at Bagram Air Base, Abu Ghraib, Guantanamo and elsewhere is a greater sacrilege against American ideals than the attack on the World Trade Center. But it is not an anomaly. These offenses against democratic principle are not a radical innovation, concocted by a rogue White House; they enlarge upon practices that are well established, but kept secret from the American people. For those having ears to hear, the torture program provides an answer to the question that echoed across the nation following September 11: 'Why do they hate us?'

The United States Military has a long tradition honoring human rights; but the same is not true for the CIA. As Chalmers Johnson explains, the CIA has become an off-budget 'private army' for the President with 'black operations' that are kept from public view, yet have a powerful impact on America's standing worldwide.[54]

A long-standing program of un-American activities—including the ouster of the democratically elected Mossadegh in Iran, the assassination of Salvadore Allende in Chile, and the operation of schools where 'friendly' regimes are taught methods of torture—has been lifted up for public consideration by the revelations concerning the Bush torture program. Yet the CIA enjoyed continuing permission from the Bush White House to carry on its projects, always on the proviso that plausible deniability be maintained for the President. Largely invisible to Americans, these ongoing programs are no secret in the societies at which they are aimed, arousing hatred that is all the more dangerous because Americans are not equipped to understand it.

The cultivation of hatred is a less ominous consequence of the American policy, however, than the destruction of hope. A truthful claim that America represents democratic freedom can inspire rising generations of leaders in the Muslim world and beyond, who are opposed to the autocratic regimes in their home countries. Yet, the torture program discredits this claim, notes Eric Haseltine, a top adviser to the Director of National Intelligence.

> I came away from my many visits to the Middle East convinced there
> is a widespread belief that if *America* abuses prisoners then there can

54. Chalmers Johnson, *Nemesis: The Last Days of the American Republic* (New York: Henry Holt & Co, 2006), pp. 90–136.

be no true freedom for anyone...It seemed to me that our greatest sin
in the eyes of Muslims was not invading the Middle East, or even our
support of Israel: our greatest sin was robbing Muslims of hope.[55]

John Conroy's comparative study concludes that the high officials
who establish and support modern torture programs are not, as a
rule, held responsible. It follows that Bush, Cheney and Rumsfeld
will get away with their crimes, even if some of their subordinates
eventually face indictments and are brought to trial.

The same need not be true for ourselves, however. Faithful and
responsible Americans have a choice, whether to face our complicity
in the misdeeds of our government, or to look the other way.

America's soul is at stake here. For its advocates, enablers and
perpetrators, American torture implicitly vindicates America's claim
to be God's chosen people, and asserts that other peoples of the
globe have only subordinate value. Those who resist American
expansion are not to be understood on their own terms, but on
terms that assert American innocence. Rejecting this fantasy does
not entail embracing the converse fantasy, in which all American
projects are wicked and all forms of resistance virtuous. 'The United
States cannot be held culpable,' Andrew Bacevich rightly observes,
'for the maladies that today find expression in violent Islamic
radicalism. But neither can the United States absolve itself of any
and all responsibility for the conditions that have exacerbated those
maladies.'[56]

The torture policy presumes there are no legitimate voices
speaking for the communities of resentment from which the
illegitimate assaults are launched. Christians in the resultant culture
of cruelty may derive a justification from the fact that God Himself
threatens the rebellious with nightmares of torment, and
demonstrated 'love' for His chosen believers by torturing Jesus in
their place. But the price of this justification is unacceptable, since it
betrays both democratic ideals and the meaning of the faith. The
career that ended in Jesus's execution is an historical source and a
spiritual validation for the claim that divine love and justice apply
impartially to all human beings, and that all possess rights that
governments cannot grant or revoke, but are obligated to respect.

---

55. Mayer, *Dark Side*, p. 331.

56. A.J. Bacevich, *The New American Militarism: How Americans are Seduced by War*
(New York: Oxford University Press, 2005), p. 198.

Coda

Hooded Man

The most haunting image from Abu Ghraib is that of 'hooded man,' standing on a box with his arms outstretched, with electrical wires hanging from his hands. The victim is compelled to maintain his balance on the narrow box, with his vision cut off. He cannot see that the wires on his hands are attached to nothing.

The wires address a problem that torturers encounter in using this method, that of compelling a victim to hold the posture, which produces severe muscular pain within fifteen minutes, and then becomes agonizing. The man under the hood is told that he is rigged to an electrical service in such a way that dropping his arms, or stepping down from the box, will cause him to be electrocuted.

In signing the memo of authorization for postural tortures, Donald Rumsfeld remarked that the four-hour limitation on this practice seemed lenient. To ease his chronic back pain, Rumsfeld used a standing desk, and pointed out in the margin of the memo that he himself was accustomed to standing eight to ten hours a day. Rumsfeld realized that he was himself free to move about, to drop his arms, to lean on the desk, and that the torture he was authorizing consisted precisely in the prisoner being forbidden to do any of these things. Rumsfeld's flippant remark caught attention, as his authorization passed down the chain of command, potentially signaling that the four-hour limitation could be set aside.[1]

In their searching discussion of the images from Abu Ghraib, Philip Gourevitch and Errol Morris comment that this picture may well be 'the most recognized emblem of the war on terror after the World Trade Center,' having 'proliferated around the globe in

---

1. Philippe Sands, *Torture Team: Rumsfeld's Memo and the Betrayal of American Values*, (New York: Palgrave MacMillan, 2008), p. 128 and Jane Mayer, *The Dark Side: The Inside Story of How the War on Terror Turned into a War on American Ideals* (New York: Doubleday, 2008), p. 223.

uncountable reproductions.'[2] The figure is especially notorious in the Middle East, where it is known as 'the Statue of Liberty.'[3] To the guards present at the scene, this exceptional interest was puzzling, since they saw 'hooded man' in the context of more severe abuses they had carried out or witnessed. Beholders worldwide found other contexts coming to bear, however, none more bluntly than that of Jesus's death by crucifixion.

I want to consider the electrical wires extending from the hands of 'hooded man' as a symbol of the religious force of this image, radiating spiritual energies outward. The humiliation inflicted on him reversed polarities and sprang back upon his tormenters, much as happened with Jesus. The Romans crucified Jesus in order to stamp out his gospel, and provided an emblem through which it spread.

'Hooded Man'—the hapless powerless victim—is an icon that reproaches the religious perversion at stake in the invasion of Iraq, in particular the misconception of America as a 'city on a hill' that is entitled to seek limitless material abundance at the expense of others, and is exempt from judgment against any standard beyond itself. In the light of this national vainglory, other peoples (with other traditions) are deemed subservient to our purposes and become demonic antagonists when they resist. 'Hooded Man' represents the shame and disgrace that have accrued to the nation from following this version of America's exemplary status, a model for other nations to abhor.

At the Puritan origins of this mythology, Roger Williams issued his fundamental challenge, claiming that the Narragansetts and other American tribes must be understood through their own language, must be honored for the virtue inherent in their customs, and must be recognized as possessing rights requiring respect. Williams also denounced the 'smoke and shadows, and dreams of earthly nothings' over which wars are fought by those who spurn authentic faith and seek the specious fulfillment promised by fantasies of ever-amplifying wealth. Williams was not a pacifist, but his version of the 'city on a hill' differs sharply from the one Ronald Reagan

2. Philip Gourevitch and Errol Morris, *Standard Operating Procedure* (New York: The Penguin Press, 2008), p. 182.

3. Thomas A. Bass, 'Counterinsurgency and Torture,' *American Quarterly*, 60.2, (June 2008), p. 237.

propounded, and poses an alternative that likewise arises from our deepest religious and historical traditions.

The catastrophe in Iraq demonstrates how vulnerable we are to the powerful and dangerous delusions about ourselves that Williams warned against. Our nation's religious backstory and its folk transformations move us directly and indirectly when we think ourselves most secular. Yet, Williams and the tradition he inaugurated also provide invaluable resources for inspiration and action. Roger Williams was a Puritan through and through, but he was capable of responding with admiration and respect to the spiritual dignity and moral strength he found in tribal communities. He bears witness to a humility that Americans greatly need to recover.

'Hooded Man' is hooded, an emblem of the mysteries that proliferate when formerly sequestered cultures, accustomed to using each other as emblems of the demonic, begin to flow together in an emerging global society. A panic-stricken flight into familiar orthodoxies offers solace for many who are disconcerted by this emerging situation, so that across the globe arise violent reactionary versions of Christianity, Islam, Judaism, Hinduism. But there is an alternative response, which sustains the turbulence and finds in it glimpses of a hitherto unimagined fulfillment. Discussions of religious conviction in this book have often turned on this contrast, between those who shoulder the burden of not-knowing, and those flee forward from anxiety into the horrific clarities of unnecessary war and bolster their shaken souls though torture.

'Hooded Man' may be taken to evoke the version of Christianity that finds refuge in hate. The figure suggests a Ku Klux Klansman in his robe and hood, consummate instance of the systemic cruelty that made African Americans a torturable class. The Klan placed a burning cross at the center of their sacred ceremonies and simultaneously made it a terroristic threat.

In the 1970s, as theologies of the blood proliferated on the Christian Right, the Klan adopted the 'blood drop cross' as its organizational emblem, for use on flags and letterhead.[4] An earlier emblem featured elements that cross horizontally, chosen to recall

---

4. 'The Mystical Insignia of a Klansman,' www.kkklan.com/mioak.htm. 6/23/2008; and Joe Johnson, 'The Skull and Cross Bones,' www.geocities/imperialkludd/Skull.html?200823. 6/23/08.

the skull and crossbones that Klan historians associate, not with pirates, but with Christian knights of the crusades. In the 'blood drop cross' the crossed elements stand erect, to recall the cross of Christ, and a comma-shaped figure is added at the center to represent a drop of blood. In 'Why We Light the Cross,' the Klan homepage explains that 'This Old Cross was bathed in the blood of our Lord Jesus Christ...Today it is used to rally the Forces of Christianity against the ever increasing hordes of the Anti-Christ and the Enemies of America.'[5] Klansmen count themselves God's chosen, exempted from the eternal punishment so richly deserved by anti-Americans.

Jesus was not crucified at God's command as a substitute for sinful mortals, however, but because the movement he headed alarmed the Roman authorities. This recognition gives 'Hooded Man' a set of meanings that strike closer to home for most of us, bringing to bear the analogies between the maltreatment administered to presumed terrorists by our government, and what Jesus endured at the hands of the Romans.

For the Romans, crucifixion was an instrument of imperial terror. Following the slave revolt led by Spartacus in 73–71 BCE, six thousand of his followers were crucified along the Appian Way. Likewise in refractory provinces like Judea, crucifixion was meant to remind subject peoples of the unstoppable Roman legions that could be sent in, if recalcitrance could not otherwise be suppressed.[6] After they assumed control of Judea in 63 BCE, the Romans sought to control the population through local collaborators drawn from the wealthy classes and the senior priesthood, but they nonetheless faced a recurrent peasant insurgency. Resentment of the crushing burden of taxation, and memories of political independence under the Hasmoneans, were given religious force by the ancient traditions of the Jews—centered in Temple worship and the literature

5. 'Why We Light the Cross,' www.cnkkkk.com. 6/23/2008.
6. Sources on the resistance in Roman Palestine and the Jesus movement include Richard A. Horsley, *Jesus and the Spiral of Violence: Popular Jewish Resistance in Roman Palestine* (Minneapolis, MN: Fortress Press, 1993); Richard A. Horsley and John S. Hanson, *Bandits, Prophets and Messiahs: Popular Movements in the Time of Jesus*, (Harrisburg, PA: Trinity Press, 1985); John Dominic Crossan, *The Historical Jesus: The Life of a Mediterranean Jewish Peasant* (New York: HarperCollins, 1991); Marcus J. Borg and John Dominic Crossan, *The Last Week: A Day-by-Day Account of Jesus's Final Week in Jerusalem* (New York: Harper Collins, 2006).

recording their sacred laws, prophecy and history. Liberation from oppressors defined that history from its outset, when Moses led the children of Israel from bondage in Egypt, and religious leaders promised that a new savior would arise amid Roman oppression, to set God's people free.

When Herod the Great died, four years before Jesus's birth, peasants went into open revolt throughout the region, and Roman legions led by Varus were dispatched from Syria to restore order. Varus's counter-insurgency tactics were particularly brutal; he razed the city of Sepphoris, just four miles from Nazareth, and crucified two thousand defenders of Jerusalem.[7]

Jesus lived in a world that was seething with incipient revolts against Rome – which included anti-Roman banditry, as well as tax resistance and mass protests – all cross-cut by Roman efforts to suppress and contain them. The temple leadership sought to put the case for Roman rule in terms plausible to the subject population, and aroused the fury of insurgents. These pious collaborators were marked for assassination by the sicarii, a cadre of urban terrorists, and both Jesus and John the Baptist denounced them.

It is important to bear in mind that Jesus and all his followers were Jews. When the gospels speak of 'the Jews' having a hand in the crucifixion of Jesus, they are referring to the elite religious professionals who perverted sacred traditions in order to serve the prevailing imperial order. The 'high priests' condemned by John and Jesus have many contemporary avatars, including Christian theologians in Nazi Germany who gave their names to virulent anti-semitism, and American Christians who provided justifications for the invasion of Iraq.[8]

The chronic turbulence in first-century Palestine came to a head in the massive revolt that broke out in 66 CE, better than three decades after Jesus's death. Vespasian and Titus led the Roman crackdown, and it took four years of hard fighting and systematic brutality to restore order. Villages and towns across Judea were

---

7. Horsley, *Jesus and the Spiral of Violence*, pp. 49–54; Borg and Crossan, *The Last Week*, pp. 14–15.

8. See Doris L. Bergen, *Twisted Cross: The German Christian Movement and the Third Reich* (Chapel Hill: University of North Carolina Press, 1996) and Robert P. Ericksen, *Theologians Under Hitler: Gerhard Kittel, Paul Althaus, Emanuel Hirsch* (New Haven, CT: Yale University Press, 1985).

devastated, their inhabitants enslaved or massacred, with a last-ditch stand taking place at Jerusalem.

The crucifixion of Jesus, on the scene, at the time of its occurrence, was incidental to this story of imperial victory over provincial recalcitrance. For the Romans, it was not the spell-binding drama the gospels describe, but standard operating procedure for disposing of popular leaders who challenged Roman claims. Among other provocative actions, Jesus staged a defiant procession through Jerusalem during Passover, which was a time when many Jews came to the city from the countryside, and was thus a promising occasion for large protest demonstrations, and the coordination of plans for revolt.[9]

Jesus's protest march expressly repudiated a tradition analogous to the one we've traced from the legend of St. George to the mythology of the American West. Many Jews who witnessed the march hoped for a 'messiah on horseback,' a military champion to liberate them from Roman oppression. Jesus rode into town on a donkey, dramatizing a salvation to be achieved through non-violent means.[10]

Jesus proclaimed a new order that would cut across the invidious hierarchies that separate classes of superior mortals from their subordinates, an order recognizing the humanity shared by all, in which all have equal value simply by virtue of being human. This seems at first glance like a harmless doctrine, since it acknowledges that imperial overlords are human too, but the Romans perceived him as a threat and crucified him in order to squelch the movement he was leading.

The result, as noted, was to provide the earliest Christians an emblem through which to assert their defiance of Roman power, as they embraced a salvation that liberated them from manifold worldly oppressions. The subordination of women to men, slaves to owners, the not-chosen to the chosen, the poor to the rich, imperial subjects to imperial masters: the religious warrant for these injustices was cancelled by the proclamation of a nondiscriminatory divine love. Jesus's gospel posed a threat not only to the Romans but to all social arrangements in which stigmatized classes of G*d's children are forced to accept a subservient place.

9. Borg and Crossan, *The Last Week*, pp. 2–5.
10. Borg and Crossan, *The Last Week*, p. 63.

As an instance of Roman imperial policy, the crucifixion evokes the systematic organization of political hatreds amid which we lead our lives, with its ceaseless jockeying of rival centers seeking a domination that is ultimately enforced through the power to inflict wholesale agony and death. Yet, followers of Jesus refused to subordinate their spirits to the requirements of this order, claiming instead that his execution was followed by the onset of a new life. His death became the talisman and promise of a blessedness that dawned upon them as mysteriously and inexorably as the coming of springtime.

'Hooded Man' serves as an emblem of America's catastrophic success in Iraq, of the evil we have done in pursuit of evil-doers, an instance of the all-too-familiar alchemy by which noble ideals are made to serve predatory enterprises. Yet this offers us an opportunity to see ourselves and our world more clearly, to repudiate nationalist vainglory and find a different path. What befell Jesus was an atrocity, but atrocity did not have the final word; on the contrary it emboldened his followers — including those who held themselves responsible for the disaster — to continue his work, gathering from tragedy and horror the promise of an indestructible redemption whose substance was theirs to live out.

The embattled cause of love and justice in our own world takes strength from this vision, and has been sustained by the spiritual authority generated across a range of religious traditions. The work of Mahatma Gandhi, Martin Luther King, Jr., and the Dalai Lama makes this clear. So for all Americans, as for American Christians, the image of 'Hooded Man' raises an age-long question. Where do you see yourself in this drama? With whom do you stand in the presence of this atrocity: the innocent crucified to serve a political order for which all of us, as citizens of a democracy, are answerable?

BIBLIOGRAPHY

Abbott, E.C., and Helena Huntington Smith, *We Pointed Them North; Recollections of a Cowpuncher* (Norman, OK: University of Oklahoma Press, 1955).

Alexander, Matthew, 'I'm Still Tortured by What I Saw in Iraq,' *The Washington Post*, 30 November 2008. www.washingtonpost.com/wp-dyn/content/article/2008/11/28.

Alexander, Matthew and John Bruning, *How to Break a Terrorist: The U.S. Interrogators Who Used Brains, not Brutality, to Take Down the Deadliest Man in Iraq* (New York: Free Press, 2008).

Ambrose, Stephen E., *Nothing Like It in the World: The Men Who Built the Transcontinental Railroad, 1863–1869* (New York: Simon & Schuster, 2000).

Amnesty International, USA Blog, 'Denounce Torture: Torture Ineffective', http://blogs.amnestyusa.org/denounce-torture/archive/2006/06/10/614w0igmvst.htm

Armbruster, Kurt E., *Orphan Road: The Railroad Comes to Seattle, 1853–1911* (Pullman, WA: Washington State University Press, 1999).

Bacevich, A.J., *The New American Militarism: How Americans are Seduced by War* (New York: Oxford University Press, 2005).

Barnes, Fred, 'Man with a Mission: George W. Bush Finds his Calling', *The Weekly Standard*, 9/30/2001. http://www.freerepublic.com/focus/f-news/536853posts.

Barrs, Jerram, *Who are the Peacemakers? The Christian Case for Nuclear Deterrence* (Westchester, IL: Crossway Books, 1983).

Bass, Thomas A., 'Counterinsurgency and Torture', *American Quarterly* 60. 2 (2008), pp. 233–40.

Baum, L. Frank, W.W. Denslow and Michael Patrick Hearn, *The Annotated Wizard of Oz: The Wonderful Wizard of Oz* (New York: Norton, 2000).

Bederman, Gail, *Manliness & Civilization: A Cultural History of Gender and Race in the United States, 1880–1917* (Chicago, IL: University of Chicago Press, 1995).

Bellavia, David, and John R. Bruning, *House to House: An Epic Memoir of War* (New York: Free Press, 2007).

Bergen, Doris L., *Twisted Cross: The German Christian Movement in the Third Reich* (Chapel Hill, NC: University of North Carolina Press, 1996).

Borg, Marcus J., and John Dominic Crossan, *The Last Week: The Day by Day Account of Jesus' Final Week in Jerusalem* (New York: Harper Collins, 2006).

Bremer, L. Paul, and Malcolm McConnell, *My Year in Iraq: The Struggle to Build a Future of Hope* (New York: Simon & Schuster, 2006).

Brodhead, Richard H., 'Sparing the Rod: Discipline and Fiction in Antebellum America', *Representations* 21 (1988), pp. 67–96.

Bromwich, David, 'The Co-President at Work,' *The New York Review of Books*, 20 November 2008, pp. 29–33.

Bumiller, Elizabeth, 'Keepers of Bush Image Lift Stagecraft to New Heights', *New York Times*, 15 May 2003.

Burgess, Dorothy Whittemore Bates, *Dream and Deed; The Story of Katharine Lee Bates* (Norman, OK: University of Oklahoma Press, 1952).

Bush, George W., Remarks by the President in Photo Opportunity with the National Security Team', The White House News and Policies, 12 September 2001. http://www.whitehouse.gov/news/releases/2001/09/20010912-4.html.

_____ 'President's Remarks at National Day of Prayer and Remembrance', The White House News and Policies, 14 September 2001. www.whitehouse.gov/news/releases/2001/09/20010914-2.html.

_____ 'Address to a Joint Session of Congress and the American People,' United States Capitol, 20 September 2001. www.whitehouse.gov/news/releases/2001/09/20010920-8.html

_____ 'President Holds Prime Time News Conference', The White House News and Policies, 11 October 2001. http://www.whitehouse.gov/news/releases/2001/10/20011011-7.html.

_____ 'President Bush Announces Major Combat Operations in Iraq have Ended', The White House News and Policies, 1 May 2003. www.whitehouse.gov/news/releases/2003/05/20030501-15.html.

_____ 'President's Remarks at the 2004 Republican National Convention', The White House News and Policies, 2 September 2004. http://www.whitehouse.gov/news/releases/2004/09/20040902-2.html.

_____ 'President Sworn-In to Second Term', The White House News and Policies, 20 January 2005. http://www.whitehouse.gov/news/releases/2005/01/20050120-1.html.

_____ 'President Bush Discusses Global War on Terror,' Address at the Pentagon, 19 March 2008. www.whitehouse.gov/news/releases/2008/03/2008039-2.html

Butler, Alban, and Kathleen Jones, *Butler's Lives of the Saints* (Tunbridge Wells, Kent: Burns & Oates, 1999).

Buzzell, Colby, *My War: Killing Time in Iraq* (New York: Berkley Caliber, 2005).

Carroll, James, *Constantine's Sword: The Church and the Jews: A History* (Boston, MA: Houghton Mifflin, 2001).

_____ *House of War: The Pentagon and the Disastrous Rise of American Power* (Boston, MA: Houghton Mifflin Co., 2006).

Carter, Dan T., *From George Wallace to Newt Gingrich: Race in the Conservative Counter-revolution, 1963–1994.* The Walter Lynwood Fleming Lectures in Southern History (Baton Rouge, LA: Louisiana State University Press, 1996). Cited in Kevin Phillips, *American Theocracy: The Peril and Politics of Radical Religion, Oil, and Borrowed Money in the 21st Century* (New York: Penguin Books, 2007).

Carter, Jimmy, 'The "Crisis of Confidence" Speech', *American Experience*, PBS. (www.pbs.org/wgbh/amex/carter/filmmore/ps_crisis.html).

Cave, Alfred A., *The Pequot War* (Amherst, MA: University of Massachusetts Press, 1996).

Chandrasekaran, Rajiv, *Imperial Life in the Emerald City: Inside Iraq's Green Zone* (New York: Alfred A. Knopf, 2006).

Channing, William E., 'Letter to Henry Clay, 1837', in John Morton Blum, William S. McFeely, Edmund S. Morgan *et al* (eds.), *The National Experience. Part One, A History of the United States to 1877* (New York: Harcourt Brace Jovanovich, 7th edn, 1989).

Chatterjee, Pratap, *Iraq, Inc.: A Profitable Occupation* (New York: Seven Stories Press, 2004).

Cheney, Richard, 'Vice President's Remarks at the United States Military Academy Commencement', The White House News and Policies, 26 May 2007. http://www.whitehouse.gov/news/releases/2007/05/print/20070526-1.html.

Cheney, Richard and Tim Russert, 'The Vice President appears on Meet the Press with Tim Russert', The White House News and Policies, 16 September 2001. www.whitehouse.gov.vicepresident/news-speeches/speeches/vp20010916.html.

Church of the National Knights of the Ku Klux Klan, 'Why We Light the Cross', www.cnkkkk.com.

Clarke, Richard A., *Against All Enemies: Inside America's War on Terror* (New York: Free Press, 2004).

Clift, Eleanor, 'Wizard of Oz Letter', *Newsweek*, 2 April 2004.

Cockburn, Andrew, *Rumsfeld: His Rise, Fall, and Catastrophic Legacy* (New York: Scribner, 2007).

Conrad, Joseph, J.H. Stape, and Michael Newton, *The Secret Agent: A Simple Tale* (London: Penguin, 2007).

Conroy, John, *Unspeakable Acts, Ordinary People: The Dynamics of Torture* (Berkeley, CA: University of California Press, 2000).

Cooper, James Fenimore, *The Pioneers: Or, the Sources of the Susquehanna: A Descriptive Tale,* with an Afterword by Robert E. Spiller (New York: Penguin Books, 1988).

Coughlin, Jack, Casey Kuhlman, and Don Davis, *Shooter: The Autobiography of the Top-ranked Marine Sniper* (New York: St. Martin's Press, 2005).

Crane, Stephen, and Bradley Sculley, *The Red Badge of Courage: An Authoritative Text: Backgrounds and Sources: Criticism* (New York: Norton, 1976).

Crossan, John Dominic, *The Historical Jesus: The Life of a Mediterranean Jewish Peasant* (New York: HarperCollins, 1991).

Danner, Mark, and Frank Rich, *The Secret Way to War: The Downing Street Memo and the Iraq War's Buried History* (New York: New York Review Books, 2006).

Donnelly, Thomas *et al*, 'Rebuilding America's Defenses', Project for a New American Century Website, September, 2000. http://www.newamericancentury.org/RebuildingAmericasDefenses.pdf.

Drake, James D., *King Philip's War: Civil War in New England, 1675–1676* (Amherst, MA: University of Massachesetts Press, 1999).

Draper, Robert, *Dead Certain: The Presidency of George W. Bush* (New York: Free Press, 2007).

Eastwood, Clint, *Dirty Harry* (New York: Warner Bros-Malpaso, 1971).

_____ *High Plains Drifter* (United Kingdom: Universal-Malpaso, 1973).

Eastwood, Clint, Michael Butler, Dennis Shryack, Michael Moriarty, Carrie Snodgress, Christopher Penn, Richard Dysart, Sydney Penny, and Richard Kiel, *Pale Rider,* Clint Eastwood Collection (Burbank, CA: Warner Home Video, 2000).

Edwards, Jonathan, 'Sinners in the Hands of an Angry God', in Jonathan Edwards and Ola Elizabeth Winslow, *Basic Writings* (New York: New American Library, 1966).

Ericksen, Robert P., *Theologians Under Hitler: Gerhard Kittel, Paul Althaus, and Emanuel Hirsch* (New Haven, CT: Yale University Press, 1985).

Falwell, Jerry, *Listen, America* (New York: Bantam, 1981).

Fattah, Hassan M., 'Symbol of Abu Ghraib Seeks to Spare Others his Nightmare', *The New York Times*, 11 March 2006. www.nytimes.com/2006/03/11/ international/middleeast/ 11ghraib.html.

Faust, Drew Gilpin, *This Republic of Suffering: Death and the American Civil War* (New York: Alfred A. Knopf, 2008).

Ferguson, Niall, *Colossus: The Rise and Fall of the American Empire* (New York: Penguin Press, 2004).

Ford, John, Max Steiner, Frank S. Nugent, John Wayne, Jeffrey Hunter, Vera Miles, Ward Bond, Natalie Wood, and Alan Le May, *The Searchers* (Burbank, CA: Warner Bros. Entertainment, 2006).

Franks, Tommy, *American Soldier* (New York: HarperCollins, 2004).

Froomkin, Dan, 'The White House Mole', White House Watch, *The Washington Post*, 4 February 2008. www.washingtonpost.com/wp-dyn/content/blog/2008/02/04/BL2008020401554.html

Fuentes, Carlos, and Alfred J. Mac Adam, *The Crystal Frontier: A Novel in Nine Stories*, (trans. Alfred Mac Adam; New York: Harcourt Brace, 1997).

Garland, Judy, Frank Morgan, Ray Bolger, Bert Lahr, Jack Haley, Noel Langley, Florence Ryerson *et al.*, *The Wizard of Oz* (Warner Bros. Family Entertainment: Turner Entertainment Co, 1999).

Gaustad, Edwin S., *Roger Williams: Prophet of Liberty* (New York: Oxford University Press, 2001).

Gordon, Michael R., and Bernard E. Trainor, *Cobra II: The Inside Story of the Invasion and Occupation of Iraq* (New York: Pantheon Books, 2006).

Gourevitch, Philip, and Errol Morris, *Standard Operating Procedure* (New York: Penguin Press, 2008).

Greenwald, Glenn, *A Tragic Legacy: How a Good vs. Evil Mentality Destroyed the Bush Presidency* (New York: Crown Publishers, 2007).

Greven, Philip J., *Spare the Child: The Religious Roots of Punishment and the Psychological Impact of Physical Abuse* (New York: Vintage Books, 1990).

Grey, Zane, *Riders of the Purple Sage* (New York: Bantam Books, 1990).

Hagee, John, *Day of Deception*, in John Hagee, *Beginning of the End; Final Dawn over Jerusalem; Day of Deception* (Nashville, TN: Thomas Nelson Publishers, 2000).

Harris, John F., 'God Gave U.S. "What We Deserve," Falwell Says', *The Washington Post*, 14 September 2001.

Hartley, Jason Christopher, *Just Another Soldier: A Year on the Ground in Iraq* (New York: HarperCollins, 2005).

Hayes, Stephen F., *Cheney: The Untold Story of America's Most Powerful and Controversial Vice President* (New York: HarperCollins, 2007).

Hedges, Chris, *War is a Force that Gives Us Meaning* (New York: Anchor Books, 2002).

_____ *American Fascists: The Christian Right and the War on America* (New York: Free Press, 2006).

Hemingway, Ernest, *A Farewell to Arms* (New York: Scribner, 1969).

Hinn, Benny, *The Blood: Its Power From Genesis to Jesus to You* (Orlando, FL: Creation House, 1993).

Hobsbawm, E.J., *On Empire: America, War, and Global Supremacy* (New York: Pantheon Books, 2008).

Hoganson, Kristin L., *Fighting for American Manhood: How Gender Politics Provoked the Spanish-American and Philippine-American Wars* (New Haven, CT: Yale University Press, 1998).

Horsley, Richard A., *Jesus and the Spiral of Violence: Popular Jewish Resistance in Roman Palestine* (Minneapolis, MN: Fortress Press, 1993).

Horsley, Richard A., and John S. Hanson, *Bandits, Prophets & Messiahs: Popular Movements in the Time of Jesus* (Harrisburg, PA: Trinity Press International, 1985).

Hughes, Karen, 'Address', Roy and Margaret Shilling Lectureship, Southwestern University, Georgetown, TX., 6 February 2003.

Hunt, Lynn Avery, *Inventing Human Rights: A History* (New York: W.W. Norton & Co., 2007).

Isikoff, Michael, and David Corn, *Hubris: The Inside Story of Spin, Scandal, and the Selling of the Iraq War* (New York: Crown Publishers, 2006).

Jewett, Robert, and John Shelton Lawrence, *Captain America and the Crusade Against Evil: The Dilemma of Zealous Nationalism* (Grand Rapids, MI: W.B. Eerdmans, 2003).

Johnson, Chalmers A., *Blowback: The Costs and Consequences of American Empire* (New York: Henry Holt & Co, 2000).

_____ *The Sorrows of Empire: Militarism, Secrecy, and the End of the Republic* (New York: Henry Holt and Co, 2004).

_____ *Nemesis: The Last Days of the American Republic* (New York: Henry Holt & Co, 2006).

Johnson, Edward, 'Wonder-Working Providence of Sion's Saviour in New England' (1654) (selection) in James E. Miller, Jr., (ed.), *Heritage of American Literature* (2 vols.; New York: Harcourt Brace, 1991).

Johnson, Joe, 'The Skull and Cross Bones', 23 June 2008, www.geocities/imperialkludd/Skull.html?200823.

Johnson, Scott and Evan Thomas, 'Still Fighting Saddam: The attacks keep coming, and the war doesn't seem over to the soldiers on the ground. With his money and his diehards, Saddam casts a long shadow — and a guerilla war may have been his strategy all along,' *Newsweek*, 21 July 2003.

Kaplan, Robert D., *An Empire Wilderness: Travels into America's Future* (New York: Vintage Books, 1999).

_____ *Imperial Grunts: The American Military on the Ground* (New York: Random House, 2005).

King Jr., Martin Luther, '"I have a dream" speech', U.S. Constitution Online, www.usconstitution.net/dream.html.

Kipling, Rudyard and Irving Howe, *The Portable Kipling*, The Viking Portable Library (Harmondsworth [Middlesex]: Penguin Books, 1982).

Kristol, William, Richard V. Allen, Gary Bauer *et al.*, 'Letter to President Bush on the War on Terrorism', Project for a New American Century Website, 20 September 2001. www.newamericancentury.org/BUshletter.htm

Ku Klux Klan, 'The Mystical Insignia of a Klansman', www.kkklan.com/mioak.htm.

LaHaye, Tim F., and Jerry B. Jenkins, *Kingdom Come: The Final Victory*, Left Behind Series (Carol Stream, IL: Tyndale House Publishers, 2007).

Last of the Independents, 'Sand Creek Massacre', www.lastoftheindependents.com/sandcreek.htm.

Lawrence, John Shelton and Robert Jewett, *The Myth of the American Superhero* (Grand Rapids, MI: W.B. Eerdmans, 2002).

Lears, T.J. Jackson, *No Place of Grace: Antimodernism and the Transformation of American Culture, 1880–1920* (New York: Pantheon Books, 1981).

Lienesch, Michael, *Redeeming America: Piety and Politics in the New Christian Right* (Chapel Hill, NC: University of North Carolina Press, 1993).

Lincoln, Bruce, *Holy Terrors: Thinking About Religion After September 11* (Chicago, IL: University of Chicago Press, 2006).

Linderman, Gerald F., *Embattled Courage: The Experience of Combat in the American Civil War* (New York: Free Press, 1987).

Linker, Damon, *The Theocons: Secular America Under Siege* (New York: Doubleday, 2006).

Maaga, Mary McCormick, *Hearing the Voices of Jonestown* (Syracuse, NY: Syracuse University Press, 1998).

Mansfield, Laura and Die Presse Vienna, 'The Hooded Man from Abu Ghraib: The Rest of the Story', Free Republic, 27 December 2005. www.freerepublic.com/focus/f-news/1547528/posts.

Mason, John, *A Brief History of the Pequot War: Some Grounds of the War Against the Pequots* (2 pages), Humanities Web Website, http://www.humanitiesweb.org/human.php?s=n&p=l&ID=20

_____ *A brief History of the Pequot War: An Epitome or Brief History of the Pequot War* (15 pages), Humanities Web Website, http://www.humanitiesweb.org/human.php?s=n&p=l&ID=20

Mayer, Jane, 'Whatever It Takes', *The New Yorker*, 19 & 26 February 2007, pp. 66–82.

_____ *Dark Side: The Inside Story of How the War on Terror Turned into a War on American Ideals* (New York: Doubleday, 2008).

McDougall, Walter A., *Promised Land, Crusader State: The American Encounter with the World Since 1776* (Boston, MA: Houghton Mifflin, 1997).

Miller, Perry, *Errand into the Wilderness* (New York: Harper, 1956).

_____ 'Roger Williams, An Essay in Interpretation', in Roger Williams, *The Complete Writings of Roger Williams* (7 vols.; New York: Russell & Russell, 1963).

Mott, Wesley T., (ed.), 'Julia Ward Howe' in *Dictionary of Literary Biography*, Vol. 235, *The American Renaissance in New England* (Third Series, NP: The Gale Group, 2001, pp. 227–34).

Murray, Andrew, *The Blood of the Cross* (Springdale, PA: Whitaker House, 1981).

_____ *The Power of the Blood of Jesus* (Springdale, PA: Whitaker House, 1993).

Neff, David, 'The Passion of Mel Gibson,' *Christianity Today*, March, 2004. http://www.christianitytoday.com/movies/commentaries/passion-passionofmel.html.

Nugent, Walter, *Habits of Empire: A History of American Expansion* (New York: Alfred A. Knopf, 2008).

Pagels, Elaine H., *Adam, Eve, and the Serpent* (New York: Random House, 1988).

Parsley, Rod, *The Backside of Calvary – Where Healing Stained the Cross* (Tulsa, OK: Harrison House, 1991).

Paul, *I Corinthians* 13:12. King James Version.

Phillips, Kevin, *American Theocracy: The Peril and Politics of Radical Religion, Oil, and Borrowed Money in the 21st Century* (London: Penguin Books, 2007).

Reagan, Ronald, 'Farewell Address to the Nation', Ronald Reagan Presidential Foundation Website, 11 January 1989. www.reaganfoundation.org/reagan/speeches/farewell.asp.

_____ 'The Shining City Upon a Hill', http://originofnations.org/books,%20papers/quotes%20etc/Reagan_The%20Shining.

Tom Regan, 'Cheney Confirms Use of Waterboarding', *Christian Science Monitor*, 26 Oct 2006. www.csmonitor.cm/2006/1026/dailyUpdate.html.

Rejali, Darius M., *Torture and Democracy* (Princeton: Princeton University Press, 2007).

Remini, Robert Vincent, *Andrew Jackson & His Indian Wars* (New York: Viking, 2001).

Rich, Frank, *The Greatest Story Ever Sold: The Decline and Fall of Truth from 9/11 to Katrina* (New York: Penguin Press, 2006).

Ricks, Thomas E., *Fiasco: The American Military Adventure in Iraq* (New York: Penguin Press, 2006).

Rieckhoff, Paul, *Chasing Ghosts: A Soldier's Fight for America from Baghdad to Washington* (New York: NAL Caliber, 2006).

Rowlandson, Mary, 'The Sovereignty and Goodness of God, together with the Faithfulness of His Promises Displayed; Being a Narrative of the Captivity and Restoration of Mrs. Mary Rowlandson', in Alden T. Vaughan and Edward W. Clark, *Puritans Among the Indians: Accounts of Captivity and Redemption, 1676–1724,* John Harvard Library (Cambridge, MA: Belknap Press, 1981).

Royster, Charles, *The Destructive War: William Tecumseh Sherman, Stonewall Jackson, and the Americans* (New York: Knopf, 1991).

Salisbury, Neal, *Manitou and Providence: Indians, Europeans, and the Making of New England, 1500–1643* (New York: Oxford University Press, 1982).

Sands, Philippe, *Torture Team: Rumsfeld's Memo and the Betrayal of American Values* (New York: Palgrave Macmillan, 2008).

Schaffner, Franklin J., George C. Scott, Karl Malden, Ladislas Farago, and Omar Nelson Bradley, *Patton* (Beverly Hills, CA: 20th Century Fox Home Entertainment, 1998).

Scherer, Michael, 'Identifying a Torture Icon', Salon Website. www.salon.com/news/ feature/2003/03/14/torture_photo/index.html.

Segal, Charles M., and David C. Stineback, *Puritans, Indians, and Manifest Destiny* (New York: Putnam, 1977).

Shakespeare, William, 'The Life of Henry the Fifth' (III.2.35) in Stephen Greenblatt *et al*, *The Norton Shakespeare: Based on the Oxford Edition* (New York: W.W. Norton And Co. Inc., 1997).

Sharansky, Natan, *The Case for Democracy: The Power of Freedom to Overcome Tyranny and Terror* (Green Forest, AR: Balfour Books, 2005).

Shenon, Philip, *The Commission: The Uncensored History of the 9/11 Investigation* (New York: Twelve, 2008).

Slotkin, Richard, *Regeneration Through Violence; The Mythology of the American Frontier, 1600–1860* (Middletown, CT: Wesleyan University Press, 1973).

_____ *The Fatal Environment: The Myth of the Frontier in the Age of Industrialization, 1800–1890* (Norman, OK: University of Oklahoma Press, 1985).

_____ *Gunfighter Nation: The Myth of the Frontier in Twentieth-century America* (Norman, OK: University of Oklahoma Press, 1998).

Slotkin, Richard, and James K. Folsom, *So Dreadfull a Judgment: Puritan Responses to King Philip's War, 1676–1677* (Middletown, CT: Wesleyan University Press, 1978).

Stiglitz, Joseph E., and Linda Bilmes, *Globalization and its Discontents* (New York: W.W. Norton, 2003).

_____ *The Three Trillion Dollar War: The True Cost of the Iraq Conflict* (New York: W.W. Norton, 2008).

Strauss, David Levi, 'Breakdown in the Grey Room: Recent Turns in the Image War', in Meron Benvenisti *Abu Ghraib: The Politics of Torture* (The Terra Nova Series; Berkeley, CA: North Atlantic Books, 2004).

Suskind, Ron, 'Faith, Certainty, and the Presidency of George W. Bush', *The New York Times Magazine,* 17 October 2004.

_____ *The Price of Loyalty: George W. Bush, the White House, and the Education of Paul O'Neill* (New York: Simon & Schuster, 2004).

_____ *The One Percent Doctrine: Deep Inside America's Pursuit of Its Enemies Since 9/11* (New York: Simon & Schuster, 2006).

The Holy Bible, Revised Standard Version, containing the Old and New Testaments. Translated from the original tongues, being the version set forth A.D. 1611, revised A.D. 1881–1885 and A.D. 1901; compared with the most ancient authorities and revised A.D. 1952 (New York: Thomas Nelson, 1953).

The Holy Bible Containing the Old and New Testaments and the Apocrypha: Translated out of the Original Tongues with the Former Translations Diligently Compared and Revised, by His Majesty's Special Command (New York: Cambridge University Press, nd).

'The War in Iraq Prophesied in the Bible: A Part of the Endtime Wars and G-d's Judgement,' http://www.templemountfaithful.org/phprint.php.

Thrapp, Dan L., *The Conquest of Apacheria* (Norman, OK: University of Oklahoma Press, 1967).

Ullman, Harlan, and James P. Wade, *Shock and Awe: Achieving Rapid Dominance* (Philadelphia, PA: Pavilion Press, 2004).

United Methodist Church (U.S.), *The Methodist Hymnal: Official Hymnal of the United Methodist Church* (Nashville, TN: Methodist Publishing House, 1966).

Utley, Robert Marshall, *The Indian Frontier of the American West, 1846–1890* (Albuquerque: University of New Mexico Press, 1984).

_____ *The Lance and the Shield: The Life and Times of Sitting Bull* (New York: Henry Holt, 1993).

_____ *The Last Days of the Sioux Nation* (New Haven, CT, London: Yale University Press, 2004).

Vaughan, Alden T., and Edward W. Clark, *Puritans Among the Indians: Accounts of Captivity and Redemption, 1676–1724* (Cambridge, MA: Belknap Press, 1981).

Walton, Rus, *Biblical Solutions to Contemporary Problems: A Handbook* (Brentwood, TN: Wolgemuth & Hyatt, 1988.

_____ *One Nation Under God* (Nashville, TN: Thomas Nelson, rev. edn, 1987).

Weisberg, Jacob, *The Bush Tragedy* (New York: Random House, 2008).

Whyte, H.A. Maxwell, *The Power of the Blood* (New Kensington, PA: Whitaker House, 2005).

Williams, Roger, 'A Key into the Language of America', in J. Hammond Trumbull (ed.), *The Complete Writings of Roger Williams* (7 vols.; New York: Russell & Russell, 1963).

_____ *The Complete Writings of Roger Williams* (7 vols.; New York: Russell & Russell, 1963).

Wills, Garry, *Lincoln at Gettysburg: The Words that Remade America* (New York: Simon & Schuster, 1992).

Wink, Walter, *Naming the Powers: The Language of Power in the New Testament* (Philadelphia, PA: Fortress Press, 1984).

_____ *Unmasking the Powers: The Invisible Forces that Determine Human Existence* (Philadelphia, PA: Fortress Press, 1986).

_____ *Engaging the Powers: Discernment and Resistance in a World of Domination* (Minneapolis, MN: Fortress Press, 1992).

Winthrop, John, 'A Model of Christian Charity' (Boston, MA: Collections of the Massachusetts Historical Society, 1838), 3rd series: 7:31–48, Hanover Historical Texts Project Website, http://history.hanover.edu/texts/winthmod.html.

Woodward, Bob, *Plan of Attack* (New York: Simon & Schuster, 2004).

_____ *State of Denial* (New York: Simon & Schuster, 2006).

_____ *State of Denial: [Bush at War, Part III]* (New York: Simon & Schuster, 2006).

Wright, Evan, *Generation Kill: Devil Dogs, Iceman, Captain America, and the New Face of American War* (New York: Berkeley Caliber, 2004).

Wright, Lawrence, *The Looming Tower: Al-Qaeda and the Road to 9/11* (New York: Knopf, 2007).

Yee, James, and Aimee Molloy, *For God and Country: Faith and Patriotism Under Fire* (New York: Public Affairs, 2005).

INDEX

Lightning Source UK Ltd.
Milton Keynes UK
31 October 2009

145685UK00001B/12/P

9 781845 531621